T0186124

Communications in Computer and Information Science 1403

Editorial Board Members

Joaquim Filipe ⓘ
  Polytechnic Institute of Setúbal, Setúbal, Portugal

Ashish Ghosh
  Indian Statistical Institute, Kolkata, India

Raquel Oliveira Prates ⓘ
  Federal University of Minas Gerais (UFMG), Belo Horizonte, Brazil

Lizhu Zhou
  Tsinghua University, Beijing, China

More information about this series at https://link.springer.com/bookseries/7899

Weizhi Meng · Sokratis K. Katsikas (Eds.)

Emerging Information Security and Applications

Second International Symposium, EISA 2021
Copenhagen, Denmark, November 12–13, 2021
Revised Selected Papers

 Springer

Editors
Weizhi Meng 🆔
Technical University of Denmark
Kongens Lyngby, Denmark

Sokratis K. Katsikas 🆔
Norwegian University of Science
and Technology
Gjøvik, Norway

ISSN 1865-0929 ISSN 1865-0937 (electronic)
Communications in Computer and Information Science
ISBN 978-3-030-93955-7 ISBN 978-3-030-93956-4 (eBook)
https://doi.org/10.1007/978-3-030-93956-4

© Springer Nature Switzerland AG 2022
This work is subject to copyright. All rights are reserved by the Publisher, whether the whole or part of the material is concerned, specifically the rights of translation, reprinting, reuse of illustrations, recitation, broadcasting, reproduction on microfilms or in any other physical way, and transmission or information storage and retrieval, electronic adaptation, computer software, or by similar or dissimilar methodology now known or hereafter developed.
The use of general descriptive names, registered names, trademarks, service marks, etc. in this publication does not imply, even in the absence of a specific statement, that such names are exempt from the relevant protective laws and regulations and therefore free for general use.
The publisher, the authors and the editors are safe to assume that the advice and information in this book are believed to be true and accurate at the date of publication. Neither the publisher nor the authors or the editors give a warranty, expressed or implied, with respect to the material contained herein or for any errors or omissions that may have been made. The publisher remains neutral with regard to jurisdictional claims in published maps and institutional affiliations.

This Springer imprint is published by the registered company Springer Nature Switzerland AG
The registered company address is: Gewerbestrasse 11, 6330 Cham, Switzerland

Preface

This book contains the papers that were selected for presentation and publication at the Second International Symposium on Emerging Information Security and Applications (EISA 2021), which was organized by the Cyber Security Section of the Technical University of Denmark, Denmark, held during November 12–13, 2021. Due to COVID-19, EISA 2021 was held online.

With the recent evolution of adversarial techniques, intrusions that may threaten the security of various assets, including information and applications, have become more complex. In addition, coordinated intrusions like worm outbreaks will continue to be a major threat to information, system, and network security in the near future. The popularity of the Internet generates a large volume of different types of sensitive information. Therefore, there is a need for emerging techniques, theories, and applications to protect information and practical security. EISA aims to provide a platform for researchers and practitioners across the world to exchange their ideas. It seeks original submissions that discuss practical or theoretical solutions to enhance information and application security in practice.

This year's Program Committee (PC) consisted of 51 members with diverse backgrounds and broad research interests. A total of 36 papers were submitted to the conference. Papers were selected based on their originality, significance, relevance, and clarity of presentation as assessed by the reviewers. Most papers were reviewed by three or more PC members. Finally, 10 full papers were selected for presentation at the conference, resulting in an acceptance rate of 27.8%. Additionally, one short paper was accepted.

EISA 2021 had seven outstanding keynote talks: "Software Vulnerability Detection: From Fuzzing to Deep Learning" presented by Yang Xiang from Swinburne University of Technology, Australia; "Highly Efficient Network Security Analysis Based on Sketches" presented by Zheng Yan from Xidian University, China, and Aalto University, Finland; "File Carving - Challenges and Research Directions" presented by Xiaodong Lin from the University of Guelph, Canada; "Passive Message Fingerprint Attacks on Challenge-based Collaborate Intrusion Detection Networks" presented by Wenjuan Li from the Hong Kong Polytechnic University, China; "On the Evolution of OCPP-based Charging Infrastructures: Threats and Countermeasures" presented by Cristina Alcaraz from the University of Malaga, Spain; "The Dumbo Protocol Family: Making Asynchronous Consensus Real" presented by Qiang Tang from the University of Sydney, Australia; and "Blockchain and Machine Learning Aided Security Framework for Internet of Things" presented by Chunhua Su from the University of Aizu, Japan. Our deepest gratitude for their excellent presentations.

For the success of EISA 2021, we would like to first thank the authors of all submissions and all the PC members for their great efforts in selecting the papers. We also thank all the external reviewers for assisting the reviewing process. For the conference organization, we would like to thank the general chairs - Liqun Chen and Jiageng Chen, the publicity chairs - Stefanos Gritzalis and Chunhua Su, and the publication chair –

Wenjuan Li. Finally, we thank everyone else, speakers and session chairs, for their contribution to the program of EISA 2021.

November 2021   Weizhi Meng
                                                          Sokratis K. Katsikas

Organization

General Chairs

Liqun Chen   University of Surrey, UK
Jiageng Chen   Central China Normal University, China

Program Chairs

Weizhi Meng   Technical University of Denmark, Denmark
Sokratis K. Katsikas   Norwegian University of Science and Technology, Norway

Publicity Chairs

Stefanos Gritzalis   University of Piraeus, Greece
Chunhua Su   University of Aizu, Japan

Publication Chair

Wenjuan Li   Hong Kong Polytechnic University, China

Steering Committee

Jiageng Chen   Central China Normal University, China
Liqun Chen   University of Surrey, UK
Steven Furnell   University of Plymouth, UK
Anthony T. S. Ho   University of Surrey, UK
Sokratis K. Katsikas   Norwegian University of Science and Technology, Norway
Javier Lopez   University of Malaga, Spain
Weizhi Meng (Chair)   Technical University of Denmark, Denmark

Technical Program Committee

Hiroaki Anada   University of Nagasaki, Japan
Raja Naeem Akram   University of Aberdeen, UK
Javier Parra Arnau   Karlsruhe Institute of Technology, Germany
Muhammad Rizwan Asghar   University of Auckland, New Zealand
Maria Bada   University of Cambridge, UK

Joonsang Baek   University of Wollongong, Australia
Gergely Biczok   Budapest University of Technology and
                                 Economics, Hungary
Francesco Buccafurri   University of Reggio Calabria, Italy
Xiaofeng Chen   Xidian University, China
Jiageng Chen   Central China Normal University, China
Chen-Mou Cheng   Kanazawa University, Japan
Bernardo David   IT University of Copenhagen, Denmark
Changyu Dong   Newcastle University, UK
Csilla Farkas   University of Southern California, USA
Yunhe Feng   University of Washington, USA
Stefanos Gritzalis   University of Piraeus, Greece
Debasis Giri   Maulana Abul Kalam Azad University of
                                 Technology, India
Debiao He   Wuhan University, China
Shoichi Hirose   University of Fukui, Japan
Julian Jang-Jaccard   Massey University, New Zealand
Qi Jiang   Xidian University, China
Romain Laborde   Paul Sabatier University, France
Costas Lambrinoudakis   University of Piraeus, Greece
Albert Levi   Sabanci University, Turkey
Wenjuan Li   Hong Kong Polytechnic University, China
Qi Lin   University of New South Wales, Australia
Giovanni Livraga   University of Milan, Italy
Leonardo Maccari   University of Venice, Italy
Mohammad Mamun   National Research Council, Canada
Sjouke Mauw   University of Luxembourg, Luxembourg
Weizhi Meng   Technical University of Denmark, Denmark
Mehrdad Nojoumian   Florida Atlantic University, USA
Chandrasekaran Pandurangan   Indian Institute of Technology, India
Davy Preuveneers   Katholieke Universiteit Leuven, Belgium
Pierangela Samarati   Università degli Studi di Milano, Italy
Jun Shao   Zhejiang Gongshang University, China
Spiros Skiadopoulos   University of Peloponnese, Greece
Ketil Stoelen   SINTEF, Norway
Chunhua Su   University of Aizu, Japan
Gang Tan   Pennsylvania State University, USA
Je Sen Teh   Universiti Sains Malaysia, Malaysia
Andreas Veneris   University of Toronto, Canada
Hao Wang   Shandong Normal University, China
Haoyu Wang   Beijing University of Posts and
                                 Telecommunications, China

Licheng Wang	Beijing University of Posts and Telecommunications, China
Qionghong Wu	Beihang University, China
Zhe Xia	Wuhan University of Technology, China
Kuo-Hui Yeh	National Dong Hwa University, Taiwan
Wun-She Yap	Universiti Tunku Abdul Rahman, Malaysia

Additional Reviewers

Norziana Jamil
Min Luo
Jing Pan

Contents

Practical and Provable Secure Vehicular Component Protection Scheme

Jixin Zhang(ID) and Jiageng Chen(✉)(ID)

Central China Normal University, Wuhan Luoyu Road 152, Wuhan, China

Abstract. With the development of the 5G technology, the realization of the Vehicular Ad Hoc Network and the automatic driving have become one step closer. The system within the vehicular itself has evolved to become rather complicated with various components. Thus, the efficient malicious components detection and integrity inspection has become an important issue. In this paper, a practical and provable secure in-vehicle components protection scheme is proposed to support the component detection, secure component replacement and software update. Security definitions are provided with the concrete schemes to meet the corresponding security, which is based on the group testing and cryptographic hash functions. We show the effectiveness of our scheme by providing the corresponding security proof and performance evaluation comparisons.

Keywords: 5G · Vehicular Ad Hoc Network · Automatic driving · Components detection · Efficiency

1 Introduction

20 years after the proposal of the concept of the Vehicular Ad-hoc Networks (VANETs), the progress of some key technologies such as IoT and 5G have made the realization of the concept one big step forward. VANETs once truly implemented can become part of the smart city to greatly improve the traffic optimization, as well as the data supply to other related areas for further various big data analysis purposes.

In response to the needs of various applications, sensors will be equipped all over the vehicle. In the traditional car system, due to the limitations of the data transmission bandwidth, real-time data access function in car communication system can no longer meet the requirements of the next generation communication. The arrival of 5G makes the data transmission ubiquitous and efficient. In the previous 20 years of research, there have been many standards proposed by different research agencies, such as Dedicated Short Range Communications (DSRC) and Cellular-Vehicle-to-Everything (C-V2X), SAE J2735 and SAE J2945, which define the information carried in the package which include sensor information from the vehicles, such as position, direction of the movement, speed and brake statistics and so on. On the other hand, with the development of the AI technologies, the automatic driving technique has already been partly

© Springer Nature Switzerland AG 2022
W. Meng and S. K. Katsikas (Eds.): EISA 2021, CCIS 1403, pp. 1–20, 2022.
https://doi.org/10.1007/978-3-030-93956-4_1

implemented by companies such as Telsa and Uber et al., which are bringing lower cost and more secure driving experience to life [27]. The recent joint efforts of academia and industry show that the paradigm shift of intelligent transportation system is taking place [26]. Especially, as the official deployment of the 5G communication [29], vehicle communication has been greatly enhanced with the help of various IoT devices. This further leads to the diversity of the component on the vehicle which is used to send and receive data from both outside and inside of the vehicles. The vehicle will be equipped with a computing and communication platform and thus the sensing capabilities will be greatly improved, such as [2,18,28].

The security model of the vehicle's interior components as a result has been changed. New vehicles launched by many manufacturers, especially in new energy vehicles, have been equipped with various sensors, and many of them support software and hardware upgrades. Subject to the sophisticated global supply chain, various sensors will come from different countries and different manufacturers. In this context, the security risks of the authentication and message integrity of sensors and other vehicle components are very different from the ones in the traditional environment such as [14,19]. V2X technology has exposed great potential of safety and efficiency, but it only focuses on the interaction between the vehicle and the outside world, neglecting the safety of the internal components of the vehicle and the messages they generate. Therefore, appropriate security protection should be carefully investigated.

In this paper, we propose an in-vehicle components protections solution based on group testing and hash based component inspection (HBCI). Sequential Aggregate MACs with Detecting Functionality (SAMD) is applied to encrypt data communicated among different agents. We build three kinds of effective HBCI for different scenarios. The security requirements are formalized including the unforgeability and identifiability. Unforgeability captures the fact that the components cannot be illegally forged, while identifiability defines that both legal and illegal components should be correctly identified. In addition, to solve the problem of data confidentiality in the process of data transmission to the agents outside of the vehicle, we also propose two effective symmetric encryption schemes. They can meet the authenticated encryption (AE) security requirements. Notice that the authentication process between the vehicle and the outside agent is beyond our discussion.

1.1   Related Work

Access infrastructure, such as Wi-Fi access points and cellular base stations (BSS), plays a crucial role in providing universal Internet services to vehicles. However, the deployment cost of different access infrastructure is different. Results of [17] and [21] provide some basic guidances for emerging vehicle network on how to choose cost-effective access infrastructure. Similarly, we study the efficient message transmission in the network of vehicles, and our goal is to protect the underlying message integrity, regardless of the network types.

[7,13,15] propose security models in 5G-enabled vehicular networks and provides the solution to address the issues of high-speed and multiple-relay in vehicular social network. The solution focuses on the network level security, while we focus more on the data security which is closely related to the upper-level applications.

There are some previous works devoted to message authentication in VSN. [11,22,25] are based on pseudonyms-based signature technology to hide partial identity information, [1,10,16,24] are based on group signature technology to provide full anonymity, and some schemes, such as [6,20] are based on the hybrid technology for the balance between efficiency and anonymity. The message integrity discussed in these schemes has been focused on the communication between vehicles and base station, so they are all digital signatures based on public key system. On the other hand, our work is based on symmetric cryptography which is more compact and efficient.

2 System Model

According to the current development of the Internet of vehicles and some relevant information, such as [14,19], it can be expected that significant changes will take place in the automotive electrical and electronic (E/E) architecture. The architecture will change from one with numerous separate Electronic Control Units (ECUs) (hundreds ECUs for complex vehicles) towards a more streamlined architecture with a few central Domain Control Units (DCUs) covering one vehicle's sub-domain each, such as chassis or infotainment. DCUs consolidate the non-time-critical functionality of multiple ECUs and process data from multiple sources centrally. For example, in a DCU-based E/E architecture, the data from multiple sensors such as cameras, radars, and LiDAR is processed centrally, e.g., for sensor fusion purpose. Functionality which remains locally is mainly related to the preprocessing of data to avoid the congestion of the vehicle bus system. Inside the vehicle, communication between the components are proceeded through the wired setting instead of the wireless transmission. And because of the closed internal environment, communication are usually not encrypted. On the other hand, messages are transmitted wirelessly between the vehicle components and the outside servers, which should be protected. For messages transmitted outside of the vehicle, we can reasonably assume that these components have shared necessary secret information with the remote servers, such as the private key. This assumption exists in many IoT systems [8]. We demonstrate the concept of the components inside the vehicle shown in Fig. 1. The system should first support the OTA update (over-the-air update), which is not intended to be covered in details here. Secondly, our solution is able to detect the validity of all components, sound the alarm regarding the malicious components and prevent the vehicle from starting. At the same time, it can also support the emergency starting in some special situation. Finally, it should be able to protect the messages communicating to the outside agents in a secure manner. In order to clarify the various application cases, our system is divided into several states, which are described as follows:

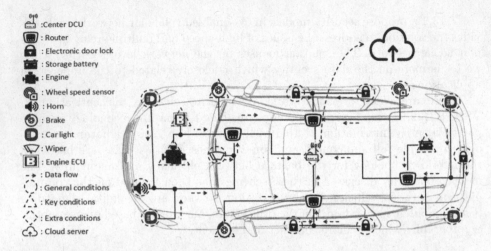

Fig. 1. Interior vehicle communication. Various components are installed inside the vehicle, and they are connected to the center DCU through the cable and routers inside the vehicle. When the center DCU receives the update information from the cloud server, it transmits the information to each component through the cable. In the start-up phase, each component will generate identity authentication information and send it to the center DCU for authentication. If the authentication is passed, the vehicle can be started normally. In case of emergency when the vehicle cannot be started, we can force it to be initiated by satisfying several key conditions configured in advance.

- **Start-Up:** This state represents the start-up process of the vehicle. In this process, the system shall check all components to ensure the correctness. The system will not be activated unless pre-specified conditions are met.
- **Running:** It indicates the status after the starting up when the vehicle is actively collecting necessary information from each components and send and receive messages from the outside. Note that the data is transmitted in plaintext form inside the vehicle.
- **Shutdown:** This state corresponds to the car stalling, which indicates that the system is off. If and only if in this state the system allows the hardware to be replaced. Read-only memory can only be written by the authorized parties in this state.

Next, we consider a system model and describe the functions of the system according to the various applications. First, when the car starts, the system should check all components to ensure their correctness, which should be one of the conditions for the normal start of the car. Moreover, the system should allow the legitimate replacement of components and should refuse to start normally when illegal components are detected. In addition, the system is able to detect all the illegal components. This is the main function we want to achieve in our system. Besides, the system should also support the detection from the remote server, software update and emergency start functions. Concretely, the cases are as follows:

Software Update: The update packet is received by the central DCU from the remote server, and then sent to the target components after detecting. This case is described in Fig. 1.

Component Inspection: At each start-up phase, all components shall send their key identification information to the central DCU for authentication. The identity information is assumed to be safe in the hardware and cannot be tampered with, that is, stored in a read-only space. If the inspection passes, one of the normal startup conditions is reached; otherwise, an error is reported to prevent the vehicle from starting. It is required that any illegal components would fail the detection phase and it is impossible to forge a legitimate component without authorization. It is described in Fig. 1, and in Sect. 3, we will introduce the HBCI scheme, which can be used to achieve this goal. We consider that the startup order of some components also needs to be guaranteed, and incorrect startup order may have serious consequences. Therefore, we also take this requirement into account. In practice, we build parallel HBCI for the case that there is no detection order required among components and the sequential HBCI for the cases that the order is of importance. Finally, we also give mixed HBCI to deal with other more complicated situations.

Component Replacement: Replace components legally so that new components can pass the component inspection process in start-up state. Note that this process should be carried out while the vehicle is in the shutdown state.

Emergency Start: After all normal starting conditions are met, the system shall start normally, except the case when the owner needs to start the car in an emergency situation and cannot reach all normal starting conditions. At this time, the system should be forced to start after meeting some necessary key conditions as well as some extra conditions. For example, the validity of the engine, ECU and storage battery should be the reasonable key conditions, and extra conditions can be given by the central DCU.

Detection from the Remote Server: In the running state, all cars in the system send their messages to the cloud server to be monitored. Cloud server will detect those messages to determine the condition of all vehicles. The messages sent to the cloud server should be authenticated and encrypted. Within the vehicle, all components send the collected information to the central DCU, which encrypts the information after detecting the integrity of the message and then sends it to the outside world. These messages are processed and forwarded by aggregator and Road-Side Units (RSU) and finally sent to the cloud server. Its aggregation process is keyless, which allows us to delegate the aggregation to an aggregator, such as RSU or other capable vehicles. In this scenario, the assumption that the end components trust central DCU is reasonable. In Sect. 4, we will introduce the Trusted Aggregation Information Transmission (TAIT) which means that the aggregator will be trusted, as well as the Untrusted Aggregation Information Transmission (UAIT) which means the opposite. In the TAIT, the encryption of the messages is also delegated to RSU. The central DCU directly sends messages to RSU, and sends MAC tags to the aggregator. MAC tags are then aggregated and sent to RSU. Finally, RSU checks the integrity and dispatches the encrypted messages. Regarding the UAIT, the whole process is similar, except that the encryption process needs to be completed by the vehicle itself.

3   Hash Based Component Inspection

We now present an efficient component inspection scheme which is unforgeable in the sense that no efficient adversary can forge a valid component. Also we will say that it is *identifiable* which means that all components can be tested correctly. Before the vehicle leaves the factory, one runs the corresponding proof generation algorithm of HBCI and stores the results in read-only memory. Every time at the start-up phase, all components send their key identification information to the central DCU. Then the central DCU applies the HBCI to complete the key identification information detection for all components. We construct sequential, parallel and mixed structures to meet the various needs of component detection. In fact, mixed structure is the combination of the first two designs.

In this paper, each component can be recognized by a set of unique elements which are used to be detected later without ambiguity. If two components have the same identification information, they should have exactly the same functionality and security level. To sound the alarm correctly, we assume that the identity information of each component contains a corresponding ID. Read-only memory can only be written by authorized personnel under specific conditions. Note that this is a weaker assumption than hardware security module (HSM), where a restricted function of the master secret can be accessed from the outside. The proof of the component is pre-formed and stored in the read-only memory.

3.1   HBCI Model

A *fundamental Hash Based Component Inspection (FHBCI)* scheme consists of three polynomial-time algorithms (G, V) as follows: let $\mathcal{P}$ be a key identification information space, Π be a proof-space,

- $\pi \leftarrow$ G(p): G is a deterministic, proof generation algorithm, which takes as input a key identification information $p \in \mathcal{P}$ and output a proof $\pi \in \Pi$.
- $accept/reject \leftarrow$ V(π, p): V is a deterministic, verification algorithm, which takes as input a proof $\pi \in \Pi$ and a key identification information $p \in \mathcal{P}$, output accept or reject.

The FHBCI must satisfy the following correctness property:

- For all $p \in \mathcal{P}$, we have $accept \leftarrow$ V(G(p), p).

Sequential Hash Based Component Inspection (SHBCI) is designed to serve the purpose that some components need to deliver messages in order. For some programs that call different components in turn, such as start-up, the correctness of message sequence from different components is required.

A **Sequential Hash Based Component Inspection (SHBCI)** scheme consists of six polynomial-time algorithms (G, V, SG_θ, DSHV) as follows: N is the number of components, Π is a proof-space, $\mathcal{P}$ is a space of key identification information, $Order = \{1, 2, ..., N\}$ is an order-space, Π_θ is a DSH proof-space.

- $\pi_\theta \leftarrow SG_\theta(KO)$: SG_θ is a deterministic proof generation algorithm, which takes as input a sequence of order/key identification information pairs $KO = ((order_1, p_1), ..., (order_N, p_N))$, where $order_i \in Order$ for any $i \in \{1, 2, ..., N\}$, and output a tuple of sequential proof $\pi_\theta \in \Pi_\theta$.
- $L/ERROR \leftarrow DSHV(KO, \pi_\theta)$: DSHV is a deterministic verification algorithm, which takes as input a sequence of order/key identification information pairs KO and $\pi_\theta \in \Pi_\theta$ and output a list L or an error messages $ERROR$, where L is a list consisting of IDs in key identification information belonged to illegal components.

The SHBCI must satisfy the following correctness properties:

- For all $p \in \mathcal{P}$, we have $accept \leftarrow V(G(p), p)$.
- For all $KO \in (\mathcal{P}, Order)^n$, we have $\emptyset \leftarrow DSHV(KO, SG_\theta(KO))$.

Different from SHBCI, Parallel Hash Based Component Inspection is designed to serve the purpose that some components do *not* need to deliver messages in order.

A **Parallel Hash Based Component Inspection (PHBCI)** scheme consists of six polynomial-time algorithms (G, V, PG_θ, DPHV) as follows: The symbols N, Π, $\mathcal{P}$, Π_θ are the same as those in SHBCI.

- $\pi_\theta \leftarrow PG_\theta(K)$: PG_θ is a deterministic proof generation algorithm, which takes as input a tuple of key identification informations $K = (p_1, ..., p_N)$, and output a tuple of proof $\pi_\theta \in \Pi_\theta$.
- $L/ERROR \leftarrow DPHV(K, \pi_\theta)$: DPHV is a deterministic verification algorithm, which takes as input a tuple of key identification information pairs K and $\pi_\theta \in \Pi_\theta$ and output a list L or an error messages $ERROR$, where L is a list consisting of IDs in key identification information belonged to illegal components.

The PHBCI must satisfy the following correctness properties:

- For all $p \in \mathcal{P}$, we have $accept \leftarrow V(G(p), p)$.
- For all $K \in \mathcal{P}^n$, we have $\emptyset \leftarrow DPHV(K, PG_\theta(K))$.

The scheme by combining SHBCI and PHBCI is called Mixed Hash Based Component Inspection, which is expected to meet any application requirements. Because the output domain of HBCI is different from the input domain, the output of HBCI needs to be transferred to the domain by using $Trans$ algorithm as the input of the next nested call.

A **Mixed Hash Based Component Inspection (MHBCI)** scheme consists of ten polynomial-time algorithms (G, V, SG_θ, DSHV, PG_θ, DPHV, Trans) as follows: The symbols N, Π, $\mathcal{P}$, Π_θ and $Order$ are the same as in SHBCI, and only new algorithm $Trans$ is demonstrated as follow.

- $p \leftarrow Trans(\pi_\theta)$: Trans is a deterministic verification algorithm, which takes as input a tuple of proof π_θ and output a key identification information.

MHBCI must satisfy the following correctness properties:

- For all $\pi_\theta \in \Pi_\theta$, we have $Trans(\pi_\theta) \in \mathcal{P}$.
- For all $p \in \mathcal{P}$, we have $accept \leftarrow V(G(p), p)$.
- For all $KO \in (\mathcal{P}, Order)^n$, we have $\emptyset \leftarrow \text{DSHV}(KO, \text{SG}_\theta(KO))$.
- For all $K \in \mathcal{P}^n$, we have $\emptyset \leftarrow \text{DPHV}(K, \text{PG}_\theta(K))$.

Specific security definitions can be found in Appendix A.

3.2 HBCI Construction

Intuitively, we can use MAC and hash chain to solve our needs. However, It is important to protect the integrity of the messages at the cost of increasing the length of the messages. Especially, this will increase the burden where real-time communication is highly expected such as the Internet of vehicles. Aggregate MAC [12] can aggregate the tags of multiple messages into one to reduce bandwidth consumption. Unfortunately, once the multiple messages are judged to be invalid related to a single tag, it is difficult to identify invalid source. In order to solve this problem, Shoichi Hirose and Junji Shikata develop a technology to detect the invalid information in Aggregate MAC [9], and later applied in Sequential Aggregate MACs with Detecting Functionality (SAMD) [23] by using group testing [3,5]. To satisfy our application, we extend their solution to support our HBCIs. Based on the same framework, according to our application, we will no longer use MAC, but use cryptographic hash function instead. The advantage is that we will no longer need to share the private key in advance as well as the security management of the key.

For FHBCI, we can simply use cryptographic hash function Hash to implement G algorithm, and use Hash(p) to verify in the verification algorithm. The correctness of FHBCI directly follows the correctness of Hash algorithm. The unforgeability of FHBCI directly follows the collision resistance of Hash algorithm. This construct and proof are simple and we omit them here.

Theorem 1 (FHBCI Unforgeability). *FHBCI meets Unforgeability if* Hash *is collision resistant and the proof is correctly stored in the read-only memory.*

Let $G_{M \times N}\{0, 1\}$ denote that G has M rows and N columns, and all elements are 0 or 1, $G(i)$ denote a set consists of column numbers with element 1 of the ith row. Let N be the number of components to be tested, $G \in \{0, 1\}_{M \times N}$ be a d-disjunct matrix, $H_1 : \{0, 1\}^* \to \Pi_\theta$ and $H_2 : \{0, 1\}^* \to \mathcal{P}$ be two hash functions.

SHBCI = (G, V, SG$_\theta$, DSHV) is given as follows:

- $\pi_\theta \leftarrow \text{SG}_\theta(KO)$: For a sequence of order/key identification information pairs $KO = ((1, p_1), (2, p_2), ..., (N, p_N))$, do as follows:
  1. For all $i \in \{1, 2, ..., N\}$, $h_i \leftarrow \text{Hash}(p_i)$.

2. $\pi_{\theta j} \leftarrow H_1((j_1, h_{j_1}), (j_2, h_{j_2}), ..., (j_x, h_{j_x}))$, where $G(j) = \{j_1, j_2, ..., j_x\}$ for all $j \in \{1, 2, ..., M\}$.
3. Write $\pi_\theta := (\pi_{\theta_1}, \pi_{\theta_2}, .., \pi_{\theta_M})$ to the read-only memory.
- $L/ERROR \leftarrow$ DSHV(KO, π_θ): For $KO = \{(order_i, p_i)\}_N$, $\pi_\theta = (\pi_{\theta_1}, \pi_{\theta_2}, ..., \pi_{\theta_M})$, do as follows:
  1. For all $i \in \{1, 2, ..., N\}$, $h_i \leftarrow$ Hash(p_i).
  2. $L \leftarrow \{id_1, id_2, ..., id_N\}$.
  3. For $j \in \{1, 2, ..., M\}$, $L \leftarrow L \backslash \{id_{order_{j_1}}, ..., id_{order_{j_x}}\}$, where $G(j) = \{j_1, j_2, ..., j_x\}$, if $\pi_{\theta_j} = H_1((j_1, h_{j_1}), ..., (j_x, h_{j_x}))$.

Theorem 2 (SHBCI Unforgeability). *If G is a d-disjunct matrix, Hash and H_1 is collision resistant, and the proof is correctly stored in read-only memory, then SHBCI satisfies the d-Unforgeability.*

Proof of Theorem 2: In order to break the unforgeability of SHBCI, if the adversary tries to replace a valid component with an illegal component, the adversary needs to replace the component p' with p^* and get the same h, which will break the collision resistant property of Hash. Otherwise, it can only expect to get the same π_{θ_i} by replacing other components in the same row of matrix G, which breaks the collision resistant property of H_1.

Theorem 3 (SHBCI Identifiability). *Suppose that the number of components whose key identification informations or their orders are invalid is at most d, G is d-disjunct, Hash and H_1 is collision resistant. We have: SHBCI meets d-message-Identifiability and d-order-Identifiability.*

Proof of Theorem 3: SHBCI meets directly *d-message-completeness* and *d-order-completeness* according the property of d-disjunct matrix and the correctness of H_1 and Hash. In order to break the *d-message-soundness* of SHBCI, the adversary needs to replace a valid component as an illegal component, which is not detected, that is to say, it will not appear in L. In order to avoid detection, this component needs to get the same π_{θ_i} as other components in the same row of matrix G, which breaks the collision resistant property of H_1 or Hash, or it avoids the detection of non-adaptive group testing, which breaks the property of d-disjunct matrix. So SHBCI meets *d-message-soundness* from the collision-resistance of H_1 and the property of d-disjunct matrix. Like above proof, for every polynomially bounded adversary A that attacks *d-order-soundness*, there exists an adversary B finding a collision of H_1 or Hash.

PHBCI = (G, Hash, V, SG$_\theta$, DSHV) is given as follows:

- $\pi_\theta \leftarrow$ PG$_\theta(K)$: For a tuple of key identification information $K = (p_1, p_2, ..., p_N)$, do as follows:
  1. For all $i \in \{1, 2, ..., N\}$, $h_i \leftarrow$ Hash(p_i).
  2. $\pi_{\theta j} \leftarrow H_1(h_{j_1}, h_{j_2}, ..., h_{j_x})$, where $G(j) = \{j_1, j_2, ..., j_x\}$ for all $j \in \{1, 2, ..., M\}$.
  3. Write $\pi_\theta := (\pi_{\theta_1}, \pi_{\theta_2}, .., \pi_{\theta_M})$ to read-only memory.

- $L/ERROR \leftarrow \text{DPHV}(K, \pi_\theta)$: For $K = (p_1, p_2, ..., p_N)$, $\pi_\theta = (\pi_{\theta_1}, \pi_{\theta_2}, ..., \pi_{\theta_M}))$, do as follows:
  1. For all $i \in \{1, 2, ..., N\}$, $h_i \leftarrow \text{Hash}(p_i)$.
  2. $L \leftarrow \{id_1, id_2, ..., id_N\}$.
  3. For $j \in \{1, 2, ..., M\}$, $L \leftarrow L \backslash \{id_{j_1}, id_{j_2}, ..., id_{j_x}\}$, where $G(j) = \{j_1, j_2, ..., j_x\}$, if $\pi_{\theta_j} = H_1(h_{j_1}, h_{j_2}, ..., h_{j_x})$.

Theorem 4 (PHBCI Unforgeability). *If G is a d-disjunct matrix, Hash and H_1 is collision resistant, and the proof is correctly stored in read-only memory, then PHBCI meets d-Unforgeability.*

Proof of Theorem 4: This proof is similar to the Unforgeability of SHBCI with the only difference being that the input of H_1 no longer contains a sequence number.

Theorem 5 (PHBCI Identifiability). *Suppose that the number of components whose key identification informations being invalid is at most d, G is d-disjunct, Hash and H_1 is collision resistant. Then we have: PHBCI meets d-message-Identifiability.*

Proof of Theorem 5: PHBCI meets directly *d-message-completeness* according the property of d-disjunct matrix and the correctness of H_1. SHBCI meets *d-message-soundness* from the collision-resistance of H_1 and the property of d-disjunct matrix. For every polynomially bounded adversary A that attacks *d-message-soundness*, there exists an adversary B finding a collision of the random oracle H_1 or Hash.

A MHBCI can be built by combining SHBCI and PHBCI. To transform the domain, we use H_2 to calculate a new Hash value for the output of SHBCI or PHBCI as the input for the next nest. It should be noted that only the output of the top-level proof generation algorithm needs to be saved in read-only memory for detecting.

MHBCI = (G, V, SG_θ, DSHV, PG_θ, DPHV, Trans) is given as follows:

- $p \leftarrow Trans(\pi_\theta)$: Output a key identification information $p \leftarrow H_2(\pi_\theta)$.

Theorem 6 (MHBCI Unforgeability). *If G is a d-disjunct matrix, Hash, H_1 and H_2 is collision resistant, and the proof is correctly stored in read-only memory, then MHBCI meets d-Unforgeability.*

Proof of Theorem 6: If competitor A is able to break the Unforgeability of MHBCI, it needs to complete 1. replace a valid component with an illegal component to obtain the same h as the original component; or 2. the component needs to obtain the same π_θ as other components in the same line of matrix G; or 3. the sub-HBCI of a detected illegal component in the nest is used to get a result by trans algorithm, which is the same as the sub-HBCI without illegal component. Otherwise, the nature of G and the correctness of Hash, H_1 and H_2

will guarantee the correctness of the test results. If the first attack is successful, there will be adversary B_1 breaking the collision resistant property of Hash. On the other hand, if the second attack is successful, there will be a collision resistant adversary B_2 to break H_1. Finally, if the third attack is successful, there will exist a B_3 to break the collision resistant property of H_2.

Theorem 7 (MHBCI Identifiability). *Suppose that the number of components whose key identification informations or their orders are invalid is at most d, G is d-disjunct, Hash, H_1 and H_2 is collision resistant. Then we have: MHBCI meets d-message-Identifiability and d-order-Identifiability.*

Proof of Theorem 7: MHBCI meets *d-Identifiability* from the properties of *d-Identifiability* of SHBCI and PHBCI and the preimage-soundness and the collision-resistance of H_2. The property of the preimage-soundness ensures that no effective adversary can find the preimage of p with all components. The collation-resistance ensures that no effective adversary can find a collision.

3.3 Component Replacement

In this system, the legal replacement of components means that new and old components can pass the component inspection, and that the replacer must have the permission to write the read-only memory. In PHBCI systems, after replacing the components, one runs the corresponding generation algorithm PG_θ to complete the entire procedure. In SHBCI systems, this process is the same as PHBCI. Note that the validity detection of components is completely based on the read-only memory, so the permission granting should be strictly managed.

3.4 Emergency Start

The emergency start procedure shall be carried out by the owner in case of emergency when the normal start-up conditions cannot all be satisfied. As shown in Fig. 1, the general conditions may include the validity of non critical components, while the key conditions should be focused on the validity of the critical components to ensure the driving safety and the validity of the owner's identification. Some of the extra conditions may need to be performed or confirmed manually.

4 Detection from the Remote Server

We build two authenticated encryption schemes based on SAMD to transmit messages to the cloud server. One is more general, which allows an untrusted aggregator but needs end components to be able to implement encryption and MAC; while the other one is more desirable for the current system, which only needs the end components to implement MAC with a trusted aggregator. In other words, the former requires the aggregator to be honest but curious, while the latter requires the aggregator to be completely trustworthy. We present two schemes to provide trade-offs for a given application. In both schemes, the tag aggregation is key-less procedure, so that it can be completed by an aggregator for high efficiency. We can assume that the central DCU and the receiver have exchanged a master key.

4.1   Detection from the Remote Server Model

In Untrusted Aggregation Information Transmission, the aggregator is not trusted. The end components send the ciphertext to the aggregator after encrypting messages. After aggregating the ciphertext tags, the aggregator sends multiple ciphertexts and the corresponding aggregation tags to the server.

A *Untrusted Aggregation Information Transmission (UAIT)* scheme consists of seven polynomial-time algorithms (G, E, D, T, V, DSA, DSAV) as follows: N is the number of the components, $\mathcal{K}_{mst}$ is a space of master key, $\mathcal{K}_e$ is a space of encryption-key, $\mathcal{K}_m$ is a space of MAC-key, $\mathcal{T}$ is a MAC-tag space, $\mathcal{M}$ is a message space, $\mathcal{C}_1$ is a ciphertext space, $\mathcal{T}_{dsa}$ is a SAMD-tag space, $\mathcal{ID} = \{id_1, id_2, ..., id_N\}$ is an ID-space, $Order := \{order_1, order_2, ..., order_N\} = \{1, 2, ..., N\}$ is an order-space.

- $key \leftarrow$ G(k_{mst}, ID): G is a probabilistic, key derivation algorithm, which takes as input a master key $k_{mst} \in \mathcal{K}_{mst}$ and a tuple of IDs $ID = (id_1, id_2, ..., id_N) \in \mathcal{ID}$ and output a set of 2N secret keys $key = \{k_{e_{id_1}}, k_{m_{id_1}}, ..., k_{e_{id_N}}, k_{m_{id_N}}\}$ such that $id_i \in ID$, $k_{e_{id_i}} \in \mathcal{K}_e$ and $k_{m_{id_i}} in \mathcal{K}_m$, for all $i \in \{1, 2, ..., N\}$.
- $c \leftarrow$ E(k_e, m): T is a probabilistic, encryption algorithm, which takes as input an encryption-key $k_e \in \mathcal{K}_e$ and a message $m \in \mathcal{M}$ and output a ciphertext $c \in \mathcal{C}_1$.
- $m \leftarrow$ D(k_e, c): T is a deterministic, decryption algorithm, which takes as input a, encryption-key $k_e \in \mathcal{K}_e$ and a ciphertext c and output a message m.
- $t \leftarrow$ T($k_m, order, c$): T is a deterministic, MAC algorithm, which takes as input a MAC-key $k_m \in \mathcal{K}_m$, an order $order \in Order$ and a ciphertext c and output a MAC-tag $t \in \mathcal{T}$.
- $accept/reject \leftarrow$ V($k_m, order, c, t$): V is a deterministic, verification algorithm, which takes as input a MAC-key k_m, an order $order$, a ciphertext c and a MAC-tag t and output $accept$ or $reject$.
- $t_{dsa} \leftarrow$ DSA(T): DSA is a deterministic, which takes as input a sequence of N MAC-tags $T = ((id_{order_i}, t_i))$ for all $(order_1, order_2, ..., order_N) \in Order$, output a tuple of SAMD-tags $t_{dsa} \in \mathcal{T}_{dsa}$. Note that this is a keyless founctoin.
- $L/ERROR \leftarrow$ DSAV(IDK, C, t_{dsa}): DSAV is a deterministic, verification algorithm, which takes as input a set of N ID/MAC-key pairs $IDK = \{(id_i, k_{m_{id_i}})\}$ and a sequence of N ID/ciphertext pairs $C = ((id_{order_i}, c_i))$ for all $i \in \{1, 2, ..., N\}$ and output a list L or an error messages $ERROR$, where L is a list consisting of IDs of components corresponding to invalid information.

The UAIT must satisfy the following correctness properties:

- For all $m \in \mathcal{M}$ and all $k_e \in \mathcal{K}_e$, we have $m \leftarrow D(E(k_e, m))$.
- For all $c \in \mathcal{C}_1$, all $order \in Order$ and all $k_m \in \mathcal{K}_m$, we have $accept \leftarrow V(k_m, order, c, T(k_m, order, c))$.
- For all $id \in \mathcal{ID}$, all $IDK = \{(id_i, k_{m_{id_i}})\}_N$ and all $C = \{(id_{order_i}, c_i)\}_N$, we have $\emptyset \leftarrow DSAV(IDK, C, t_{dsa})$, where $t_{dsa} \leftarrow DSA((id_{order_i}, T(k_{m_{id_{order_i}}}, order_i, c_i)))$, $order_i \in Order$.

In the Trusted Aggregation Information Transmission, the aggregator is trusted. End components send the message plaintext to the aggregator directly. After aggregating the message tag, the aggregator encrypts multiple messages and sends ciphertext with the aggregated tag.

A **Trusted Aggregation Information Transmission (TAIT)** scheme consists of seven polynomial-time algorithms (G, T, V, DSA, DSAV, E, D) as follows: The symbols $N, \mathcal{K}_{mst}, \mathcal{K}_e, \mathcal{K}_m, \mathcal{T}, \mathcal{M}, \mathcal{T}_{dsa}, \mathcal{ID}, Order$ are the same as those in UAIT, $\mathcal{C}_2$ is a ciphertext space.

- $key \leftarrow G(k_{mst}, ID)$: G is a probabilistic, key derivation algorithm, which takes as input a master key $k_{mst} \in \mathcal{K}_{mst}$ and a tuple of IDs $ID = (id_1, id_2, ..., id_N) \in \mathcal{ID}$ and output a set of N + 1 secret keys $key = \{k_e, k_{m_{id_1}}, k_{m_{id_2}}, ..., k_{m_{id_N}}\}$ such that $id_i \in ID$, $k_e \in \mathcal{K}_e$ and $k_{m_{id_i}} in \mathcal{K}_m$, for all $i \in \{1, 2, ..., N\}$.
- $t \leftarrow T(k_m, order, m)$: T is a deterministic, MAC algorithm, which takes as input a MAC-key $k_m \in \mathcal{K}_m$, an order $order \in Order$ and a message $m \in \mathcal{M}$ and output a MAC-tag $t \in \mathcal{T}$.
- $accept/reject \leftarrow V(k_m, order, m, t)$: V is a deterministic, verification algorithm, which takes as input a MAC-key $k_{m'}$, an order $order$, a message m and a MAC-tag t and output $accept$ or $reject$.
- $t_{dsa} \leftarrow DSA(T)$: DSA is a deterministic, which takes as input a sequence of N MAC-tags $T = ((id_{order_i}, t_i))$ for all $(order_1, order_2, ..., order_N) \in Order$, output a tuple of SAMD-tags $t_{dsa} \in \mathcal{T}_{dsa}$. Note that this is a keyless founctoin.
- $L/ERROR \leftarrow DSAV(IDK, m, t_{dsa})$: DSAV is a deterministic, verification algorithm, which takes as input a set of N ID/MAC-key pairs $IDK = \{(id_i, k_{m_{id_i}})\}$ and a sequence of N ID/message pairs $C = ((id_{order_i}, m_i))$ for all $i \in \{1, 2, ..., N\}$ and output a list L or an error messages $ERROR$, where L is a list consisting of IDs of components corresponding to invalid information.
- $c \leftarrow E(k_e, m')$: T is a probabilistic, encryption algorithm, which takes as input an encryption-key $k_e \in \mathcal{K}_e$ and a tuple of messages/SAMD-tag pairs $m' = ((m_1, m_2, ..., m_N), t_{dsa}) \in \mathcal{M}^N \times \mathcal{T}_{dsa}$ and output a ciphertext $c \in \mathcal{C}_2$.
- $m \leftarrow D(k_e, c)$: T is a deterministic, decryption algorithm, which takes as input an encryption-key $k_e \in \mathcal{K}_e$ and a ciphertext c and output a message m.

The TAIT must satisfy the following correctness property:

- For all $m' \in \mathcal{M}^N \times \mathcal{T}_{dsa}$ and all $k_e \in \mathcal{K}_e$, we have $m \leftarrow D(E(k_e, m'))$.
- For all $m \in \mathcal{M}$, all $order \in Order$ and all $k_m \in \mathcal{K}_m$, we have $accept \leftarrow V(k_m, order, m, T(k_m, order, m))$.

– For all $id \in \mathcal{ID}$, all $IDK = \{(id_i, k_{m_{id_i}})\}$ and all $M = ((id_{order_i}, m_i))$, we have $\emptyset \leftarrow \mathrm{DSAV}(IDK, M, t_{dsa})$, where $t_{dsa} \leftarrow \mathrm{DSA}((id_{order_i}, \mathrm{T}(k_{m_{id_{order_i}}}, order_i, m_i)))$, for all $order_i \in Order$.

4.2 Instantiation

Let N be the number of components to send message, $G \in \{0,1\}_{M \times N}$ be a d-disjunct matrix, $H : \{0,1\}^* \to \mathcal{T}$ be random oracle, ctr is a counter kept by an aggregator and updated after sending an aggregated tag, the initial value of counter is 1.

UAIT = (G, E, D, T, V, DSA, DSAV) is given as follows:

– $key \leftarrow \mathrm{G}(k_{mst}, ID)$: Output a set of 2N secret keys $key \leftarrow \mathrm{HKDF}(k_{mst}, ID)$, where $key = \{k_{e_{id_1}}, k_{m_{id_1}}, ..., k_{e_{id_N}}, k_{m_{id_N}}\}$.
– $c \leftarrow \mathrm{E}(k_e, m)$: Output $c \leftarrow E_{k_e}(m)$.
– $m \leftarrow \mathrm{D}(k_e, c)$: Output $m \leftarrow D_{k_e}(c)$.
– $t \leftarrow \mathrm{T}(k_m, order, c)$: Output $t \leftarrow MAC(k_m, order \parallel c)$.
– $accept/reject \leftarrow \mathrm{V}(k_m, order, c, t)$: Output $accept$ if $MAC(k_m, order \parallel c) = t$, otherwise output $reject$.
– $t_{dsa} \leftarrow \mathrm{T}(k_m, order, c)$: For $T = ((id_{order_i}, t_i))$, do as follows:
  1. $t_{dsa_j} \leftarrow H(ctr, t_{j_1}, t_{j_2}, ..., t_{j_x})$, where $G(j) = \{j_1, j_2, ..., j_x\}$ for all $j \in \{1, 2, ..., M\}$.
  2. $t_{dsa} := t_{dsa_1}, t_{dsa_2}, ..., t_{dsa_M}$, output t_{dsa}, and $ctr \leftarrow ctr + 1$.
– $L/ERROR \leftarrow \mathrm{DSAV}(IDK, C, t_{dsa})$: For $IDK = \{(id_i, k_{m_{id_i}})\}$ and $C = ((id_{order_i}, c_i))$ for all $i \in \{1, 2, ..., N\}$ do as follows:
  1. Output $ERROR$ if $ctr \neq ctr_v$.
  2. For all $i \leftarrow \{1, 2, ..., N\}$, $t_i \leftarrow MAC(k_{m_{id_{order_i}}}, order_i, c_i)$.
  3. $L \leftarrow \{id_1, id_2, ..., id_N\}$.
  4. For $j \in \{1, 2, ..., M\}$, $L \leftarrow L \backslash \{id_{order_{j_1}}, ..., id_{order_{j_x}}\}$, where $G(j) = \{j_1, j_2, ..., j_x\}$, if $t_{dsa_j} = H(ctr, t_{j_1}, t_{j_2}, ..., t_{j_x})$.
  5. Output L, and $ctr_v \leftarrow ctr_v + 1$.

Theorem 8 (UAIT AE-security). *Suppose that the number of components whose key identification information or their orders being invalid is at most d, G is d-disjunct, SAMD meets the UF-CMA security, E is a CPA-secure symmetric encryption scheme. In the random oracle model, we have: UAIT satisfies the AE-security.*

Proof of Theorem 8: This proof follows directly from Theorem 9.2 of Sect. 9.4.1 in [4].

TAIT = (G, T, V, DSA, DSAV, E, D) is given as follows:

– $key \leftarrow \mathrm{G}(k_{mst}, ID)$: Output a set of N + 1 secret keys $key \leftarrow \mathrm{HKDF}(k_{mst}, ID)$, where $key = \{k_e, k_{m_{id_1}}, ..., k_{e_{id_N}}, k_{m_{id_N}}\}$.
– $t \leftarrow \mathrm{T}(k_m, order, m)$: Output $t \leftarrow MAC(k_m, order \parallel m)$.
– $accept/reject \leftarrow \mathrm{V}(k_m, order, m, t)$: Output $accept$ if $MAC(k_m, order \parallel m) = t$, otherwise output $reject$.

- $t_{dsa} \leftarrow \mathrm{T}(k_m, order, m)$: For $T = ((id_{order_i}, t_i))$, do as follows:
    1. $t_{dsa_j} \leftarrow H(ctr, t_{j_1}, t_{j_2}, ..., t_{j_x})$, where $G(j) = \{j_1, j_2, ..., j_x\}$ for all $j \in \{1, 2, ..., M\}$.
    2. $t_{dsa} := t_{dsa_1}, t_{dsa_2}, ..., t_{dsa_M}$, output t_{dsa}, and $ctr \leftarrow ctr + 1$.
- $L/ERROR \leftarrow \mathrm{DSAV}(IDK, M, t_{dsa})$: For $IDK = \{(id_i, k_{m_{id_i}})\}$ and $C = ((id_{order_i}, m_i))$ for all $i \in \{1, 2, ..., N\}$ do as follows:
    1. Output $ERROR$ if $ctr \neq ctr_v$.
    2. For all $i \leftarrow \{1, 2, ..., N\}$, $t_i \leftarrow MAC(k_{m_{id_{order_i}}}, order_i, c_i)$.
    3. $L \leftarrow \{id_1, id_2, ..., id_N\}$.
    4. For $j \in \{1, 2, ..., M\}$, $L \leftarrow L \backslash \{id_{order_{j_1}}, ..., id_{order_{j_x}}\}$, where $G(j) = \{j_1, j_2, ..., j_x\}$, if $t_{dsa_j} = H(ctr, t_{j_1}, t_{j_2}, ..., t_{j_x})$.
    5. Output L, and $ctr_v \leftarrow ctr_v + 1$.
- $c \leftarrow \mathrm{E}(k_e, m')$: Output $c \leftarrow E_{k_e}(m')$.
- $m \leftarrow \mathrm{D}(k_e, c)$: Output $m \leftarrow D_{k_e}(c)$.

Theorem 9 (TAIT AE-security). *Suppose that the number of components whose key identification information or their orders being invalid is at most d, G is d-disjunct, SAMD meet UF-CMA security, E is a CPA-secure symmetric encryption scheme without message padding, the inputs of the aggregator are secret. In random oracle model, we have: TAIT meets AE-security.*

Proof of Theorem 9: Let E happen to implement AES counter mode. Then, CPA security of the system follows immediately from CPA security of AES counter mode. For ciphertext integrity, polynomially bounded adversary $\mathsf{A_{ci}}$ makes Q encryption queries. Each query consists of a message m_i, to which the challenger replies a ciphertext $c_i = (x_i, u_i)$, where x_i is a random IV, u_i is a one-time pad encryption of (m_i, t_{dsa_i}), where the pseudo-random pad r_i derived from IV x_i, and t_{dsa_i} is SAMD tag of m_i. We can replace the pseudo-random pad with a truly random pad, adversary $\mathsf{A_{ci}}$ will not notice any difference, otherwise there exists a polynomially bounded adversary $\mathsf{B_{aes}}$ that can break the pseudo-random of AES. We then consider two different ways that $\mathsf{A_{ci}}$ wins by outputting (x, u): one output x of $\mathsf{A_{ci}}$ is not among x_i, and the other is. For the first case, the pad r is truly random and never used, so the probability of $\mathsf{A_{ci}}$ winning is negligible. For the second one, the value u is decrypted under r_j for some $j = 1, 2, ..., Q$. Moreover, because of $(x, u) \neq (x_j, u_j)$, (m, t_{dsa}) must not equal to (m_j, t_{dsa_j}). So if $\mathsf{A_{ci}}$ wins, there exists a polynomially bounded adversary $\mathsf{B_{samd}}$ that can successfully forge a SAMD tag.

5 Comparison

In this section, we compare all the component inspection schemes that we have constructed with the related techniques such as the Merkle trees and SAMDs. Comparisons are shown in Table 1. Note that the underlying algorithm of SAMD is different from other schemes. The corresponding algorithm is MAC, while the other schemes apply cryptographic hash function.

Table 1. Scheme comparison

Scheme	Time complexity	Space complexity	Read-only memory	Secret key
SHBCI	$O(d^2 log^2 N T_H + dT_H)$	$O(d)$	✓	✗
PHBCI	$O(d^2 log^2 N T_H + dT_H)$	$O(d)$	✓	✗
MHBCI	$O(d^2 log^2 N T_H + dT_H)$	$O(d)$	✓	✗
Merkle tree	$O((N-1)T_H)$	$O(N)$	✓	✗
SAMD	$O(d^2 log^2 N T_M + dT_H)$	$O(d)$	✗	✓

Compared with the other schemes, SAMD does not need read-only memory, but its security goal is relatively more difficult to achieve. At the same time, because hash computing speed is faster than MAC, which as a result leads to the fact that SAMD is more computational expensive. Also as we have demonstrated, reasonable use of aggregator can shift the burden of computation to some extra computing devices.

Unlike other schemes, which use disjoint matrix, Merkle tree uses tree structure to provide membership proof for some elements by using a small amount of calculation and memory. But once the membership proof for all elements is required, the amount of calculation and memory required will be greatly increased, and thus lose its advantage. In addition, for mixed structure, the logical structure of tree is very complex, and non-adaptive group testing is suitable for this scenario.

6   Conclusion

In this paper, we propose a vehicle component protection scheme, and give the concrete design and security analysis of its key functional modules. In the component inspection module, we present three HBCI schemes to fit the needs of different real world requirements. The unforgeability property is partially guaranteed by read-only memory and we demonstrated the provable security for other properties as well. In addition, we give the corresponding component replacement scheme and general emergency start scheme. For the detection from the remote server module, two encryption schemes based on SAMD are given, which can meet the AE security. UAIT is the more universal one, and the security is easier to achieve, but on the other hand needs more expensive hardware costs. TAIT is more suitable for the vehicle component protection system, but the security is more difficult to achieve and less efficient than UAIT. Lastly, we compare all component inspection schemes that we have built with the related solutions from the point of view of both security and performance.

A   Security Definition of HBCI

Regarding all HBCIs, we define UF-CMA security and identifiability along with our model, which is similar to [23]. Note that the number of all participants should be determined before HBCI starts.

Let T be a tuple, $\{T\}$ denote a set containing all elements in T. π is a proof of an elements p, π^* is a proof of a set P, we define $\pi_i \odot \pi_\theta^*$ to indicate that proof π and proof π^* satisfy $p \in P$. Let G is a matrix, $G_{M \times N}\{0, 1\}$ denote that G has m rows and N columns, and all elements are 0 or 1, $G(i)$ denote a set consists of column numbers with element 1 of the ith row.

A.1   Security Definition of SHBCI

Definition 1 (SHBCI Unforgeability). *A SHBCI = (G, V, SG_θ, DSHV) scheme is d-unforgeable if no polynomially bounded adversary A has a non-negligible advantage against the Challenger in the following game:*

- *Setup* : Qur $\leftarrow \emptyset$.
- *Challenge query* : *The adversary A makes a sequence of queries. Each query consists of a sequence of order/key identification information pairs $KO = ((1, p_1), (2, p_2), ..., (N, p_N))$, to which the challenger replies $\pi_\theta \leftarrow$ SG(KO). Challenger sets* Qur $\leftarrow$ Qur $\cup (KO, \pi_\theta)$.
- *Verification query* : *A outputs $KO^* = ((1, p_1^*), ..., (N, p_N^*))$ and π_θ^* such that $(KO', \pi_\theta^*) \in$ Qur and $(KO^*, \pi_\theta^*) \notin$ Qur, Challenger computes $L^* \leftarrow$ DSHV(KO^*, π_θ^*). A wins if it holds that $L^* \neq ERROR$, $|L^*| \leq d$ and $\exists ID \notin L$ such that $ID \in \{KO^*\}\backslash\{KO^*\} \cap \{KO'\}$.*

Definition 2 (SHBCI Message-Identifiability). *A SHBCI = (G, V, SG_θ, DSHV) scheme is d-Message-Identifiability if it satisfies message-completeness and message-soundness. It holds that if no polynomially bounded adversary A has a non-negligible advantage against the Challenger in the following game:* A *outputs $((1, p_1^*, \pi_1^*), (2, p_2^*, \pi_2^*), ..., (N, p_N^*, \pi_N^*))$ and π_θ^*, then Challenger computes $L^* \leftarrow$ DSHV(KO^*, π_θ^*). If $|L^*| \leq d$,*

1. A *wins message-completeness game if it holds that $L^* \cap \{ID \mid ID \in p_i, accept \leftarrow$ V(π_i, p_i)$, \pi_i \odot \pi_\theta^*, 1 \leq i \leq N\} \neq \emptyset$.*
2. A *wins message-soundness game if it holds that $\{ID \mid ID \in p_i, reject \leftarrow$ V(π_i, p_i)$, \pi_i \odot \pi_\theta^*, 1 \leq i \leq N\}\backslash L^* \neq \emptyset$.*

Definition 3 (SHBCI Order-Identifiability). *A SHBCI = (G, V, SG_θ, DSHV) scheme is d-order-Identifiable if it satisfies order-completeness and order-soundness. It holds that if no polynomially bounded adversary A has a non-negligible advantage against the Challenger in the following game:*

- *Setup* : Qur $\leftarrow \emptyset$.
- *Challenge query* : A *makes a sequence of queries. Each query consists of a sequence of order/key identification information pairs $KO = ((1, p_1), (2, p_2), ..., (N, p_N))$, to which the challenger replies $\pi_\theta \leftarrow$ SG(KO). Challenger sets* Qur $\leftarrow$ Qur $\cup KO$.
- *Output* : A *outputs $KO^* = ((1, p_1^*), (2, p_2^*), ..., (N, p_N^*))$ and π_θ^*, Challenger computes $L^* \leftarrow$ DSHV(KO^*, π_θ^*). If $|L^*| \leq d$,*

1. A *wins order-completeness game if it holds that* $KO^* \notin$ Qur*, there exists* $\{p_1^\#, ..., p_N^\# \mid ((1, p_1^\#), (2, p_2^\#), ..., (N, p_N^\#)) \in$ Qur$\} = \{p_1^*, ..., p_N^*\}$, $\pi_\theta^* = \pi_\theta^\#$ *and* $L^* \cap \{ID \mid ID \in p_i, (i, p_i^*) \neq (i, p_i^\#), accept \leftarrow V(\pi_i, p_i^\#), accept \leftarrow V(\pi_i, p_i^*), \pi_i \odot \pi_\theta^*, 1 \leq i \leq N\} \neq \emptyset$.

2. A *wins order-soundness game if it holds that* $KO^* \notin$ Qur*, there exists* $\{p_1^\#, ..., p_N^\# \mid ((1, p_1^\#), ..., (N, p_N^\#)) \in$ Qur$\} = \{p_1^*, ..., p_N^*\}$, $\pi_\theta^* = \pi_\theta^\#$ *and* $\{ID \mid ID \in p_i, (i, p_i^*) = (i, p_i^\#), accept \leftarrow V(\pi_i, p_i^\#), accept \leftarrow V(\pi_i, p_i^*)), \pi_i \odot \pi_\theta^*, 1 \leq i \leq N\} \setminus L^* \neq \emptyset$.

A.2   Security Definition of PHBCI

Definition 4 (PHBCI Unforgeability). *A PHBCI = (G, V, PG$_\theta$, DPHV) scheme is d-unforgeable if no polynomially bounded adversary* A *has a non-negligible advantage against the Challenger in the following game:*

- *Setup :* Qur $\leftarrow \emptyset$.
- *Challenge query :* A *makes a sequence of queries. Each query consists of a tuple of key identification informations* $K = (p_1, p_2, ..., p_N)$, *to which the challenger replies* $\pi_\theta \leftarrow$ PG(K). *Challenger sets* Qur $\leftarrow$ Qur $\cup (KO, \pi_\theta)$.
- *Verification query :* A *outputs* $K^* = (p_1^*, p_2^*, ..., p_N^*)$ *and* π_θ^* *such that* $(K', \pi_\theta^*) \in$ Qur *and* $(K^*, \pi_\theta^*) \notin$ Qur*, Challenger computes* $L^* \leftarrow$ DPHV(K^*, π_θ^*). A *wins if it holds that* $L^* \neq ERROR$, $|L^*| \leq d$ *and* $\exists ID \notin L^*$ *such that* $ID \in \{K^*\} \setminus \{K^*\} \cap \{K'\}$.

Definition 5 (PHBCI Message-Identifiability). *A PHBCI = (G, V, PG$_\theta$, DPHV) scheme is d-Message-Identifiability if it satisfies message-completeness and message-soundness. It holds if no polynomially bounded adversary* A *has a non-negligible advantage against the Challenger in the following game:* A *outputs* $((p_1^*, \pi_1^*), (p_2^*, \pi_2^*), ..., (p_N^*, \pi_N^*))$ *and* π_θ^*, *then Challenger computes* $L^* \leftarrow$ DPHV(K^*, π_θ^*). *If* $|L^*| \leq d$,

1. A *wins message-completeness game if it holds that* $L^* \cap \{ID \mid ID \in p_i, accept \leftarrow V(\pi_i, p_i), \pi_i \odot \pi_\theta^*, 1 \leq i \leq N\} \neq \emptyset$.

2. A *wins message-soundness game if it holds that* $\{ID \mid ID \in p_i, reject \leftarrow V(\pi_i, p_i), \pi_i \odot \pi_\theta^*, 1 \leq i \leq N\} \setminus L^* \neq \emptyset$.

A.3   Security Definition of MHBCI

Definition 6 (MHBCI Unforgeability). *A MHBCI = (G, V, SG$_\theta$, DSHV, PG$_\theta$, DPH, DPHV, Trans) scheme is d-unforgeable if no polynomially bounded adversary* A *has a non-negligible advantage against the Challenger in the following game:*

- *Setup :* Qur $\leftarrow \emptyset$.
- *Challenge query :* A *makes a sequence of queries. Each query consists of a sequence of Structured key identification information pairs* KS*,such as* $(((1, (p_1, p_2)), (2, p_3))..., p_N)$, *to which the challenger replies* π_θ *corresponding* SG$(*)$ *and* PG$(*)$. *Challenger sets* Qur $\leftarrow$ Qur $\cup (KS, \pi_\theta)$.

– *Verification query* : A *outputs* KS^* *and* π_θ^* *such that* $(KS', \pi_\theta^*) \in$ Qur *and* $(KS^*, \pi_\theta^*) \notin$ Qur, *Challenger computes* L^* *corresponding* DPHV$(*)$ *and* DSHV$(*)$. A *wins if it holds that* $L \neq ERROR$, $|L^*| \leq d$ *and* $\exists ID \notin L^*$ *such that* $ID \in \{KS^*\} \backslash \{KS^*\} \cap \{KS'\}$.

Finally, we say that A issues at most Q signing queries.

For MHBCI's Identifiability consists of the Identifiability of SHBCIs and PHBCIs.

References

1. Bayat, M., Barmshoory, M., Rahimi, M., Aref, M.R.: A secure authentication scheme for VANETs with batch verification. Wirel. Netw. **21**(5), 1733–1743 (2015). https://doi.org/10.1007/s11276-014-0881-0
2. Chan, K.Y., Dillon, T.S., Chang, E.: An intelligent particle swarm optimization for short-term traffic flow forecasting using on-road sensor systems. IEEE Trans. Ind. Electron. **60**(10), 4714–4725 (2013)
3. Cheraghchi, M.: Improved constructions for non-adaptive threshold group testing. Algorithmica **67**(3), 384–417 (2013). https://doi.org/10.1007/s00453-013-9754-7
4. Dan Boneh, V.S.: A graduate course in applied cryptography (2020). https://crypto.stanford.edu/~dabo/cryptobook/
5. Du, D.Z., Hwang, F.K.: Combinatorial Group Testing and Its Applications. Series on Applied Mathematics, 2nd edn, vol. 12. World Scientific (2000)
6. Guo, H., Yu, F., Zhang, Z., Wong, W., Ma, M., Wu, Y.: HASVC: an efficient hybrid authentication scheme for vehicular communication. In: Proceedings of IEEE International Conference on Communications, ICC 2011, Kyoto, Japan, 5–9 June 2011, pp. 1–5. IEEE (2011)
7. Gupta, N., Manaswini, R., Saikrishna, B., da Silva e Silva, F.J., Teles, A.S.: Authentication-based secure data dissemination protocol and framework for 5G-enabled VANET. Future Internet **12**(4), 63 (2020). https://doi.org/10.3390/fi12040063
8. He, H., Yan, J.: Cyber-physical attacks and defences in the smart grid: a survey. IET Cyper-Phys. Syst. Theory Appl. **1**(1), 13–27 (2016)
9. Hirose, S., Shikata, J.: Non-adaptive group-testing aggregate MAC scheme. In: Su, C., Kikuchi, H. (eds.) ISPEC 2018. LNCS, vol. 11125, pp. 357–372. Springer, Cham (2018). https://doi.org/10.1007/978-3-319-99807-7_22
10. Horng, S., et al.: b-SPECS+: batch verification for secure pseudonymous authentication in VANET. IEEE Trans. Inf. Forensics Secur. **8**(11), 1860–1875 (2013)
11. Jo, H.J., Kim, I.S., Lee, D.H.: Reliable cooperative authentication for vehicular networks. IEEE Trans. Intell. Transp. Syst. **19**(4), 1065–1079 (2018)
12. Katz, J., Lindell, A.Y.: Aggregate message authentication codes. In: Malkin, T. (ed.) CT-RSA 2008. LNCS, vol. 4964, pp. 155–169. Springer, Heidelberg (2008). https://doi.org/10.1007/978-3-540-79263-5_10
13. Lai, C., Lu, R., Zheng, D., Shen, X.S.: Security and privacy challenges in 5G-enabled vehicular networks. IEEE Netw. **34**(2), 37–45 (2020)
14. Li, W., Song, H., Wei, Y., Zeng, F.: Toward more secure and trustworthy transportation cyber-physical systems. In: Sun, Y., Song, H. (eds.) Secure and Trustworthy Transportation Cyber-Physical Systems. SCS, pp. 87–97. Springer, Singapore (2017). https://doi.org/10.1007/978-981-10-3892-1_5

15. Liao, D., Li, H., Sun, G., Zhang, M., Chang, V.: Location and trajectory privacy preservation in 5G-enabled vehicle social network services. J. Netw. Comput. Appl. **110**, 108–118 (2018)

16. Lin, X., Sun, X., Ho, P., Shen, X.: GSIS: a secure and privacy-preserving protocol for vehicular communications. IEEE Trans. Veh. Technol. **56**(6), 3442–3456 (2007)

17. Lu, N., Zhang, N., Cheng, N., Shen, X., Mark, J.W., Bai, F.: Vehicles meet infrastructure: toward capacity-cost tradeoffs for vehicular access networks. IEEE Trans. Intell. Transp. Syst. **14**(3), 1266–1277 (2013)

18. Naranjo, P.G.V., Shojafar, M., Mostafaei, H., Pooranian, Z., Baccarelli, E.: P-SEP: a prolong stable election routing algorithm for energy-limited heterogeneous fog-supported wireless sensor networks. J. Supercomput. **73**(2), 733–755 (2017). https://doi.org/10.1007/s11227-016-1785-9

19. Munich, O.B., Stuttgart, J.D., Munich, J.P.S.: Automotive software and electronics 2030 (2019). https://www.gsaglobal.org/wp-content/uploads/2019/07/McKinsey-Report-with-GSA-Logo.pdf

20. Rajput, U., Abbas, F., Eun, H., Oh, H.: A hybrid approach for efficient privacy-preserving authentication in VANET. IEEE Access **5**, 12014–12030 (2017)

21. Ramírez-Reyna, M.A., Cruz-Pérez, F.A., Castellanos-Lopez, S.L., Hernández-Valdez, G., Rivero-Angeles, M.E.: Performance analysis of dynamic spectrum leasing strategies in coordinated cognitive radio networks. EURASIP J. Wirel. Commun. Netw. **2018** (2018). Article number: 242. https://doi.org/10.1186/s13638-018-1266-3

22. Raya, M., Hubaux, J.: Securing vehicular ad hoc networks. J. Comput. Secur. **15**(1), 39–68 (2007)

23. Sato, S., Hirose, S., Shikata, J.: Sequential aggregate MACs with detecting functionality revisited. In: Liu, J.K., Huang, X. (eds.) NSS 2019. LNCS, vol. 11928, pp. 387–407. Springer, Cham (2019). https://doi.org/10.1007/978-3-030-36938-5_23

24. Shao, J., Lin, X., Lu, R., Zuo, C.: A threshold anonymous authentication protocol for VANETs. IEEE Trans. Veh. Technol. **65**(3), 1711–1720 (2016)

25. Sun, Y., Lu, R., Lin, X., Shen, X., Su, J.: An efficient pseudonymous authentication scheme with strong privacy preservation for vehicular communications. IEEE Trans. Veh. Technol. **59**(7), 3589–3603 (2010)

26. Wu, W.-C., Liaw, H.-T.: The next generation of Internet of Things: internet of vehicles. In: Hung, J.C., Yen, N.Y., Hui, L. (eds.) FC 2017. LNEE, vol. 464, pp. 278–282. Springer, Singapore (2018). https://doi.org/10.1007/978-981-10-7398-4_29

27. Xin, X., et al.: A literature review of the research on take-over situation in autonomous driving. In: Marcus, A., Wang, W. (eds.) HCII 2019. LNCS, vol. 11585, pp. 160–169. Springer, Cham (2019). https://doi.org/10.1007/978-3-030-23538-3_12

28. Yang, B., Lei, Y.: Vehicle detection and classification for low-speed congested traffic with anisotropic magnetoresistive sensor. IEEE Sens. J. **15**(2), 1132–1138 (2014)

29. Yang, F., Li, J., Lei, T., Wang, S.: Architecture and key technologies for Internet of Vehicles: a survey. J. Commun. Inf. Netw. **2**(2), 1–17 (2017)

NEEX: An Automated and Efficient Tool for Detecting Browser Extension Fingerprint

Ting Lyu[✉], Liang Liu, Fangzhou Zhu, Jingxiu Yang, Simin Hu,
and Yanxi Huang

Nanjing University of Aeronautics and Astronautics, Nanjing 210000, Jiangsu, China
{tinglv,liangliu,fangzhouzhu,jingxiuyang,siminhu,hyx}@nuaa.edu.cn

Abstract. Browser extensions have gradually replaced plug-ins as auxiliary tools to enhance browser features, such as ad-blocking, image favorites, user agent randomization, etc. While improving user browsing experience, it also provides a new idea for web tracking. In recent years, researchers have proposed browser extension fingerprinting, which uniquely identifies a user by obtaining the list of browser extensions user-installed to realize user tracking.

In order to fully comprehend the detectability of browser extensions, we design NEEX, an automated tool to judge whether the extension can be fingerprinted. It uses extension fingerprinting based on DOM modification of a web page and our newly proposed JavaScript-based extension fingerprinting which utilizes the changes in properties of JavaScript objects caused by the implementation of extension functions. In addition, we use NEEX to conduct a comprehensive analysis of extensions on Google Chrome, which provides the largest number of extensions. In our collected data set containing 91,147 extensions, we can detect the existence of 17.68% extensions. Finally, the superiority of NEEX is proved through comparative experiments with existing works.

Keywords: Web tracking · Browser extensions · Fingerprinting · Detectability

1 Introduction

Since the emergence of the Internet, various network technologies have gradually jumped into the public's view, and people's lives have become more closely connected with the network. Among them, web technology has brought great convenience to our lives. According to statistics [4], as of December 2020, Chinese netizens alone have reached 989 million. It also carries a wider variety of

This work is supported by the National Natural Science Foundation of China under Grant No. 61402225 and the Science and Technology Funds from National State Grid Ltd. (The Research on Key Technologies of Distributed Parallel Database Storage and Processing based on Big Data).

© Springer Nature Switzerland AG 2022
W. Meng and S. K. Katsikas (Eds.): EISA 2021, CCIS 1403, pp. 21–35, 2022.
https://doi.org/10.1007/978-3-030-93956-4_2

services, such as online shopping, search engine, online video, social network, etc. While the popularization of web technology brings benefits, security and privacy issues also follow. In recent years, many scholars are committed to the research of web tracking technology and provide a lot of available countermeasures.

Traditional web tracking uses state identifiers (such as cookies) to identify a user uniquely. To combat it, the browser's privacy mode and some extensions (such as Cookie AutoDelete) automatically delete cookies and clear storage at the end of the session. In this way, the effectiveness of identification technology is reduced [7]. Eckerlsey et al. [6] proposed a stateless identification technique (i.e., browser fingerprinting), which utilizes eight attributes related to browser and system configuration, such as time zone and browser plug-in. The method does not require anything to be stored on the user's device and becomes difficult to detect. Since then, researches on user identification technology based on recessive characteristics such as browser extension list, HTML5 Canvas, CPU's clock frequency [8–10,23,24], and so on have also appeared.

Browser extensions are third-party programs written using HTML, CSS, and JavaScript to enhance the browser's functionality, which can track users like websites [11]. Some extensions directly disclose sensitive information, such as user access history and search requests to third parties [2,11,21], while others can achieve cross-domain access, which facilitates user tracking. In addition, the list of browser extensions installed by users can also be used to track users, which is called browser extension fingerprinting. Many researchers have proposed to use implicit features such as web page's DOM(Document Object Model) [5,12,13,18] and extension's WAR(Web Accessible Resources) [17] to identify different extensions, thereby infer the presence of extensions in user's browser. However, they either manually analyzed a small number of browser extensions or just tested popular extensions with a large number of users.

In order to comprehensively analyze the actual performance of browser extension fingerprinting in detecting the existence of extensions, this paper, for the first time, carries out large-scale research on the fingerprintability of browser extensions. We identify different extensions by their modification behavior of web page's DOM and their effect on the properties of JavaScript objects. On the one hand, previous work [18] shows that extensions may operate on the DOM of the browsing page, such as adding new DOM elements or removing existing DOM elements. We fingerprint the browser extension by taking advantage of how different extensions operate on the web page's DOM.

On the other hand, some extensions strengthen user privacy and enrich browsing features by requesting specific network resources or overwriting the browser's built-in functionality. This behavior changes the parsing results of the browser rendering engine and the JavaScript parsing engine, which alters the values of JavaScript properties. To this end, we propose a new method for determining the existence of extensions, that is, using the effects of different extensions on JavaScript properties to confirm whether the extensions can be fingerprinted or not.

To widely analyze whether or not browser extensions are fingerprintable, we design an automated tool called NEEX(Netting Extensions) that utilizes the extension's operations on the DOM of the accessed page and its impact on JavaScript properties. It automatically collects changes in the web page's DOM and JavaScript properties before and after the browser extension is loaded to uniquely identify an extension. In addition, we collect the largest data set of extensions on Chrome browser (65.27% market share [1]) to date and use NEEX to perform a comprehensive analysis of the fingerprintability of extensions.

In conclusion, the main contributions of this paper are as follows:

- We propose a new browser extension fingerprinting technique for determining the existence of the extensions, which identifies different extensions by their different effects on the properties of JavaScript objects.
- We design an automated tool, NEEX, to capture browser extension fingerprints, which combined extension fingerprinting based on DOM modification and extension fingerprinting based on JavaScript properties.
- We collect the largest extension database so far and conduct the first comprehensive analysis of browser extensions using NEEX. The results show that 17.68% of extensions can be fingerprinted.

The remainder of this paper is organized as follows: In Sect. 2, we introduce the relevant background of browser extension fingerprinting technology and the attack model used in this paper. Section 3 shows NEEX, an automated tool we design, and explains our proposed browser extension fingerprinting technologies. Section 4 describes the collection of experimental data, the specific implementation of the experiments, and the explanation of the results. We discuss future work in Sect. 5, and a summary is given in Sect. 6.

2 Background

Browser extensions provide additional functionality to facilitate user browsing and enhance the protection of security. However, while it provides convenience, it also brings many security risks. First, the browser grants too high permission to the extension so that it can realize cross-domain access, read the user's browsing history, and some extensions can even execute arbitrary scripts in the context of the web page [2]. This undoubtedly poses threats to users' security and privacy. Secondly, in order to realize its function, the extension may modify the information sent to the server (e.g., anti-web tracking extension User-Agent Switcher and Manager), change the web page's DOM (e.g., ad-blocking extension), etc. Finally, some extensions themselves imply sensitive information, such as Joe Biden to Joe Budden, an extension that blocks political figures, which can be alluding to the user's political leanings. And the extension Parental Control - Adult Block, which protects minors from adult sites, can expose users' age. Therefore, in recent years, the research of browser extensions has attracted more and more attention. Among them, browser extension fingerprinting that can be used for user tracking is also becoming popular.

As we all know, a web page can use JavaScript to access the navigator.plugins object to get a list of plug-ins currently installed in the user's browser.

But unlike plug-ins, browsers don't provide any API to allow pages to get the list of user-installed extensions directly. In spite of this, many researchers proposed to use the side-channel analysis technology [14–17] to indirectly obtain extensions installed on the user's browser, which can be divided into two types: DOM-based and WAR-based.

Literature [18] developed an automated system, XHound, for the first time to capture the side effects of extensions on the DOM of web pages. DOM here refers mainly to the HTML DOM, which expresses HTML documents in a tree structure. We can determine whether an extension is fingerprintable by grabbing the DOM of the web page before and after the extension is loaded.

For security reasons, browsers require extensions to declare resources (such as images, HTML, CSS, or JavaScript) accessible to web pages in their configuration file manifest.json. Pages are able to access resources through the URL:*chrome-extension://<your-extension-id>/<path/to/resource>*. The <your-extension-id> is the unique identifier of the extension and does not change once it is published in the Chrome browser.The WAR-based extension fingerprinting mainly uses <your-extension-id> to identify an extension.

2.1   Threat Model

In this paper, the attacker builts a well-designed web page or website to identify extensions installed by the current browsing user and then uniquely identify the user. The above identification can be realized by dynamically obtaining the extension's related operations on the page.

Actually, an extension that implements its function by modifying features of a web page requires certain preconditions. Take extensions of modifying the web page's DOM as an example, some of them require the page to contain specified elements or only apply to a specific domain name such as twitter.com. For the latter, XHound [18] uses the local DNS stub parser to resolve the domain name of Alexa top 50 to the localhost and uses Apache to rewrite the URL, thus capturing the fingerprint of the extension designed for the specified domain name. However, in the actual attack scenario, the attacker cannot manipulate the user host to achieve the redirection of domain name. And this measure has become infeasible, so this paper does not focus on extensions that only works for certain domain names.

On the other hand, previous studies have shown that extension fingerprinting technology using extensions' unique identifiers offers the largest number of detected extensions. However, Firefox randomly generates an extension ID for each browser instance to prevent websites from fingerprinting browsers by checking for installed extensions [22]. Although Chrome browser has not yet given specific solutions, Trickel et al. [19] has provided it with a scheme of randomization processing to extensions' unique identifiers. Therefore, extension fingerprinting based on WAR ID is not within the scope of this paper.

3   NEEX

This section mainly introduces NEEX, an automated tool we design to detect extensions. It captures the extension's operation on the DOM and JavaScript properties. Then it uses the above information to generate the fingerprint of the browser extension and uniquely identifies it. NEEX consists of three steps: preparation, fingerprint information acquisition, and fingerprint database generation. Specifically, (1) we first crawl IDs of all extensions in Chrome Web Store, along with the text of their overview that contains the introduction information to each extension. (2) The browser load extensions one by one based on the collected IDs and access our pre-built Honey Page, capturing the page's DOM and JavaScript properties. (3) Ultimately, we compare the obtained fingerprint information of each extension with the DOM and JavaScript properties of the original page. If the comparison result shows no change, the extension is undetectable. Otherwise, it is fingerprintable. We extract the changes in DOM and JavaScript properties as the extension fingerprint and store it in the fingerprint database. The overview of NEEX architecture is shown in Fig. 1 for details.

Preparation. To determine whether an extension can be detected by extension fingerprinting based on DOM modification and extension fingerprinting based on JavaScript properties, it is necessary to get the complete list of extensions to be analyzed in advance. As mentioned earlier, when a new extension is released, the Google Chrome assigns an unique ID associated with it. The unique ID is made up of 32-bit characters that do not change with updates and so on. So, we design and implement a crawler that automatically gets the IDs of all extensions on the Chrome Web Store.

Second, to ensure the integrity and comprehensiveness of Honey Page, for each extension, we visit the detailed page based on its ID and extract the first paragraph of its overview. At the same time, to eliminate the burden of text redundancy on page loading, we preprocess the text.

Capture of Fingerprint Information. To determine if an extension is detectable, we need to know whether it modifies the DOM of a web page or JavaScript properties. Therefore, we need to get the original information of the page as well as its relevant information after installing the extension. The specific steps are as follows:

(1) We download installation files of extensions from Google Chrome based on the obtained list of IDs. (2) Launch a Chrome browser using Selenium ChromeDriver and install the specified extension in the browser by adding the launch option add_extension (installation_package.crx). The parameter in brackets is the installation file captured in the first step. (3) Visit the URL of our customized Honey Page, capture the HTML DOM and JavaScript properties of the web page, and store them in different files (id_dom.html and id_js.txt). It should be noted that the HTML DOM of a web page can be captured directly by DOM APIs, while JavaScript properties are captured by injected additional JavaScript scripts into the web page. We also parse the DOM and JavaScript properties of the original page without any extensions installed as a baseline for our comparison.

Generation of Fingerprint Database. We utilize the fingerprint information captured in the previous stage to generate extension fingerprints. Specifically, we use Python difflib library to compare the .html file and .txt file of each extension with corresponding files of the original page. Then we get two diff files, that is, the comparison results of the web page's DOM and JavaScript properties. If both of them are empty, the extension is not fingerprintable. In other words, it neither modifies the DOM of the web page nor affects the properties of JavaScript objects. Otherwise, we will process the comparison results according to Sects. 3.1 and 3.2 to obtain the DOM fingerprint and JS fingerprint of the extension. Finally, the DOM fingerprint and JS fingerprint of the extension are stored in our extension fingerprint database, including the extension's ID, the addition and deletion of DOM elements, and the addition and deletion of JavaScript properties.

In the following sections, we will introduce two extension fingerprinting techniques in NEEX: DOM-based extension fingerprinting and JavaScript-based extension fingerprinting.

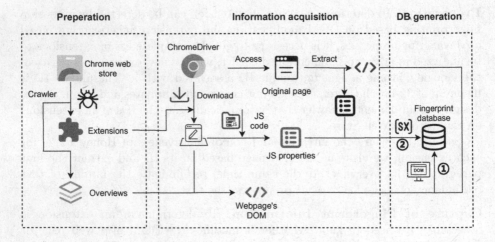

Fig. 1. Overview of NEEX architecture

3.1 DOM-Based Extension Fingerprinting

The extension implements a series of operations on the web page to realize its own functions. For example, The extension of Dark Reader modifies the web page's background color, the ad-blocking extension AdBlock filters advertisements on web pages, etc. The DOM-based extension fingerprinting identifies the extension based on the DOM changes caused by different extensions operations on the web page. The DOM modification behaviors can be divided into four categories: (1) add new DOM elements, (2) delete existing DOM elements, (3) re-assign values to existing DOM elements, and (4) replace the text content of the web page.

First, most of extensions add new DOM elements, for instance, LastPass adds an icon of password management to the HTML <input> tag, which is implemented by inserting a <style> attribute. This extension modifies the HTML DOM of a web page only if the user visits a page that contains a <input> tag. Moreover, using Grammarly, the grammar and spell checker, will add a green icon to the <textarea> of the web page.

Second, extensions deleting DOM elements mainly are used for ad blocking. Meanwhile, some of them delete specific contents like Obama Blocker. It is a filter that removes Barack Obama from pages. Such extensions we think of them as extensions modifying the text content. Third, some extensions re-assign values to existing DOM elements. For example, Trump your friend changes all images of the web page to Trump.

Finally, for extensions that replace the text content of a web page, they usually change the word or phrase specified by themselves. For example, 'Joe Biden to Joe Budden' changes all instances of the phrase 'Joe Biden' on a web page to 'Joe Budden'.

To sum up, the extension's behavior of modifying the web page's DOM requires certain triggering factors. Therefore, in order to detect as many extensions as possible, we need to design a web page. It should contain a variety of rich HTML elements that trigger the extension's action on the DOM, so as to detect the presence of extensions.

Construction of Honey Page. As mentioned above, to expand the number of detectable extensions, a Honey Page is built. We first add all tags contained in HTML5 and the basic attributes corresponding to each tag to the page. At this point, for the above four types of extensions modifying the DOM, the page can basically meet the trigger conditions of the extensions adding DOM elements or re-assign values to existing DOM elements. What's more, for extensions deleting existing DOM elements, we add advertising code into the Honey Page.

Extensions of Replacing Text Content. To trigger such extensions to modify the web page's DOM, we need to add the text content to be replaced into the web page. Because the language, length, and content of the text to be replaced by each extension are different, getting the specified text becomes a challenge.

We found that the detailed page for each extension in the Chrome Web Store contains an "overview" section that describes the functions, source address, author information, instructions for using the extension, etc. We have done a manual analysis of some extensions, and it turns out that the first paragraph of an extension overview is usually a basic description of what the extension can do. For example, the first paragraph of NOOT NOOT's overview is "Replaces swear words with NOOT NOOT". We can capture extensions that modify the particular text of the web page by simply taking the first paragraph of each extension's overview and adding it to the Honey Page. What's more, to remove text redundancy, we preprocess the obtained text: use regular expressions to remove punctuation marks and delete terminating words through natural language processing. After that, the final text content is added to Honey Page.

Extensions of Re-assigning Value of Attributes. Besides, in our manual analysis experiments, we found that some extensions modify the specified values of HTML elements. For example, the HTML5 Autoplay Blocker, which disables autoplay of all HTML5 audio and video, will modify the DOM only if the autoplay="autoplay" are included in the tag of <audio> or <video>. And the Docomplete re-enables autocomplete for password fields on websites that intentionally disable it (autocomplete=off). To capture such extensions' behaviors, we 1) get all attributes with enumerable values in HTML. 2) Similarly, use the first paragraph of the extension's overview to iterate over all the attributes obtained. 3) For an attribute that appears in the overview, add it and all of its optional values to Honey Page.

Finally, we also embed domain-specific content such as Facebook dynamic shares and YouTube videos into our Honey Page to expand the number of detectable extensions. After the above series of processing, We finally completed the construction of the Honey Page, which is used to crawl extension fingerprints based on DOM modification.

Composition of DOM-Based Fingerprint. Although Starov O et al. [18] have proved that 9.6% of the 10000 most popular extensions on Google Chrome could modify the page's DOM on any domain, thus illustrating the effectiveness of extension fingerprint based on DOM modification. However, due to the security and privacy issues of the extension program (see Sect. 2 for details), more and more researchers devote themselves to the defense research of extension fingerprinting in recent years. For instance, CloakX [19] implements extension diversification by randomizing the values of class and id attributes of HTML tags to resist DOM-based extension detection. Specifically, the scheme confuses the extension's DOM fingerprint to make the fingerprint of the same extension different for different accessing users.

In this regard, we propose an improved scheme to break the defense of CloakX by ignoring the specific values of DOM attributes. Specifically, we segment the collected extension fingerprints in tag pairs. For each tag, we only keep the tag name, the attribute name, and the text content and filter out the values of attributes. Then, the extension fingerprint based on DOM modification mainly consists of two parts: added DOM elements and deleted DOM elements, both of them are collections of tags.

3.2   JavaScript-Based Extension Fingerprinting

The researchers have put forward several effective defense measures against the WAR-based extension fingerprinting, making it invalid (see Sect. 2 for details). Although DOM-based extension fingerprinting can still detect the presence of some extensions, the number of detectable extensions is limited. To improve the detection performance of NEEX, we propose a JavaScript-based extension fingerprinting, which takes advantage of the differences in how different extensions modify JavaScript properties.

As a matter of fact, Schwarz M [20] indicates that different hardware and software environments used by different users (for example, operating systems, CPU architectures, and browsers) lead to differences in their JavaScript accessibility properties that can be used to distinguish users.

With this in mind, we conducted some experiments and found that some extensions request specific network resources or rewrite the browser functionality in order to enhance user privacy and enrich browsing features. These behaviors will cause the properties of JavaScript objects to change. To this end, we propose an extension fingerprinting technology based on JavaScript properties to detect extensions that do not modify the web page's DOM.

Collection of JavaScript Properties. To get the different effects of extensions on JavaScript properties, we first need to obtain the properties of JavaScript objects. To do this, we build a list of properties, including property names and their corresponding values. Property types mainly include function, number, string, boolean, array, and object, all of which can be captured by JavaScript.

In particular, (1) for simple properties such as number, string, and boolean, we can read the property name and the corresponding individual value directly. (2) The structure of array and object is more complicated, and their values are usually composed of the above basic types. For them, we go through their values in depth until the value is the basic data type. (3) The function is more personalized. The contents of functions are often different, and the specific call determines the result. In this regard, we get some information by properties of itself (e.g., name, length) and the source string of the function through toString().

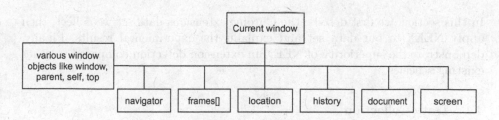

Fig. 2. Browser object model

Other objects on the client can be accessed by using the window object. This relationship constitutes the browser object model. The window object represents the root node, and the relationship between browser objects is shown in Fig. 2 [3]. Based on the browser object model, we use the reflect.ownkeys() function to traverse all JavaScript objects and their properties to build our property list.

In addition, to capture more extension fingerprints, we add some additional object properties to the property list. WebGL Fingerprint Defender and Canvas Fingerprint Defender, for example, prevent attackers from capturing information related to graphics cards by rewriting the browser's function for fingerprint recognition. This can affect the results of canvas rendering and result in WebGL and Canvas related properties change. However, they are not objects directly accessible to JavaScript, so we instantiate WebGL through HTML5 Canvas and take it as a window object to facilitate us to read its properties.

As mentioned above, the accessible HTML DOM is either referenced in the window object or exists in its child elements. Avira Password Manager, for example, modifies the (user, password) input box by adding the <svg> tag into it. What's more, it also can cause JavaScript properties to change, such as window.canvas.previousElementSibling.lastElementChild.style.style.cssText. So, we extend the Honey Page from Sect. 3.1 to capture as many extension fingerprints based on JavaScript properties as possible. We additionally inject JavaScript code into the page to get JavaScript properties.

Composition of JavaScript-Based Fingerprint. The extension fingerprint based on JavaScript properties mainly includes the newly added JavaScript properties and the deleted JavaScript properties, which are the collection of JavaScript properties and their values.

Furthermore, for some time-related properties, take the property of window.performance.timing.domLoding as an example, it returns the Unix millisecond timestamp when the DOM structure of the current web page is parsed. Obviously, its value changes dynamically according to the time when the page is loaded. Consequently, we filter this type of property through regular expressions to ensure the reliability and stability of extension fingerprints.

4   Experiment

In this section, we first descibe the Chrome extensions data set we collect, then apply NEEX to our data set and explains the experimental results. Finally, demonstrate the superiority of NEEX in extension detection compared to other existing schemes.

4.1   Data Collection

To traverse all extensions on the Chrome Web Store, we write an automated crawler. A data set containing 91,147 extensions (as shown in Table 1) is collected on Google Chrome 83.0.4103.116. It is made up of 11 categories of extensions: blogging, shopping, developer tools, photos, etc.

The following experiments are all based on this data set. We divide the above data set into 16 groups with 6,000 extensions of each, among which the last group contains 1,147 extensions. In addition, to save time and cost, we parallel our experiments on four identical servers configured with a 4-core Intel Xeon E5-2682 v4 CPU, 8 GB RAM, and Windows 2016 x64 operating system.

Table 1. Composition of extension data set

Categories	Number
Blogging	2166
Shopping	5060
Development	10729
Communication	9860
Productivity	19036
Search	5531
Sports	1561
Accessibility	8973
News	2375
Fun	13848
Photos	12008
Total	**91147**

4.2 Fingerprintability of Extensions

In this section, we apply NEEX to our data set in order to fully analyze the finger-printability of Chrome extensions. NEEX makes use of extension fingerprinting based on DOM modification and extension fingerprinting based on JavaScript properties to identify extensions, so the experiment is divided into two parts.

In the first part, we split the experiment into two phases: (1) we test extensions modifying the text of the web page. Use the first paragraph in the "overview" section of the extension's installation page to extract the text content that may trigger the modification behavior of the extension to the page's DOM. Meanwhile, we obtain the final trigger text by comparing the changes of the text content before and after loading the extension. (2) Because CloakX randomizes the values of class and ID attribute of web elements, we improve the existing DOM-based extension fingerprinting by ignoring attributes' values and keeping only the tag name, attribute name, and text to counter the defense. We evaluated the fingerprintability of extensions under CloakX's defense by crawling changes in the web page's DOM before and after the extension was loaded.

In the second part, we conduct experiments to evaluate whether the extension can be fingerprinted based on the changes of JavaScript properties before and after loading the extension, in order to verify the effectiveness of our proposed JavaScript-based extension fingerprinting technology.

The final results are shown in Fig. 3. A total of 16,166 extensions (17.68% of the entire data set) can be fingerprinted, of which 5,805 have DOM fingerprint, and 11,856 have JavaScript fingerprint. In particular, for extensions that modify the DOM of a web page, we captured 5,805 extensions that can implement DOM modification behaviorto web page without triggering conditions, 1,211 extensions operate on the web page when it contains certain specified DOM elements, and

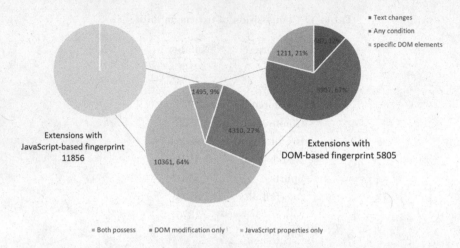

Fig. 3. Browser object model

687 extensions modify the text of the web page. Furthermore, 4,310 extensions have only DOM fingerprint, 10,361 extensions have only JavaScript fingerprint, and 1,495 extensions have both. It can be seen that our proposed extension fingerprinting based on JavaScript properties effectively expands the number of fingerprintable extensions, providing a solid foundation for web tracking based on the list of browser extensions.

4.3   Performance of Extension Detection

Based on the collected 91,147 extensions, we install a single extension on the browser in turn, collect the DOM fingerprint and JavaScript fingerprint, and count the fingerprintable extensions. In this section, in order to verify the effectiveness of NEEX in Chrome extension detection, we compare it with Xhound [18] and CloakX [19]. The detectable rate of the extension (the percentage of fingerprintable extensions in the data set) is used as the evaluation criterion.

XHound: The first fully automated system of fingerprinting browser extensions for analyzing the side effects of extensions on the DOM of the web page. The top 10,000 Chrome extensions were investigated and XHound detected that 9.2% of them introduce changes on any URL, such as adding new DOM elements and removing existing DOM elements.

CloakX: A multiphase tool is designed to diversify extensions while maintaining functional equivalence. In detail, it adds a dynamic proxy (Droxy) that dynamically intercepts DOM requests and replaces the original ID and class name of web page elements with its random counterpart. At the same time, it statically analyzes and overwrites the DOM ID and class name that Droxy cannot intercept dynamically. Although this is a defense solution for browser extension fingerprinting, Trickel E et al. experimented with the detectability of extensions using technologies such as XHound to evaluate its effectiveness. We take the results of this experiment as one of the comparison references.

Table 2 shows the experimental results of NEEX and two existing works. All of them are tested on the Chrome platform. To the best of our knowledge, this paper provides the largest data set of extensions so far, about 1.5 times that of CloakX and more than 9 times that of XHound. The NEEX's performance of extension detection is almost twice that of the two comparison schemes above. This result is mainly due to: (1) our proposed JavaScript-based extension fingerprinting. It can detect 73.34% of the total fingerprintable extensions (see Fig. 3). (2) For the extension based on DOM modification, we additionally consider the extension of modifying the value of a specific attribute, which was not covered in the previous study. (3) We conduct a separate experiment on extensions that modify a web page's text to ensure that as many such extensions as possible can be detected.

Table 2. Comparison with prior works

Attack	Platform	Extensions	Detectable	Percentage
[18]	Chrome	10000	920	9.2%
[19]	Chrome	59255	5323	8.98%
NEEX	Chrome	91147	16166	17.68%

5   Discussion and Future Work

During the implementation of NEEX, especially the capture of extension fingerprint based on DOM modification, we encountered several problems as follows. One is to catch exceptions, and the other is to load exceptions. First of all, we found that for some extensions, there is a time limit for the modification of the web page. Take the extension of Mr. Macintosh as an example, a cartoon will randomly appear anywhere on a web page and disappear in a flash when the page is loaded in a browser with the extension installed. For this type of extension, we usually have no time to catch its modifications to the page. Second, when installing some extensions into the browser, an error window will appear, indicating that the extensions cannot be loaded. Although these problems will reduce the number of detectable extensions to some extent, such extensions are only a tiny part of our data set.

In addition, for the collected extension fingerprints, we found that some extensions have similar or identical fingerprints. For instance, the extensions of ad blocking have the same modification to the page's DOM. Similarly, JavaScript-based extension fingerprints also have collisions. In this paper, we comprehensively utilize multiple browser extension fingerprints, which improved the uniqueness of fingerprints.

In real browsers, users often install multiple extensions at the same time. In this case, the fingerprint information captured is not for a single extension but the mixed fingerprint for multiple extensions. Multiple extensions'behaviors to the web page will affect each other to varying degrees. How to infer the list of extensions installed by users from the mixed fingerprints of multiple extensions is still an open problem.

6   Conclusion

To keep the browser alive in the mobile Internet era, extensions came into being. An extension is a component that extends browser functionality. It works at the browser level and is developed using HTML, CSS, and JavaScript. The convenience is accompanied by some security and privacy issues. In this paper, we focus on browser extension fingerprinting, which takes advantage of a list of extensions installed by the user to achieve the purpose of user tracking.

We propose a new JavaScript-based extension fingerprinting technology. It fingerprints different extensions using their impact on JavaScript properties. In order to analyze the detectability of browser extensions on a large scale, we design a system called NEEX, which combines extension fingerprinting based on DOM modifications and extension fingerprinting based on JavaScript properties to automatically install extensions on the browser and determine their fingerprintability. Meanwhile, we collect the largest database of extension fingerprints and carry out experiments on it with NEEX. The results show that 16,166 extensions can be fingerprinted.The NEEX's detectable rate of extensions is almost twice as much as two existing works.

References

1. Browser Market Share Worldwide. https://gs.statcounter.com/browser-market-share. Accessed 14 Jul 2021
2. Somé, D.F.: EmPoWeb: empowering web applications with browser extensions. In: 2019 IEEE Symposium on Security and Privacy (SP), pp. 227–245. IEEE (2019)
3. JS Window Object Details. http://c.biancheng.net/view/5832.html. Accessed 19 Jul 2021
4. Statistical Report on the Development of China's Internet. http://www.cnnic.net.cn/hlwfzyj/hlwxzbg/hlwtjbg/202102/t20210203_71361.htm. Accessed 19 Feb 2021
5. Acar, G., et al.: FPDetective: dusting the web for fingerprinters. In: Proceedings of the 2013 ACM SIGSAC conference on Computer and Communications Security, pp. 1129–1140 (2013)
6. Eckersley, P.: How unique is your web browser? In: Atallah, M.J., Hopper, N.J. (eds.) PETS 2010. LNCS, vol. 6205, pp. 1–18. Springer, Heidelberg (2010). https://doi.org/10.1007/978-3-642-14527-8_1
7. Vastel, A., Laperdrix, P., Rudametkin, W., Rouvoy, R.: Fp-Scanner: the privacy implications of browser fingerprint inconsistencies. In: 27th USENIX Security Symposium (USENIX Security 2018), pp. 135–150 (2018)

8. Sanchez-Rola, I., Santos, I., Balzarotti, D.: Clock around the clock: time-based device fingerprinting. In: Proceedings of the 2018 ACM SIGSAC Conference on Computer and Communications Security, pp. 1502–1514 (2018)
9. Cao, Y., Li, S., Wijmans, E., et al.: (Cross-) browser fingerprinting via OS and hardware level features. In: NDSS (2017)
10. Wu, S., Li, S., Cao, Y., Wang, N.: Rendered private: making GLSL execution uniform to prevent WebGL-based browser fingerprinting. In: 28th USENIX Security Symposium (USENIX Security 2019), pp. 1645–1660 (2019)
11. Starov, O., Nikiforakis, N.: Extended tracking powers: measuring the privacy diffusion enabled by browser extensions. In: Proceedings of the 26th International Conference on World Wide Web, pp. 1481–1490 (2017)
12. Mowery, K., Bogenreif, D., Yilek, S., Shacham, H.: Fingerprinting information in JavaScript implementations. Proc. W2SP 2(11), 180–193 (2011)
13. Nikiforakis, N., Kapravelos, A., Joosen, W., Kruegel, C., Piessens, F., Vigna, G.: Cookieless monster: exploring the ecosystem of web-based device fingerprinting. In: 2013 IEEE Symposium on Security and Privacy, pp. 541–555. IEEE (2013)
14. Gulyas, G.G., Some, D.F., Bielova, N., Castelluccia, C.: To extend or not to extend: on the uniqueness of browser extensions and web logins. In: Proceedings of the 2018 Workshop on Privacy in the Electronic Society, pp. 14–27 (2018)
15. Sanchez-Rola, I., Santos, I., Balzarotti, D.: Extension breakdown: security analysis of browsers extension resources control policies. In: 26th USENIX Security Symposium (USENIX Security 2017), pp. 679–694 (2017)
16. Sjösten, A., Van Acker, S., Picazo-Sanchez, P., Sabelfeld, A.: Latex gloves: protecting browser extensions from probing and revelation attacks. Power 57 (2018)
17. Sjösten, A., Van Acker, S., Sabelfeld, A.: Discovering browser extensions via web accessible resources. In: Proceedings of the Seventh ACM on Conference on Data and Application Security and Privacy, pp. 329–336 (2017)
18. Starov, O., Nikiforakis, N.: XHOUND: quantifying the fingerprintability of browser extensions. In: 2017 IEEE Symposium on Security and Privacy (SP), pp. 941–956. IEEE (2017)
19. Trickel, E., Starov, O., Kapravelos, A., Nikiforakis, N., Doupé, A.: Everyone is different: Client-side diversification for defending against extension fingerprinting. In: 28th USENIX Security Symposium (USENIX Security 2019), pp. 1679–1696 (2019)
20. Schwarz, M., Lackner, F., Gruss, D.: JavaScript template attacks: automatically inferring host information for targeted exploits. In: NDSS (2019)
21. Borgolte, K., Feamster, N.: Understanding the performance costs and benefits of privacy-focused browser extensions. In: Proceedings of The Web Conference 2020, pp. 2275–2286 (2020)
22. Development Guide of Mozilla Add-ons. https://developer.mozilla.org/en-US/docs/Mozilla/Add-ons/WebExtensions/manifest.json/web_accessible_resources. Accessed 21 Jul 2021
23. Nakibly, G., Shelef, G., Yudilevich, S.: Hardware fingerprinting using HTML5. arXiv preprint arXiv:1503.01408 (2015)
24. Salo, T.J.: Multi-factor fingerprints for personal computer hardware. In: MILCOM 2007-IEEE Military Communications Conference, pp. 1–7. IEEE (2007)

APHC: Auditable and Privacy Preserving Health QR Code Based on Blockchain

Pujie Jing[1] , Shixiong Yao[1,2(✉)] , and Yueyue He[1]

[1] Central China Normal University, Wuhan, China
yaosx@ccnu.edu.cn
[2] Key Laboratory of Aerospace Information Security and Trust Computing
(Wuhan University), Ministry of Education, Wuhan 430072, China

Abstract. The outbreak of COVID-19 has brought great pain to people around the world. As the epidemic continuing, prevention and control measures become particularly important. Then, the health QR code has been designed to tracing and controlling the epidemic. Through the health code, the confirmed cases and close contacts will be traced quickly. However, the health code records a great deal of residents' privacy information and if it is leaked, the consequences will be severe. Although some existing health code schemes preserve the privacy, but most of them either do not support fine-grained auditability or are centralized health code storage. Therefore, we propose an auditable and privacy-preserving health QR code scheme based on blockchain.

Keywords: Health QR code · Blockchain · CP-ABE

1 Introduction

COVID-19 erupted around the globe at the beginning of 2020. The virus has attacked more than 177 million people so far [15]. Standardized epidemic prevention has become the main task in some countries. How to identify the health status of a person, facilitate the close contacts traceability of an infected person are the significant problems at present. In order to prevent the spread of the COVID-19, many countries or businesses around the world have adopted mobile technologies to trace close contacts. China, Singapore, Australia [6] and Israel [11] were the first countries to require their citizens to use apps to trace close contacts. The technologies of close contacts tracing attract more attention, and some epidemic prevention and control methods have been proposed, such as Health QR Code (HC). As a new tool to record the health status, HC records personal and visiting information of residents. Preserving the private information behind the HC has also become an urgent issue in the adoption of health code.

Currently, the main health code schemes are classified into two categories. The first kind of scheme is based on *close contact tracing*, and the other is based on the *centralized health code management*. The representative research work of

© Springer Nature Switzerland AG 2022
W. Meng and S. K. Katsikas (Eds.): EISA 2021, CCIS 1403, pp. 36–49, 2022.
https://doi.org/10.1007/978-3-030-93956-4_3

the former includes GAEN [8] and Joseph [9] schemes. These schemes record the health code information of someone who they have recently been in contact with. The advantage of these schemes is that the close contacts can be traced via a chain or tree searching from the confirmed cases. What's more, they are not conducive to the regular epidemic audit and control by government departments. The representative research work of the latter includes COVIDSafe [6] and HaMagen [11] schemes. In this type of schemes, the data behind the health code is encrypted and stored centrally, thus, it is beneficial to audit private information. However, the centralized storage method faces with the risk of health code's privacy leakage and the single point of failure.

In order to solve the problems mentioned above, we design a privacy preserving, efficient auditable and traceable health code scheme based on blockchain for epidemic control and prevention. The main contributions include:

- We propose a non-contact health code scheme based on blockchain. It supports efficient audit and trace about the private information of the confirmed case and close contacts. It achieves efficient epidemic prevention and control.
- In order to preserve the private information behind the HC, we put forward an attribute-based encryption method to protect residents' information, such as ID, name, phone number, location etc., and to achieve fine-grained access control by audit institutions.
- For the sake of efficient auditability and traceability, we design a keyword search method to achieve multi-dimensional information audit such as ID, location, and timestamp.
- At last, we implement the prototype of this system, and proof the feasibility of this scheme through security analysis and performance evaluation.

The remainder of this paper is organized as follows. Related work will be discussed in Sect. 2. In Sect. 3, we will review the related techniques used in this paper. The system model, threat model and design goals are given in Sect. 4. In Sect. 5, we describe the specific algorithm design of this scheme. In Sect. 6 and 7, through security analysis and performance evaluation, we proof this scheme is feasible. Finally, we draw a conclusion about this paper.

2   Related Work

Currently, the main methods to prevent and control the epidemic are divided into two categories: the schemes dominated by government and industrial or academic community. Next, we will give an overview of these schemes.

The HC schemes dominated by government often belong to centralized scheme. For example, the South Korean government's scheme requires residents to provide real identity information, and the device's GPS permissions must be turned on to ensure that the government can trace these residents' locations at any time. Government can fully obtain residents' location information. Furthermore, in the TraceTogether [4] scheme proposed by the Singapore government, the government agency generates an anonymous-id for each resident.

When the residents interact in close proximity, their devices share the anonymous-id through a communication protocol (such as Bluetooth). If one of the residents is infected, the government will decrypt its stored anonymous-ID to trace their close contacts. Although the private information is stored in local device, the government is fully aware of all private information. A similar application called COVIDSafe [6] has been established by the Australian government. In addition, a contact tracing app named HaMagen was proposed by the Israeli Health Department [11]. This application downloads the infected resident's GPS information periodically from the government cloud server, and compares the location information with the location list information visited by the owner of the device. However, the centralized HC management may easily suffer the leakage of residents' private information and single point of failure.

Aimed at epidemic prevention, some commercial companies have also put forward their own schemes. Some European and American countries adopt the GAEN proposed by Apple and Google to achieve close contact tracing [8]. The device will broadcast the EphID through the Bluetooth device, and the close contacts will record their EphID from each other. When a device owner is infected, according to its EphID, the system finds close contacts for reminders. However, this scheme cannot prevent malicious residents from submitting the wrong data and causing misjudgment.

On this basis, a large number of mobile apps have also been derived, such as the Covid-watch [16] team's scheme. Each user carries a device to hold a random number and maintain a random number list. In a close contact scenario, each device updates their random list to record the close contacts. If a user is confirmed, his (her) random number will be public visible. Then, anyone can check whether he (she) has been in contact with the confirmed patient by traversing the random number list. In [9], Joseph et al. proposed a secure scheme, in which, all users can check whether they have been in contact with the confirmed patient without learning their private information. This scheme effectively avoids the false positive attack of malicious users and protects personal information. However, this scheme is not conducive to the government's epidemiological investigation.

Some scholars have proposed that the blockchain framework can be used to build contact tracing schemes. Torky and Hassanein proposed a blockchain-based framework [14] and Choudhury et al. proposed a blockchain-based scheme called CovidChain [3]. These schemes provide a concrete COVID-19 protection framework. However, these schemes are still based on close contact tracing, so health authorities (HA) can audit part of the information from blockchain rather than trace close contacts based on key information, such as time, location, etc. Therefore, they are inefficient in epidemic traceability by government department.

3   Preliminaries

In this section, we will introduce some basic technologies used in our scheme, and review the applications of these technologies.

3.1   BlockChain

Blockchain technology is a decentralized distributed storage technology [12]. Blockchain is a time-stamp-based chained data storage structure. It is generally composed of five layers [17].

The *data layer* describes the data structure of the blockchain that is a structure of "block + chain". Blocks are generally composed of a block header and a block body [13]. All blocks are linked into a chain through the hash function in chronological order. In *network layer*, the blockchain nodes communicate with each other by peer-to-peer protocols. *Consensus layer* solves the issue of data consistency. So far, the popular consensus mechanisms include PoW, PoS, DPoS, PBFT and so on. In *contract layer*, smart contracts are some script codes or protocols which do not require third-party trust endorsement. They can execute automatically when the certain condition has been triggered. The *top layer* is about the concrete application that is a privacy preserving and auditable health code in this paper.

Currently, blockchain is divided into public, consortium and private chain. The public chain is openness without permission. It is difficult to audit and supervise the data on the chain. The private chain is not suitable for multi-participation and dynamically changed membership. The consortium chain is based on a certain access mechanism such as PKI system. Only authorized nodes can join it. Therefore, we choose the consortium chain to implement our system.

3.2   Ciphertext Policy-Attribute Based Encryption (CP-ABE)

In 2007, Sahai and Waters proposed an attribute-based encryption (ABE) method [1]. After that, Goyal et al. introduced two kinds of ABE schemes [5], namely encryption based on ciphertext policy attributes (CP-ABE) and encryption based on key policy attributes (KP-ABE). The essence of ABE is a method of adding the access structure to the identity-based encryption scheme [2]. An access control policy is added to the resident's private key or ciphertext, so that some authorized residents with attributes can satisfy the access control policy.

The algorithm of CP-ABE mainly includes the following steps:

- $(Psk, Msk) \leftarrow Setup(k)$: input the security parameter k, output system public key Psk and master key Msk.
- $Usk \leftarrow KeyGen(Psk, Msk, \mathbf{A})$: input system public key Psk, master key Msk and the attribute set $\mathbf{A}$ of the data owner, output the private key Usk of the data owner.
- $CT \leftarrow Encrypt(Psk, T, A_{cp})$: input the system public key Psk, the plaintext T and the access control policy A_{cp} associated with the access policy, output the ciphertext CT.
- $T \leftarrow Decrypt(Psk, Usk, CT)$: input the system public key Psk, resident's private key Usk and the ciphertext CT, output the plaintext T.

3.3 Bilinear Mapping

Assuming $e : G \times G \rightarrow G_t$, G and G_t are two cyclic groups of prime order P, and g is the generator of G. If the following three properties are satisfied, e is a bilinear map [5].

- **Bilinear:** $\forall g, h \in G, \forall a, b \in Z_p, e(g^a, h^b) = e(g, h)^{ab}$.
- **Non-degenerate:** $e(g, g) \neq 1$.
- **Computability:** $\forall g, h \in G, e(g, h)$ can be calculated effectively in polynomial time.

4 APHC Design

4.1 System Model

In this section, we give the system model of APHC, and briefly describe the entities and workflow involved in this model. As shown in Fig. 1, this scheme includes four entities.

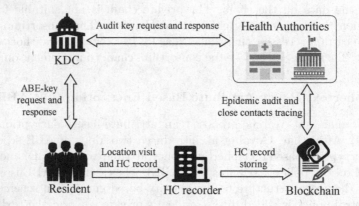

Fig. 1. The system model of APHC.

- **Key Distribution Center (KDC).** The KDC is a trusted third party. In reality, it can be the related government agency in various regions. It is responsible for the key generation and distribution.
- **Resident.** Each resident holds a health code. He (or she) registers from the authorized KDC and obtains a public key, which is used to encrypt the *personal information* in health code, such as ID, phone number or home address.
- **Health Authorities (HA).** HA mainly initiates the auditing and tracing of data. The audit institutions can decrypt, audit and trace the health code private information.
- **HC Recorder.** In practice, schools, supermarkets or business districts act as the HC recorders. They record residents' *visiting information* such as location and timestamp by scanning the health code. This information will be encrypted and uploaded to the blockchain.

The threat model is designed as follows. We assume all parties follow the cryptographic primitives in this scheme. We do not consider network security attacks (DDos attacks, etc.), computer virus attacks, and hardware attacks (destroying servers and other smart devices, powering off, etc.). We suppose that the KDC must be a trusted third party. The HC resident who can be authenticated by the KDC. The key can only be held by each entity and cannot be shared with others. HC recoders may be honest but curious. They honestly pass the ciphertext of the private health code information, but they are also curious about the content of health code ciphertexts and hope to decrypt it.

4.2   Design Goals

– **Privacy preservation.** The health code private information should not be leaked or tampered during sharing and storage. Any unauthorized data auditor cannot acquire the private information, including the personal and visiting information of the residents.
– **Auditability.** HA can audit the close contacts. When a confirmed patient appears, only those HA with corresponding authority can decrypt, view and audit.
– **Efficient traceability.** HA can upload search keywords, perform keywords matching, and obtain the new keywords (HC residents' previous locations and scan-time) in next round. Then, HA can use new keywords for multi-dimensional matching to achieve breadth and depth contact tracing.

4.3   The Workflow of APHC

In this section, we will give a description of the health code workflow in the epidemic prevention and control. The main four stages throughout this workflow are described as flows. Note that the algorithms involved in these workflows are described in Sect. 5.

(1) Entities Registration and Key Distribution
At the beginning of this scheme, all the entities should register with the KDC to request key pairs (attribute-based public and private key pairs) for health code information encryption. Besides, it needs to complete the key distribution for the authenticated residents and HAs.

(a) *Resident's ABE keys request*
A resident u_i initiates a registration request $Req = \{pID, S_{(.)}\}$ to KDC for the ABE key. KDC calls the KeyGen algorithm to generate the key (Pk_{u_i}, Sk_{u_i}). Then, the KDC will record the Resident's anonymous-ID pID and the key pairs, and respond with the Pk_{u_i} to u_i. Pk_{u_i} is used to encrypt a resident's personal information when residents scan the HC for a HC's entrance permission.

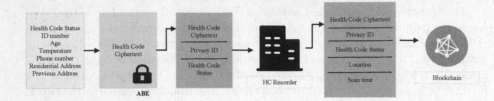

Fig. 2. The workflow of Health code private information upload

(b) *HA's auditable and traceable key request*

When a confirmed patient appears, HA can audit the epidemic according to the location and timestamp. It also can trace a confirmed patient's visited location and then zone the High-risk area. The HA with particular attribution can request sk_{u_i} from KDC to obtain residents' personal information.

(2) HC Record and Upload

When a resident visited any commercial district (HC recorder), he (she) must scan the HC code to submit his (her) personal information. And then, the HC recorder will collect this visitor's anonymous ID and visiting information, and then upload it to the Hyperledger Fabric network.

In detail, the resident executes `Encrypt` algorithm to encrypt his (her) own personal information locally, and upload $ABE - Ciphertext$ to the HC recorder through HC scanning. This process is shown in Fig. 2. Finally, HC recorder executes `Upload` algorithm to upload the encrypted result $ABE - Ciphertext$ and searches keywords on the blockchain through Smart Contract (SC).

(3) Epidemic Audit

The government, hospital, healthcare commission and some organizations serve as the HA who can audit the status of epidemic prevention and control.

In detail, HA calls the `Match` algorithm to do the match of keywords (such as location and scan time) and search keywords on the blockchain. After obtaining the matching ciphertext, HAs with different permissions can apply to KDC for different ABE decryption keys based on their audit attributes. Therefore, HAs can perform epidemic audits on health code plaintext.

HAs have different access rights to obtain the ABE decryption keys. Such as commercial security inspector, doctors, and government audit agencies.

- **Security inspector** can only obtain residents' health code status. If the red status appears, they can request the corresponding keys from KDC to access the personal information of the resident with red status.
- **Doctors** can not only obtain the health code status, but also get the residents' temperature, symptoms and so on. Therefore, doctors can obtain the decryption authority direct at those residents with red status or yellow status but with abnormal temperature.

- **Government audit agency** can investigate whether residents access high-risk areas or not. The personal information of these residents who visit a high-risk area should be traced by an audit institution regardless of their health code status.

(4) Close Contacts Tracing

When a HA discover a confirmed patient, it needs to trace close contacts based on the information of confirmed patient.

Firstly, HA calls `Decrypt` algorithm to obtain the patient's personal and visiting information, which is regarded as keywords (ID, location and timestamp and so on) for breadth search, so the close contact tracing can be realized.

Secondly, When HA needs to trace close contacts, it needs to apply to KDC for an audit and trace key, and then implements keywords match on the blockchain with `Match`. Therefore, HA will obtain the health code information of the matched close contacts. Subsequently, HA can call the `Decrypt` function to decrypt the close contact's health code ciphertext, so as to obtain a wider range of close contact information and achieve diffusion of close contact tracing.

5 Algorithms

In order to achieve the "one-to-many" relationship between the resident and the HA, this scheme uses the access control policy to perform ABE to achieve the security of the health code information. What's more, for the purpose of efficient diffusion search based on specified keywords, we design the keywords uploading and matching algorithms in the form of chaincode. The variables used in our scheme are denoted in Table 1.

Table 1. Notations used in algorithm design

Notation	Description
U	Resident set
A	Attribute set
A_{cp}	Access control policy
φ_i	Resident U_i's attribute, include: health code status ($S_{(.)}$), COVID-19 symptoms (Sym_{C-19}) Temperature anomaly ($T_{anomaly}$)
λ	Security parameter
Msk	Master system key
(Pk_{U_i}, Sk_{U_i})	Resident's public and private key pairs
M	Health code plaintext
CT	Health code ciphertext
pID	resident's anonymous-ID
W_s	Search keywords
W	Keywords
$S_{(.)}$	Health code status S_{red}, S_{yellow}, S_{green}

5.1 System Initialization Algorithm

Setup(k): The initialization algorithm executed by KDC, takes security parameter k as input, and selects a group G with prime number p as the order, where the generator is g. Next, KDC generates the attribute set $\mathbf{A} = \{\varphi_1, \varphi_1, \ldots, \varphi_n\}$ and a series of random numbers are set $\alpha, t_1, t_2, \ldots, t_n \in \{Z_p^*\}$, then $y = e(g, g)^\alpha$ and $T_j = g^{t_j}$ are obtained. Finally, KDC gets global security parameters $GP = (g, y, T_i)$ and master key $Msk = (\alpha, t_j)$, where $1 \leq j \leq n$.

5.2 System Function Algorithms

(1) KeyGen(GP, Msk, U_i, A): executed by KDC, with the input of the global security parameter GP, system master key Msk, the resident identity U_i, the attribute set $\mathbf{A}$ corresponding to U_i, output the public and private key pairs (Pk_{U_i}, SK_{U_i}). KDC selects some random numbers $\gamma, \in Z_p^*$. Then it can be calculated $d_0 = g^{\alpha - \gamma}$, , for each attribute φ_i in the $\mathbf{A}$, compute $d_j = g^{\gamma t_j^{-1}}$, then output the key of the resident U_i, $Sk_{u_i} = (d_0, d_j | \varphi_i)$, $Pk_{u_i} = g$.

(2) Encrypt(M, Pk_{u_i}, A_{cp}): executed by resident with the input of public key Pk_{u_i}, the plaintext M (HC personal data), and access control policy A_{cp}, output the CT ($ABE - ciphertext$). The algorithm process is as follows:

- Choose a random number $s \in Z_p^*$, and compute $C_0 = g^s$, $C_1 = M \cdot y^s$.
- The access control tree T corresponding to the access control policy A_{cp} as shown in Fig. 3 and Fig. 4, set the value of the root node of this access control tree to be s, and the logical parent node and child node relationship "AND" or "OR" of the access control tree can be set:
  "OR" relationship: the value assigned to the child node is also s.
  "AND" relationship: for each child node except the last one, assign a random value s_i, the last child node is s_t.

$$s_t = s - \sum_{i=1}^{t-1} s_i \tag{1}$$

The access control tree leaf values used to generate ciphertext elements. For each attribute $\varphi_{i,j} \in A_{cp}$, $C_{j,i} = T_j^{s_i}$ (i represent the index of the attribute in access control tree, $T_{anomaly}$ is 1, Sym_{C-19} is 2). Therefore, the ciphertext $CT = \{T, C_0, C_1, C_{j,i}\}$ of the plaintext M can be obtained.

(3) Decrypt(CT, Sk_{u_i}, A_{u_i}): After the HA obtains the ciphertext set, which can use the private key Sk_{u_i} to decrypt the CT. If the attribute set $\mathbf{A}_{u_i} = \{\varphi_1, \varphi_2, \ldots, \varphi_i\}$ satisfy the access control policy A_{cp}, the plaintext M can be obtained.

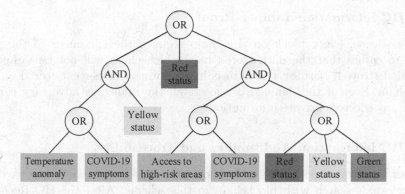

Fig. 3. Access control tree.

$$S_{red} \text{ OR } ((T_{anomaly} \text{ OR } Sym_{C-19}) \text{ AND } S_{yellow}) \text{ OR }$$
$$((Acc_{hr} \text{ OR } Sym_{C-19}) \text{ AND } (S_{red} \text{ OR } S_{yellow} \text{ OR } S_{green}))$$

Fig. 4. Access control policy

(4) `Upload((`CT, W, W_s`)`)**: HC recorder uses this algorithm to append the content ($(ABE-Ciphertext\ (CT)$ and the keywords (W)) or search keywords (W_s)) to the ledger.

(5) `Match(`W, W_s`)`**: It is a deterministic algorithm run by HA by the way of smart contract. This algorithm triggers the keywords match in smart contract, which takes keywords W and search keywords W_s as input and returns a set of corresponding $ABE - ciphertext\ (CT)$.

6   Security Analysis

In this section, we analyze the security of this scheme from the following aspects. We have proved that this scheme can achieve the prospective security goal.

6.1   HC Information Privacy Preservation

The security storage of health code data is an important feature of the auditable and privacy preserving health code scheme. In this scheme, it can be ensured that the health code information is secure during the process of encryption, storage, and auditing. Any operation on the blockchain will be recorded, so only authorized HAs can obtain the health code ciphertext, and the HA with the corresponding attribute set can decrypt it. The attribute-based encryption algorithm used in this scheme is proved to be secure in [7], so the ciphertext of the HC information is privacy-protected.

6.2   HC Information Tamper-Proof

In this scheme, every block on the chain requires the consensus of the peer nodes to ensure that the data stored in the blockchain will not be tampered with or destroyed. Besides, the data is in the form of ciphertext stored on the blockchain. Even if the damage is successful, the malicious adversary cannot obtain any effective private information.

6.3   HC Information Auditability and Traceability

In order to achieve the search for the anonymity-ID, location, and time, we combine keywords search with blockchain in this scheme. After the HC Recorder obtains the $ABE-ciphertext$ and the keywords (the health code, anonymity-ID, location, and time information), it will upload the combine of $ABE-Ciphertext$ and keywords. Malicious adversary cannot obtain any plaintext information through keywords, ensuring that the HC information cannot be leaked during the trace process.

7   Performance Evaluation

In this paper, we have implemented the prototype of APHC, and we will give a performance evaluation in this section. Based on the simulation implementation on the Hyperledger Fabric blockchain platform, the computation and storage cost of the scheme are analyzed.

7.1   Implementation

In order to verify the design in this scheme, we test the practical performance of APHC through experimental evaluation on a real blockchain platform. We build this scheme model on Ubuntu, using Docker as the chaincode management environment, and Docker-compose to configure the Docker container. Hyperledger Fabric v1.4 develops the blockchain system. As shown in Fig. 5, a consortium blockchain network based on the HLF platform is designed to audit and trace the health code information. This blockchain network includes information sharing organizations, **HC Recorder**, and **HA**.

Install chaincode (including UploadHC(), MatchHC(), DownloadHC() functions), etc. into peer and initialize. After the initialization is complete, different peers will use chaincode to complete logical operations. The HC information keywords search operation in HLF as shown in Fig. 6.

UploadHC(): This chaincode function is mainly responsible for uploading $ciph-ertext$ and $keyword$. HC recorder calls it to upload $ABE-Ciphertext$ and $keywords(W)$, and HA calls it to upload $searchkeywords(W_s)$.

MatchHC(): This chaincode function mainly completes the matching operation between the search keyword uploaded by HA and the keyword content uploaded by HC recorder. After the matching is completed, it will return the corresponding $ABE-Ciphertext$.

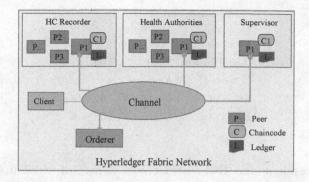

Fig. 5. Health code blockchain network based on HLF

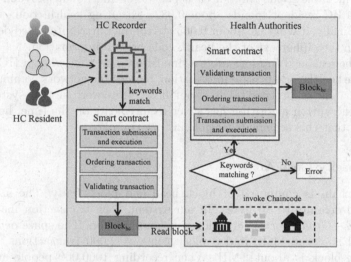

Fig. 6. Health code ciphertext search in blockchain network

`DownloadHC()`: This chaincode function mainly completes the operation of reading data from the blockchain, reading the $ABE - Ciphertext$ returned by `MatchHC()`.

7.2   Computation Cost Measurement

In APHC, pairing-based cryptography (PBC) [10] is utilized to generate the keys and the HLF blockchain platform to test the scheme, uses the discrete logarithmic difficulty equivalent to 1024 bit for the test.

Assume that a KDC contains 1000000 HC users, 500 HC Recorders, and 50 HAs. There are 3 keywords for each HC resident, 8 attributes of the HC user, and 9 leaf nodes of the access control tree.

According to the experimental data, simulation test can be conducted, and the test results are as follows:

Table 2. Computation analysis

Phase	Operation	Time
Initialization	*Setup*	0.01 s
	KeyGen	
Encryption	*Encryption*	0.082 s
Decryption	*Decrypt*	0.065 s

Each HC resident and HC recorder hold a pair of attribute-based keys. The keys are updated every day, and 50000000 pairs of keys will be generated. As shown in Table 2, the time of each pair executing Setup+KeyGen is about 0.01 s; each HC resident spends about 0.082 s executing health code encryption Encrypt; Finally, it will take about 0.065 s to conduct attribute based decryption Decrypt on the ciphertext of the health code private information.

It can be reckoned from the above simulation data that when a HC resident uploads the health code private information, besides the network communication process, the entire process takes about 0.1 s. Moreover, in this system, only the ABE encryption algorithm has strict requirements on the time, hence, it is considered that this scheme is feasible in time complexity.

7.3   Capacity Cost Analysis

The blockchain is composed of block head and block body. The size of the block head defaults to 80 bytes. In our system, each transaction mainly contains $ABE - Ciphertext$, encryption time and location. The space occupied by one record is about 1 KB, and a block contains 2,000 transactions, then the size of one block is about 2 MB. When recording 1000,000 people every day, suppose everyone visited 10 HC recorders every day, the space occupied by the health code data generated every day is about 10 GB. Thus, during three periods (the latency period of COVID-19 is 14 days [4]), 420 GB of health code privacy data will be generated. The blockchain storage can satisfy the capacity demand. Therefore, this scheme is feasible in space complexity.

8   Conclusion

In this paper, we propose a new health code privacy preserving and auditable scheme. In this scheme, we integrate attribute-based encryption, and blockchain to achieve epidemic prevention and control. It supports fine grained access control on residents' personal information and visiting information. While ensuring the privacy preserving of health code information, it ensures the efficiency of health code tracing. What's more, through the security analysis and performance evaluation, we verified the feasibility of the scheme.

References

1. Bethencourt, J., Sahai, A., Waters, B.: Ciphertext-policy attribute-based encryption. In: 2007 IEEE Symposium on Security and Privacy (SP2007), pp. 321–334. IEEE (2007)
2. Boneh, D., Franklin, M.: Identity-based encryption from the Weil pairing. SIAM J. Comput. **32**(3), 586–615 (2003)
3. Choudhury, H., Goswami, B., Gurung, S.K.: CovidChain: an anonymity preserving blockchain based framework for protection against COVID-19. arXiv preprint arXiv:2005.10607 (2020)
4. Government of Singapore: Tracetogether. https://www.tracetogether.gov.sg/
5. Goyal, V., Pandey, O., Sahai, A., Waters, B.: Attribute-based encryption for fine-grained access control of encrypted data. In: Proceedings of the 13th ACM Conference on Computer and Communications Security, pp. 89–98 (2006)
6. Australian Government Department of Health: COVIDSafe app (2020). https://www.health.gov.au/resources/apps-and-tools/covidsafe-app
7. Ibraimi, L., Tang, Q., Hartel, P., Jonker, W.: Efficient and provable secure ciphertext-policy attribute-based encryption schemes. In: Bao, F., Li, H., Wang, G. (eds.) ISPEC 2009. LNCS, vol. 5451, pp. 1–12. Springer, Heidelberg (2009). https://doi.org/10.1007/978-3-642-00843-6_1
8. Apple & Goole: Contact Tracing-Cryptography Specification v1.1, 23 April 2020. https://blog.google/documents/56/Contact_Tracing_-_Cryptography_Specification.pdf/
9. Liu, J.K., et al.: Privacy-preserving COVID-19 contact tracing app: a zero-knowledge proof approach. IACR Cryptol. ePrint Arch. **2020**, 528 (2020)
10. Lynn, B.: The pairing-based cryptography (PBC) library (2010)
11. Ministry of Home Affairs, Government of India: Hamagen (2020). https://govextra.gov.il/ministry-of-health/hamagen-app/download-en/
12. Nakamoto, S.: Bitcoin: A peer-to-peer electronic cash system. Technical report, Manubot (2019)
13. Risius, M., Spohrer, K.: A blockchain research framework. Bus. Inf. Syst. Eng. **59**(6), 385–409 (2017). https://doi.org/10.1007/s12599-017-0506-0
14. Torky, M., Hassanien, A.E.: COVID-19 blockchain framework: innovative approach. arXiv preprint arXiv:2004.06081 (2020)
15. COVID-19 Map-Johns Hopkins Coronavirus Resource Center. https://coronavirus.jhu.edu/map.html
16. COVID watch: Slowing the spread of infectious diseases using crowdsourced data. https://www.covid-watch.org/article
17. Zheng, Z., Xie, S., Dai, H., Chen, X., Wang, H.: An overview of blockchain technology: architecture, consensus, and future trends. In: 2017 IEEE International Congress on Big Data (BigData Congress), pp. 557–564. IEEE (2017)

AMLChain: Supporting Anti-money Laundering, Privacy-Preserving, Auditable Distributed Ledger

Yueyue He and Jiageng Chen(✉)

Central China Normal University, Wuhan 430079, Hubei, China
jiageng.chen@mail.ccnu.edu.cn

Abstract. Anti-money laundering (AML), as an important measure to ensure financial security and social stability, has attracted more and more attention. However, due to customer privacy protection, market competition, and other reasons, the current regulatory authorities and financial institutions have not yet formed a customer information sharing mechanism, which makes it difficult to monitor suspicious transactions. In paper, we use the distributed digital identity based on the blockchain to improve over the traditional know your customer (KYC) authentication process by combining KYC and suspicious transaction identification. With the help of cryptographic tools such as zero-knowledge proofs, suspicious interbank transactions can be effectively identified while the legal privacy is preserved.

Keywords: Anti-money laundering · Blockchain · Distributed digital identity · Zero-knowledge proofs

1 Introduction

"Money laundering" is the criminal act of legalizing illegal income and it is carried out in ways such as by providing financial accounts, facilitating the transfer of property forms, facilitating the transfer of funds, or remitting money abroad to evade legal sanctions. Money laundering is one of the most common and severe financial crimes in the financial industry. According to the statistics of the International Monetary Fund, the amount of illegal money laundering accounts for about 2% to 5% of the world's GDP every year [22]. Money laundering not only destroys the fair principle of economic activities but also destroys the market economy and orderly competition, damage the reputation of financial institutions and normal operation. It is usually associated with drug trafficking, smuggling, terrorism, corruption, tax evasion, and other serious criminal offenses, and it poses a serious threat to the economic system.

Anti-money laundering (AML) is a systematic project in which the government uses legislative and judicial forces to mobilize relevant organizations and commercial institutions to identify possible money laundering activities, deal with relevant funds and punish relevant institutions and individuals in order to prevent criminal activities. The formulation and implementation of AML are

© Springer Nature Switzerland AG 2022
W. Meng and S. K. Katsikas (Eds.): EISA 2021, CCIS 1403, pp. 50–67, 2022.
https://doi.org/10.1007/978-3-030-93956-4_4

conducive to the elimination of potential financial risks and legal risks brought by money laundering to financial institutions and the maintenance of financial security, which is of great significance to the healthy and orderly development of the world economy and society in the future [19].

1.1 Currently Existing Problems

With the deepening of international anti-terrorism and AML, Know Your Customer (KYC) has been paid more attention. Thus it makes KYC become an essential regulatory measure for this financial business scene. But for now, KYC is time-consuming and laborious, repeated authentication costs are high, and customer information privacy is difficult to guarantee [7]. On average, banks spend more than 40 million euros on KYC compliance reviews each year. Taking into account the trend of increasingly severe global supervision, some banks have invested nearly 300 million euros in increasing the KYC compliance review, AML investigations, and customer due diligence (CDD) [13]. Besides, the security and privacy of customer's authentication information can not be guaranteed, which can easily cause the leakage of customer identity information and in turn lead to the illegal use by criminals, and harm the banks and customers' interests.

Another critical step in AML is the identification of suspicious transactions [12]. However, the procedure of suspicious transaction details and the correlation with customer identification is insufficient. The suspicious transaction monitoring and analysis systems and customer information management systems of some financial institutions are independent and incompatible. The transaction also failed to effectively use the CDD results in the screening and analysis of abnormal data. Besides, various financial institutions' current customer information is not interoperable, and customers can open different accounts in different banks for money laundering. Identifying this type of suspicious transaction often has the consequence of underreporting because a single bank cannot know the complete transaction record of the customer, and the upper-level supervisory agency can only identify such suspicious transactions by accepting the routine report of the bank, which lacks real-time effect.

1.2 Contribution

To address the above problems to provide transaction integrity, confidentiality, and support secret audit, we design an AMLChain based on a consortium blockchain. In AMLChain, we use zero-knowledge proof, digital signature, and other security primitives to provide privacy protection for user identity, transaction details, and transaction accounts. Besides, according to the real-world evaluation scenario, we have defined specific privacy-preserving auditing rules to enable the regulators to monitor users' identity to identify suspicious transactions, which significantly accelerates the efficiency of suspicious interbank transactions transaction identification. Also, it changes the existing KYC certification process by effectively connecting islands of data among agencies, which can reduce the cost of KYC effectively and meet multiple regulatory requirements.

1.3   Organization

The rest of this paper is organized as follows. Related work is introduced in Sect. 2. In Sect. 3, cryptographic primitives that will be used in our scheme are introduced. In Sect. 4, the entities, threat models, and workflows in AMLChain are introduced. The specific implementation methods are introduced in Sect. 5. Then we discuss the security in Sect. 6. We compared AMLChain to the previous work in Sect. 7. Finally, we conclude our paper in Sect. 8.

2   Related Work

The emergence of distributed digital identity provides a new way to solve the existing problems of KYC authentication. It is usually represented by an identity identifier and its associated attribute declaration. Distributed digital identity includes distributed digital identity identifier (did) and verifiable claim (VC)[8]. Generally, an entity can have multiple identities, and there is no associated information between different identities, thus effectively avoiding the collection of owner identity information. VC is a descriptive statement issued by a did that endorse certain attributes of another did and attaching its digital signature to prove these attributes' authenticity. On May 30, 2008, the Canadian bankers association released the white paper on the future of Canadian digital identity authentication – joint identity authentication [23]. The system can reduce the additional cost of double submission of information and sharing information between departments, reducing fraud and misinformation. In the future, digital identity authentication would subvert the existing Internet identity entrance pattern and change people and society's connections. At present, Microsoft, WeIdentity, uPort, lifeID, and other companies have developed related projects in this field [11,16].

Blockchain is a new application model of computer technologies involving distributed data storage, consensus mechanism and widely used in the financial field. Satoshi Nakamoto proposed this concept in 2008 as Bitcoin [14]. Bitcoin is generally considered to be an anonymous payment network. But in fact, Bitcoin may be the most transparent payment network in the world. Bitcoin provides an unprecedented level of transparency, and most people have not yet adapted to such a mechanism. All Bitcoin transactions are public, traceable, and permanently stored in the Bitcoin network. The Bitcoin address is the only information needed to define the distribution and transfer destination of Bitcoin. These addresses are generated anonymously by the user's wallet. However, once the address is used, all transaction histories related to it are publicly opened and thus violate the confidentiality requirement [1]. Anyone can view the balance and all transactions of any address. Since users usually need to reveal their identities to receive services or goods, Bitcoin addresses cannot remain completely anonymous. To protect transaction privacy, Monero uses Stealth Address to hide the address of the payee, protect the privacy of the payee, use Ring Signature to hide the address of the sender, protect the privacy of the sender, and use Ring Confidential Transactions (RCT) to hide the transaction amount [20]. Zcash is based on the zk-SNARK protocol and adopts the zero-knowledge proof to protect users' privacy [18]. Solidus is a distributed ledger system that uses ORAM to hide transaction graphs and amounts between banks and customers [4]. zkLedger uses a multi-column general ledger structure to provide fast and rich audit support by using a new proof scheme using Schnorr-type non-interactive zero-knowledge proof [15]. FabZk has made improvements based on zkLedger and deployed it on the Hyperledger Fabric [10]. To implement the audit function based on privacy, PAChain [24] uses three separate modules: sender, recipient, and transaction privacy modules. All three modules provide auditability. Authentication of the sender privacy and receiver privacy modules allows it to analyze each module's security clearance. However, none of the above studies has the function of suspicious transaction identification.

3 Preliminaries

In this section, we will introduce several cryptographic tools. First introduce a mathematical assumption, bilinear groups. $\mathcal{G}$ is an algorithm, which takes as input a security parameter λ and outputs a tuple $(p, \mathbb{G}_1, \mathbb{G}_2, \mathbb{G}_T, \hat{e})$, where $\mathbb{G}_1, \mathbb{G}_2$ and $\mathbb{G}_T$ are multiplicative cyclic groups with prime order p, and $\hat{e}$: $\mathbb{G}_1 \times \mathbb{G}_2 \rightarrow \mathbb{G}_T$ is a map, which has the following three properties. The first is bilinearity: $e(A^x, B^y) = e(A, B)^{xy}$ for all $A \in \mathbb{G}_1, B \in \mathbb{G}_2$ and $x, y \in \mathbb{Z}_p$. The second is non-degeneracy: $e(u, g) \neq 1$, where 1 is the identity of $\mathbb{G}_T$. And the last is efficient computability: there exists an algorithm that can efficiently compute $e(A, B)$ for all $A \in \mathbb{G}_1$ and $B \in \mathbb{G}_2$. We use Elliptic Curve Digital Signature (ECDSA) [9] for user authorization. The three algorithms involved are as follows. $(SK, PK) \leftarrow$ KeyGen (λ) where λ is a security parameter. $\sigma \leftarrow$ Sign (SK, m) and $accept/reject \leftarrow$ Verify (PK, σ, m). In addition, we use the hidden public key signature to ensure the user's account privacy, which uses the ElGamal encryption algorithm. We also used zero-knowledge proofs when constructing specific agreements, which are described in detail below.

3.1 ElGamal Encryption

The ElGamal algorithm (Gen, Enc, Dec) is as follows:

- $(pk, sk) \leftarrow Gen()$: $x \xleftarrow{s} \mathbb{Z}_p, sk \leftarrow x, pk \leftarrow g^x$
- $(\alpha, \beta) \leftarrow Enc(pk, m)$: if $\neg(m, pk \in G)$, output $\bot; r \leftarrow \mathbb{Z}_p, \alpha \leftarrow m \cdot pk^r, \beta = g^r$
- $\alpha/\beta^{sk} \leftarrow Dec(sk, (\alpha, \beta))$ |: if$\neg(sk \in \mathbb{Z}_p \wedge \alpha, \beta \in G)$, output $\bot$; output α/β^{sk}

The ElGamal encryption is semantically secure if the Decisional Diffie-Hellman (DDH) problem is hard for $\mathbb{G}$ [21].

3.2 Hidden Public Key Signature

Solidus utilizes a hidden-public-key (HPK) signature scheme in order to authenticate transactions without exposing the sending recipient. This simple system allows a signer to sign a public key pk, which is ElGamal encrypted under the public key of a bank PK, i.e., a ciphertext $c \xleftarrow{\$} \text{Enc}\ (PK, pk)$. An HPK signature scheme (hGen, hSign, hVer) with public key PK is as follows:

- $(sk, pk) \leftarrow \text{hGen}()$: $sk \xleftarrow{\$} \mathbb{Z}_p, pk \leftarrow g^{sk}$
- $\sigma \leftarrow hSign(sk, PK, m)$: $r \xleftarrow{\$} \mathbb{Z}_p, (\alpha, \beta) \leftarrow (pk \cdot PK^r, g^r)$ construct a NIZK:
  $pf = PoK((sk, r) : (g^{sk} \cdot PK^r = \alpha) \wedge$
  $(g^r = \beta))$ with tag m. Output $\sigma = (c = (\alpha, \beta), pf)$.
- $accept/reject \leftarrow \text{hVer}(PK, \sigma, m)$: Parse $\sigma = (c, pf)$ and verify pf with PK, m, c.

3.3   Zero-Knowledge Proof

We used the Pederson Commitment to hide the amount of the transaction, and in order to satisfy the subsequent suspicious transaction identification, we used a series of non-interactive zero-knowledge proofs (NIZK). Under the random oracle model, a Σ-protocol can be converted into a NIZK statement using the Fiat-Shamir heuristic [6].

In a nutshell, zero-knowledge proofs include two parties: the prover, who has access to private data, and the verifier, who wants to be persuaded of property about that data. For example, the prover may be aware of the commitment com's opening and wishes to persuade the verifier that the committed value v is within a certain range. The prover can create a binary string p, the proof, that simultaneously persuades the verifier while revealing nothing else about v using NIZKs. The prover does not need to communicate with the verifier to verify p, and the prover can append p to the ledger, where any party in the system can validate it.

NIZK proof systems are particularly efficient for algebraic properties in cyclic groups, such as equality of values committed in Pedersen Commitments or similar.

4   AMLChain Overview

4.1   Entities

We first introduce the entities involved in our system here. They include:

Identity Authentication Center (IAC): The identity authentication center is used to confirm the true identity of the user. After determining that the identity is legal, it will issue a verifiable claim to the distributed digital identity used for authentication. An identity authority is actually a collection of trusted authorities that can issue verifiable credentials, not a single authority. For example, it can be a collection of police centers, government agencies, and universities.

User: Users manage their own distributed digital identity and verifiable claims. The user can have multiple dids, but one will be selected as the main did for subsequent suspicious transaction identification.

Regulator: The regulator will verify the user's main did, and only after the verification is passed will it issue a verifiable claim for the user's other did. The regulator will also identify suspicious transactions.

Bank: Banks can record transactions on public ledgers, and they can also perform necessary audits on transactions.

4.2 Workflow

There are 5 phases in AMLChain and the specific architecture is shown in Fig. 1.

In the setup phase, each organization will generate its own public and private key pairs, public parameters and their main did.

In the identity authentication phase, each user generates a pair of public and private key pairs, and then a main did. Then uploads the public key and main did to the IAC for registration. The IAC can authenticate the user's real-name information, and the legality of did, a user can only have one main did. The IAC then generates a VC for the main did submit by the authenticated user and uploaded its hash digest to the blockchain.

In the dedicated identity generation phase, users will generate a series of dids for their registered banks to communicate with other banks to prevent identities from being associated. After users generate these new dids, they need to submit them to the regulators for registration. When registering, the user will hand over the newly generated dids, main did, and the VC of the main did to the regulator. The regulator will issue VC for the newly generated dids after verification. After that, the user delivers the main did, new dids, and corresponding VCs to the registered bank, and the bank will open an account after verification. If the user loses the VC, he can issue an approve claim (AC) to the blockchain, allowing the verification agency to pull the VC from the backend that issued the VC.

In the transfer phase, the user will initiate the transaction. After verifying the transaction's legitimacy, the sending bank will upload the transaction record into the blockchain. The receiving bank can restore the receiving account and the transfer amount.

In the suspicious transaction identification phase, the regulator will review and identify records on the blockchain.

4.3 Algorithm Definition

We use the following algorithms to briefly describe the working mechanism of distributed digital identity.

- $(param, SK_n, PK_n) \leftarrow$ Setup(λ): Inputs security parameter λ, and outputs public parameters param and key pairs (SK_n, PK_n) for the orgnazation n.
- $did_n \leftarrow$ DIDCreate(PK_n): The did document is stored in the distributed storage, and the correspondence between the did and the public key is recorded in the document. The corresponding relationship of these identity data is anchored on the blockchain. Therefore, the user or organization n needs to upload their own public key when generating their own did.

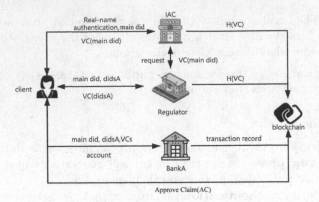

Fig. 1. AMLChain architecture

- $PK_n \leftarrow$ DIDResolve (did_n): Did resolver provides did resolution services, and can query the corresponding did document based on the did. Because the corresponding relationship between the public key and the did is recorded on the did document, the PK can be directly extracted from the did document.
- $VC_{user} \leftarrow$ VCCreat (info, did_{user}, did_{issuer}): The generation of a verifiable claim requires the issuing party to use its own did and the user's did and the related information info.
- $did_{issuer/user} \leftarrow$ FindIssuer (VC): The did of the issuer or user can be queried from the verifiable claim VC.

4.4   Threat Model

We believe that banks will respect the privacy of users but do not act honestly. For example, banks may illegally transfer money to others, manipulate account balances, and forge transactions. Besides, the bank also wants to know the customer privacy or transaction information of other banks. Our threat model only includes cryptographic attacks and does not consider other attacks such as network traffic attacks. For example, an adversary can use network traffic to determine which two banks are trading. This kind of adversary is considered beyond the scope of this article.

Identity Privacy: Except for the Identity Authentication Center, no one can associate a user's real identity with a digital identity. Nor can it be collected through trading behavior. The cryptographic adversary here attempts to associate the user's identity information through the user's transaction behavior.

Transaction Privacy: Except for the parties involved in the transaction (sending account, receiving account, and the bank they belong to), no one can know the specific amount of the transaction. Other banks cannot know the participating banks of the transaction. The adversary here includes other banks on the blockchain. They are trying to analyze the frequency of certain businesses and transactions that each bank is handling.

Account Privacy: In addition to regulatory agencies, there is no way to determine if two transactions involving the same bank involved the same account. The adversary here refers to the bank involved in the transaction, and they try to know the specific account sent to the other bank.

User Safety: Without the user's explicit permission (in the form of a signature), the balance of any user shall not be reduced, and other organizations shall not illegally use the user's digital identity. The adversary here tries to forge the user's signature to conduct an improper transaction.

Transaction Identification Integrity: The system should identify four types of suspicious transactions and suspicious behaviors: frequent transactions, large or cumulative large transactions, frequent interbank transactions, and bank collusion in money laundering behavior. Banks' collusion in money laundering refers to banks can steal assets to satisfy money laundering by uploading incorrect data and identifying this kind of behavior by auditing transactions. At the same time, the above privacy requirements should be met in the suspicious transaction identification phase.

5 Detail Description

We describe our proposed system in details here.

Setup Phase: In this phase, each organization will generate it's main did and upload it to the blockchain. Here we use the IAC as an example. Other organizations run the same function.

-Setup: The IAC first calls the Setup algorithm to get its key pair (PK_{IAC}, SK_{IAC}). Let $H : \{0,1\}^* \to \mathbb{Z}_p$ be a cryptographic hash function. IAC publishes the public parameters param. After that, IAC generates its main did did_{IAC} using the DIDCreate algorithm, associates the PK_{IAC} with the did, and finally uploads it to the blockchain.

Identity Authentication Phase: In this phase, the user registers a main did. The IAC records the user and his real identity.

-User: The user chooses a secret key as $SK_{user} \in \mathbb{Z}_p$ and computes the public key $PK_{user} = h^{SK_{user}}$, and then generates their main did through the DIDCreate algorithm, did_{user}. And after the generation is completed, the public key and main did are given to the IAC.

-IAC: After the IAC has verified the user's identity information, it will generate a VC, VC_{did} for its main did by using the VCCreate algorithm. And attach its own signature, $\sigma_{vc} \leftarrow Sign(VC, SK_{IAC})$. Finally, calculate the hash digest H(VC) for the VC and upload it to the blockchain.

Dedicated Identity Generation Phase: In this phase, the user will generate new dids for the bank and submit them to the regulator for registration. The identity information held by each agency is shown in Fig. 2. Note that the user needs to generate n new dids, where the letter n denotes the number of banks in the consortium chain. Because a bank can conduct business with other banks on the blockchain, different dids are required for the business of different banks to avoid information being collected.

-User: The user first sends his main did to the regulator and at the same time sends the VC of the main did. After the verification is passed, the user will create key pairs for generating new dids. After the generation is completed, the public keys and new dids are given to the regulator. If the user loses his VC, he can issue an AC and upload it to the blockchain.

-Regulator: First, the regulator will verify the identity of the user through the main did by the user. Then it extracts the issuer's did did_{issuer} from the VC sent by the user through the FindIssuer algorithm. And then calls the DIDResolve algorithm to extract its public key PK_{issuer} to verify the signature in the VC. $accept/reject \leftarrow$ Verify $(PK_{issuer}, \sigma, VC)$. If a user loses his own VC, the regulator can request the user to issue an AC and send it to IAC to obtain the user's VC from the IAC background. After the regulator verifies the legitimacy of the user's main did, the user-generated did, and corresponding pk are registered. In addition, the regulator will also generate a hash digest for it and upload it to the blockchain.

-IAC: When IAC receives the AC from the regulator, it will verify its legitimacy. First, IAC will find the issuer's did did_{issuer} from the AC through the FindIssuer algorithm. And then, it will extract the public key PK_{issuer} through the DIDResolve algorithm. Next, IAC will check the correctness of AC. $accept/reject \leftarrow$ Verify (PK_{user}, σ, AC). If the verification is passed, the IAC will send the user's VC offline to the regulator, and the regulator can check the hash digest recorded on the blockchain to verify its correctness.

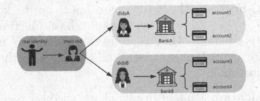

Fig. 2. Identity map

The red area is the identity information known by the IAC, indicating that the IAC can associate the user's real identity with the main did. The yellow and green areas represent the identity information known to $Bank_A$ and $Bank_B$, indicating that the bank can only see the user's main did and the dids generated for itself. The regulator can know the corresponding information of main did and dids. As for this picture, the regulator knows the relationship between main did, $dids_A$ and $dids_B$.

Transfer Phase: In this phase, users will transfer money, here is the analysis of interbank transfer. Suppose the did that Alice generated for $Bank_A$ for the business between $Bank_A$ and $Bank_B$ is recorded as is did_{AB}. The did that Bob generated for $Bank_B$ for the business between $Bank_B$ and $Bank_A$ is recorded as is did_{BA}. Alice wants to use her account in $Bank_A$ $account_1$ transfers money to Bob's $account_2$ at $Bank_B$. The transfer process and the contents of the blockchain public ledger are shown in Fig. 3.

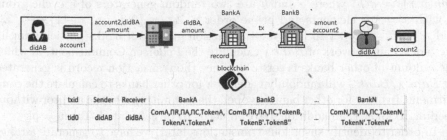

txid	Sender	Receiver	BankA	BankB	...	BankN
tid0	didAB	didBA	ComA,ПR,ПA,ПC,TokenA, TokenA'.TokenA"	ComB,ПR,ПA,ПC,TokenB, TokenB'.TokenB"	...	ComN,ПR,ПA,ПC,TokenN, TokenN'.TokenN"

Fig. 3. Transaction flow chart

-Sender: When Alice initiates a transaction, she hides Bob's account from $Bank_A$, and cannot expose her account to $Bank_B$. Each account has its own public and private key pair, and the public key is used to represent the account.

First, generate random unique txid. Since Alice's bank can only know that Alice wants to transfer the money to an account in $Bank_B$, but does not know who to transfer to, Alice needs to use $Bank_B$'s public key to hide Bob's account. Encrypt $c_r = Enc(PK_{Bank_B}, PK_{account_2})$ and she also needs to hide the specific amount v, $c_v = Enc(PK_{Bank_A}, v)$. The signature of the hidden public key allows $Bank_B$ to know that it is an account of $Bank_A$ that transfers money to it. $\sigma = hSign(SK_{account_1}, PK_{Bank_A}, (txid, (c_r, c_v))$. And finally, Alice send $(txid, did_{AB}, did_{BA}, PK_{Bank_B}, c_r, c_v, \sigma)$ to $Bank_A$.

-Sending bank: After receiving the transaction information from the sender, it will be verified, processed and sent to the receiving bank, and the required information will be uploaded to the public ledger.

$Bank_A$ will receive $(txid, did_{AB}, did_{BA}, PK_s, c_v, c_r, \sigma)$ from Alice. First, $Bank_A$ will verify this transaction: assert txid is unique $\land hVer(PK_{Bank_A}, (txid, c_v, c_r), \sigma) \land (((\alpha, \beta), \_) \leftarrow \sigma : Dec(SK_{Bank_A}, (\alpha, \beta)) = PK_{account_1})$. Finally, the bank will decrypt the transfer amount and check whether there is enough money in the user's account for this transaction. $v = Dec(SK_{Bank_A}, c_v)$. After that, the bank checks to see if there is enough balance in the user's account to make the transaction.

After verification, $Bank_A$ will generate the transaction information sent to $Bank_B$. It will encrypt the actual amount with $Bank_B$'s public key. Since a user-generated signature is attached, $Bank_B$ can verify whether $Bank_A$ has tampered with the amount. $c_v' = Enc(PK_{Bank_B}, v)$. Generate txdata $(txid, (c_v, c_r), \sigma, c_v')$. $Bank_A$ will also attach its signature. $\sigma_s = sign(SK_{Bank_A}, txdata)$. Finally,

$Bank_A$ *will* send (txid, did_{AB}, did_{BA}, txdata, σ_s) to $Bank_B$. Next, $Bank_A$ will generate a transfer record and record it in the public ledger of the blockchain for audit.

Here we use Pedersen Commitment to hide the transaction amount. Com = $com(v, r) = g^v h^r$ where g and h are two random generators of a cyclic group $\mathbb{G}$ with $s = |\mathbb{G}|$ elements and prime order p, $\mathbb{Z}_p = \{0, 1, \cdots, s - 1\}, v \in \mathbb{Z}_p$, and $r \in \mathbb{Z}_p$. In order to hide the transaction graph, all banks participating in the blockchain network of $Bank_A$ calculate the Pedersen Commitment, in which the amount of other banks is set to 0. Since the transaction record is generated by $Bank_A$, $Bank_A$ will randomly generate r for other banks to calculate the commitment. In order for other banks to open the commitment to the auditor without needing to know r, an additional Token needs to be calculated, Token = pk^r.

In order to identify suspicious transactions later, we have to generate a range proof for each transaction which is constructed with bulletproof [3]. First, the upper and lower limits of the transaction amount will be determined by $Bank_A$, which are represented by l and r respectively. In this way, the regulator can know the type of the transaction. $\Pi_R = ZK(v, r' : \text{Com} \wedge l \leqslant v \leqslant r)$. Where $ZK(v, r' : \text{Com})$ is a zero-knowledge proof of v such that Com = $g^v h^r$, g and h are known to the verifier, r' is a random number different from the r above. We also need to produce a range proof for the remaining balance of the spending bank: $\Pi_A = ZK(v_A, r_A : \text{Com}_A \wedge l \leqslant v_A \leqslant r)$. Where $ZK(v_A, r_A : \text{Com}_A)$ is a zero-knowledge proof of v_A such that $\text{Com}_A = g^{v_A} h^{r_A}$, g and h are known to the verifier, $v_A = \sum_{i=0}^m v_i$, r_A is a random number different from the r above, l and r are two bound values, m is the number of rows.

The above proof is based on a hypothetical premise, com(v,r) and $Token = PK^r$ use the same r. Therefore, we must make the transaction initiator ensure that the two r are equal when constructing the data. So the sending bank need to construct a proof of consistency expressed as Π_C, and save this proof in each cell so that other orgnazations can authenticate. In addition, two tokens need to be generated $Token'$ and $Token''$ help to construct the proof. The proof here is constructed with a variant of Chaum-Pedersen [5]. For the spending orgnization, $Token' = PK^{r_A}$, $Token'' = t \cdot (\text{Com}_A / s)^{SK}$. For other orgnization, $Token' = Token \cdot (\text{Com}_A / s)^{SK}$, $Token'' = PK^{r_A}$. $s = \prod_{i=0}^m \text{Com}_i = g^{\sum_{i=0}^m v_i} h^{\sum r_i}$ and $t = \prod_{i=0}^m Token_i = h^{SK \sum_{i=0}^m r_i}$.

Finally, the information to be recorded on the public ledger is
$\langle did_{AB}, did_{BA}, \text{Com}_i, Token_i, \Pi_R, \Pi_A, \Pi_C, Token'_i, Token''_i \rangle$.

-Receiving bank: After receiving (did_A, did_B, txid, txdata, σ_s) from $Bank_A$, $Bank_B$ will verify the transaction: assert txid is unique $\wedge Verify(PK_{Bank_A}$, txdata, $\sigma_s) \wedge$ all proofs in txdata are valid. Retrieve $(txid, (c_v, c_r), \sigma, c'_v)$ from txdata. $v \leftarrow Dec(SK_{Bank_B}, c'_v)$; $PK_{account_2} = Dec(SK_{Bank_B}, c_r)$.

Suspicious Transaction Identification Phase: In this phase, the regulator will perform transaction identification based on the contents of the public ledger.

-Frequent transactions: Frequent transactions here refer to more than 20 transactions per day. Because the regulator can know the relationship between the user's main did and other dids. Each user has only one main did. In other words, the regulator can identify the behavior of the same user conducting transactions in different banks.

-Large transaction: The large amount here does not necessarily mean that a single transaction exceeds the limit. Still, it can also mean that the same user performs multiple small transactions within a certain period to make the total amount exceed the limit. Since we have generated a range proof Π_R for each transaction, the regulator here can know the range of the transaction. The specific method is as follows. Since the range proof is constructed with bullet-proof, and the construction is non-interactive proof. The proof include a Pederson Commitment $Com = com(v, r')$. Two pedersen vector commitments A, S with a binding value mu. Two linear vector polynomials are denoted by $\vec{t}$ with a binding value τ and an inner-product proof IPP. Two pedersen commitments to the two coefficients of $\vec{t}$ denoted by T_1 and T_2. Three challenges are x, y, z. Because it is non-interactive, all random challenges are replaced by hash functions, such as y = H(A, S) and z = H(A, S, y). Besides, since the regulator can know the user's main did through the did on the ledger, the regulator can identify accumulated large transactions by recording the number of transactions and the range of transactions of the same person.

-Frequent interbank transactions: Since the user will go to the regulator to register when registering the dids for the bank, the regulator knows the bank to which they belong, so it can identify whether it involves frequent multi-bank transfers through the did record the public ledger.

-Bank conspiracy to launder money: This kind of money laundering method is relatively rare, mainly to prevent the bank from registering the wrong transaction information on the blockchain, to achieve money laundering.

First, make sure that the transaction is in balance when registering the transaction and there is no negative amount, otherwise the bank can steal the amount from it. Since the transaction initiator limits all blinding factors when generating pederson commitments, namely $\sum_{i=1}^{N} r_i = 0$. Due to the homomorphism promised by pederson, com = $com(v1, r1) * com(v2, r2) = \left(g^{v1}h^{r1}\right) * \left(g^{v2}h^{r2}\right) = g^{v1+v2}h^{r1 \cdot r2}$. If in a row, the sum of all the amounts v and all the blinding factors r are all 0, then the result of the commitment multiplication should be 1. So the regulator only need to verify whether the result of $\prod_{i=1}^{N} Com_i = \left(g^{\sum_{i=1}^{N} v_i}\right) \cdot \left(h^{\sum_{i=1}^{N} r_i}\right)$ is 1 where N is the number of columns. In this way, the regulator can ensure that the amount spent is equal to the amount received. Combined with the range proof for each transaction, it can also ensure that the amount is not negative.

Due to the use of the table structure, the records of other banks are also recorded by the transaction initiating bank, so it is necessary to ensure that the assets of other banks are not stolen. The specific method is as follows Token $_n \cdot g^{SK \cdot v_n} = (Com_n)^{SK}$, where SK is the bank's private key and v_n is its transaction amount.

Simultaneously, the regulator should check that the bank has sufficient assets through Π_A. Since the bulletproof is used, it will not be detailed here. In the previous section, we know that all these proofs are implemented under the premise of using the same parameters, which can be checked by Π_C. The specific method is as follows.

$$\Pi_C = \mathrm{ZK}_1 \left(g_1^{x_1}, y_1^{x_1} \wedge g_1^{ran_1}, y_1^{ran_1}, \mathrm{CHA}_1, RES_1 \right)$$
$$\wedge \mathrm{ZK}_2 \left(g_2^{x_2}, y_2^{x_2} \wedge g_2^{ran_2}, y_2^{ran_2}, \mathrm{CHA}_2, \mathrm{RES}_2 \right)$$

ZK stands for non-interactive zero-knowledge proof, $g_1^{x_1}$ and $g_2^{x_2}$ are two generalized Schnorr proofs, ran_1 and ran_2 are two random numbers, $\mathrm{CHA}_1 = \mathrm{Hash}\,(\mathrm{Token}')$, $\mathrm{CHA}_2 = \mathrm{Hash}(\mathrm{Token}'')$ $\mathrm{RES}_1 = ran_1 + x_1\,\mathrm{CHA}_1$, $\mathrm{RES}_2 = ran_2 + x_2\,\mathrm{CHA}_2, g_1 = \left(\prod_{i=0}^{m} \mathrm{Com}_i \right) / \mathrm{Com}_A, y_1 = \left(\prod_{i=0}^{m} \mathrm{Token}_i \right) / \mathrm{Token}', g_2 = \mathrm{PK}, y_2 = \mathrm{Token}/\mathrm{Token}''$ $\left(\prod_{i=0}^{m} \mathrm{Com}_i \right) / \mathrm{Com}_A, y_1 = \left(\prod_{i=0}^{m} \mathrm{Token}_i \right) / \mathrm{Token}', g_2 =. \mathrm{PK}, y_2 = \mathrm{Token}/\mathrm{Token}''$ the verifier first checks if $g^{\mathrm{RES}} = (g^x)^{\mathrm{CHA}} g^{ran}$ and if $y^{\mathrm{RES}} = (y^x)^{\mathrm{CHA}} y^{ran}$ for the two non-interactive Σ protocols ZK_1 and ZK_2. The specific proof process is as follows.

For the transaction initiator:

$$g_1^{\mathrm{SK}} = \left(\prod_{i=0}^{m} \mathrm{Com}_i \right)^{\mathrm{SK}} / (\mathrm{Com}_A)^{\mathrm{SK}} = (g^{\sum_{i=0}^{m} u_i} h^{\sum_{i=0}^{m} r_i})^{\mathrm{SK}} / (g^{\sum_{i=0}^{m} u_i} h^{r_A})^{\mathrm{SK}}$$

$$= (h^{\sum_{i=0}^{m} r_i})^{\mathrm{SK}} / (h^{r_A})^{\mathrm{SK}} = t/\mathrm{PK}^{r_A} = y_1$$

$$g_2^{r-r_A} = \mathrm{PK}^{r-r_A} = \left(\prod_{i=0}^{m} \mathrm{Com}_i \right)^{\mathrm{SK}} / (\mathrm{Com}_A)^{\mathrm{SK}} = \mathrm{Token}/\mathrm{Token}''$$

$$= y_2$$

For other Banks:
$$g_1^{\mathrm{SK}} = (s/\mathrm{Com}_A)^{\mathrm{SK}} = t/\mathrm{Token}' = y_1$$
$$g_2^{r-r_A} = \mathrm{PK}^{r-r_A} = \mathrm{Token}/\mathrm{Token}'' = y_2$$

6 Security Discussion

We now discuss the security of our system, according to the threat model we defined in Sect. 4.4.

Lemma 1. *AMLChain can provide identity privacy, if the digital identity complies with the W3C issued decentralized identifier specification.*

We believe that the identity authentication center is credible and will not disclose the real information of users. The user will register a main did. Through parsing, the attacker can find the did document corresponding to the did on the blockchain. The did document includes the did's unique identification code, the public key list and the detailed information of the public key (holder, encryption algorithm, key status, etc.), and the did holder's description of other personal attributes. But no information can reveal the actual identity of the user. Therefore, the attacker cannot determine the real identity of the user from the did. In addition, for each bank, the user will generate n dedicated dids, where n is the number of banks joining the blockchain. In this way, the interaction between different banks uses different did, which can avoid other banks knowing which two banks are conducting transactions, thus ensuring the bank's identity privacy.

Lemma 2. *AMLChain can provide transaction privacy, if the homomorphic commitment used is secure.*

When the originating bank uploads the transaction record to the blockchain, it will hide the amount with a commitment during registration. The AMLChain uses Pederson Commitment which is a secure homomorphic commitment. And the commitment to a value v is com = COM(v,r) = $g^v h^r$. The value v is private because it satisfies the hiding property.

Since the transaction registration party will generate commitments for all banks on the blockchain, there is a $size-n$ vector for each bank, $\vec{coin}$, committing values to $\vec{v}$. Each commitment uses a new randomness r_k. Most of the entries will contain the commitment of value 0, but this is not obvious to an outside observer for banks that are not involved in the transaction.

Lemma 3. *The system provides account privacy if the Decisional Diffie-Hellman (DDH) problem is hard for $\mathbb{G}$ and the zero-knowledge proof in HPK is sound.*

AMLChain uses the HPK in Solidus to authenticate the transaction without exposing the sending account. This method allows a signer to sign for the public key pk of a signing account called ElGamal encrypted under the public key PK of a bank. Hence, the recipient only knows that a valid signature has been created with respect to some account in the sending bank but does not learn anything about it. The specific algorithm is as follows.
-Proof Generation

1. Randomly choose $r \in \mathbb{Z}_p$
2. Compute $(\alpha, \beta) \leftarrow \text{Enc}(PK, pk)$
3. Compute the challenge e = $\text{H}(\alpha, \beta, PK, m)$
4. Compute z = r + eSK
5. Output the proof pf

-Proof Verification

1. Compute e = $H(\alpha, \beta, PK, m)$
2. Accept the proof if and only if $g^z = \beta PK^e$

As we use the NIZK to generate the hSign function, so it satisfies these properties, completeness and Zero-knowledge. As to the completeness, we can see it simply from the hSign equation. As to the zero-knowledge, the simulator first chooses a random z and then computes $\beta = g^z PK^{-e}$. In this way, the simulator can respond to any challenge.

Since the user's account pk is ElGamal encrypted by the sending bank, only the sending bank can know the specific account. When the receiving bank verifies, through NIZK's zero-knowledge, it can only know that it is a legitimate account belonging to the sender's bank conducting transactions. Still, it does not know the specific account.

Lemma 4. *AMLChain provides account privacy under the random oracle model.*

Pointcheval and Stern have proved that based on the elliptic curve discrete logarithm problem and the hash function used is a random function, ECDSA is unforgeable under the existing circumstances for selected plaintext attacks [17]. Browl proved that ECDSA itself is safe under the premise that a basic group is an ordinary group, and the hash function used is anti-collision [2]. Therefore, the adversary cannot forge the signature for authorization or transaction.

Lemma 5. *AMLChain provides transaction identification integrity if the non-interactive zero-knowledge proofs in equation above are sound.*

In the previous sections, four types of suspicious transaction identification methods have been explained. Therefore, this part mainly analyzes how to ensure users' and banks' privacy in the process of identifying transactions.

The identification of frequent transactions, large transactions, and frequent interbank transactions is completed by monitoring the did on the public ledger through the smart contract. When a user opens an account in a bank, multiple dids will be generated to process transactions between the bank and different banks. Therefore, other organizations on the blockchain can't get their business by associating did with their banks. There is a basic premise that banks will not disclose their own did information to other banks. Besides, due to the use of table structure to record transactions, other organizations can not observe which two banks are trading to ensure bank privacy.

The special suspicious transaction is the collusive transaction between banks, which is equivalent to a privacy audit.

First of all, the regulator must ensure the balance between income and expenditure. The regulator only needs to add up all the commitment values in a row and then verify that the total amount is equal to 1 to prove that the transaction is balanced. There is no need to open the commitment during the verification process, so it will not divulge additional information.

Secondly, each bank must ensure that its asset registration is correct. For the banks that are not involved in the transaction, the registered amount should be 0. They can use their Token to check whether the transaction is correct. Token $m \cdot g^{\text{SK} \cdot v_m} = (\text{Com}_m)^{\text{SK}}$. T. So once the registered amount is wrong, fraud can be detected by the bank.

Regulators will need to know if the bank has adequate funds to carry out the transaction. The prover generates a range proof for the remaining balance of the spending organization: $\Pi_A = \text{ZK}(v_A, r_A : \text{Com}_A \wedge r \leqslant v \leqslant l)$ where $\text{ZK}(v_A, r_A : \text{Com}_A)$ is a zero-knowledge proof of v_A. And use the BulletProofs internal-product range proof to prove that the remaining assets of an account. Here the attacker wants to know more than verify the correctness of the asset. A simulator is used to prove zero-knowledge, which provides a distribution of proofs for $(g, h \in \mathbb{G}, \mathbf{g}, \mathbf{h} \in \mathbb{G}^{n \cdot m}, \mathbf{V} \in \mathbb{G}^m)$. The simulator uniformly selects all proof elements and challenges from their respective domains at random or explicitly calculates them as defined in the protocol. According to the verification equations, S and T_1 are computed.

Table 1. Comparison with existing schemes

Schemes	Sender privacy	Recipient privacy	Transaction privacy	Privacy audit	Transaction graph	Transaction identification	Efficiency
Bitcoin	weak	weak	nonsupport	nonsupport	nonsupport	nonsupport	-
Monero	medium	strong	strong	nonsupport	support	nonsupport	-
PAChain	medium	strong	strong	strong	support	nonsupport	-
Zcash	strong	strong	strong	strong	nonsupport	nonsupport	-
Solidus	strong	strong	strong	strong	nonsupport	nonsupport	-
zkLedger	-	-	strong	strong	support	nonsupport	weak
FabZK	-	-	strong	strong	support	nonsupport	medium
This Paper	strong	strong	strong	strong	support	support	medium

○: nonsupport; ◔: weak; ◑: medium; ◕: strong; ●: support; - : uninvolved

$$S = \left(h^{-\mu} \cdot A \cdot \mathbf{g}^{-z-1} \cdot \mathbf{h}'^{z \cdot \mathbf{y}^{n \cdot m} - \mathbf{r}} \prod_{j=1}^{m} \mathbf{h}_{[(j-1) \cdot m : j \cdot m]}^{z^{j+1} \cdot 2^n} \right)^{-x^{-1}}$$

$$T_1 = \left(h^{-\tau_x} g^{k(y,z) + z \cdot \langle \mathbf{1}^{n \cdot m}, \mathbf{y}^{n \cdot m} \rangle - t} \cdot \mathbf{V}^{z^2} \cdot \mathbf{z}^m \cdot T_2^{x^2} \right)^{-x^{-1}}$$

The simulator runs the inner-product argument with the simulated witness (l, r). Both components in the evidence are either randomly distributed independently, or the verification equations completely describe their relationship. As we can simulate the witness effectively, the inner-product statement remains zero information. But it won't leak details.

The regulator also needs to ensure that banks have not generated proofs with different parameters, which can prevent malicious banks from tampering with data. The AMLChain uses a variant of Chaum-Pedersen's zero-knowledge proofs to construct the proof. Since the NIZK is correct, the following equation should hold.

1. for the spending bank
$g_1^{SK} = \left(\prod_{i=0}^{m} \mathrm{Com}_i \right)^{SK} / (\mathrm{Com_A})^{SK}$; $g_2^{r - r_A} = \left(\prod_{i=0}^{m} \mathrm{Com}_i \right)^{SK} / (\mathrm{Com_A})^{SK}$
2. for other banks
$g_1^{SK} = (s / \mathrm{Com_A})^{SK}$; $g_2^{r - r_A} = \mathrm{Token} / \mathrm{Token}''$

7   Compare with Related Work

In this section, the AMLChain proposed in this article is compared with the financial applications of several blockchains. The selected functions are sender privacy, recipient privacy, transaction privacy, hidden transaction graph, privacy audit, and suspicious transaction identification, which are shown in Table 1.

In Sect. 2, we have analyzed that Bitcoin does not guarantee the privacy of users. Among the three digital currencies, Zcash has the strongest privacy. PAChain can conduct a privacy audit on the premise of providing user privacy. zkLedger and FabZK use table structure to hide transaction graphs, but they only analyze the flow direction of the transaction at the bank level. Although

Solidus analyzes the flow of transactions at the user level, it cannot hide the transaction graph. Due to the use of distributed digital identities, AMLChain protects user privacy from the source. At the same time, the table structure is used to hide the transaction graph, and on this basis, it also provides a suspicious transaction identification function. As AMLChain deals with transactions between banks, we mainly compare the efficiency with Solidus, zkLedger, and FabZK. Solidus is a privacy-preserving distributed ledger with online authentication that can process 3–4 transactions per second. zkLedger and Solidus have similar performances. zkLedger can generate verifiable correct answers to auditor queries for 100,000 transactions in less than ten milliseconds. FabZK has lower latency by improving the validation scheme. FabZK has a throughput of up to 180 times that of zkLedger. The performance of AMLChain is comparable to that of FabZK.

8   Conclusion

In this paper, we focus on the existing problems in AML supervision in the banking industry. The consortium blockchain is applied to the AML system with the help of cryptographic knowledge such as zero-knowledge proofs to achieve user privacy. Simultaneously, we use distributed digital identity to improve the traditional KYC authentication process to combine customer identity and suspicious transaction identification, which can help improve interbank suspicious transaction identification efficiency. The blockchain-based architecture provides a strong guarantee for data integrity and availability. As a result, our solution has several advantages over the previous ones regarding privacy functionalities and efficiency.

References

1. Androulaki, E., Karame, G.O., Roeschlin, M., Scherer, T., Capkun, S.: Evaluating user privacy in bitcoin. In: Sadeghi, A.-R. (ed.) FC 2013. LNCS, vol. 7859, pp. 34–51. Springer, Heidelberg (2013). https://doi.org/10.1007/978-3-642-39884-1_4
2. Brown, M., Hankerson, D., López, J., Menezes, A.: Software implementation of the NIST elliptic curves over prime fields. In: Naccache, D. (ed.) CT-RSA 2001. LNCS, vol. 2020, pp. 250–265. Springer, Heidelberg (2001). https://doi.org/10.1007/3-540-45353-9_19
3. Bünz, B., Bootle, J., Boneh, D., Poelstra, A., Wuille, P., Maxwell, G.: Bulletproofs: short proofs for confidential transactions and more. In: 2018 IEEE Symposium on Security and Privacy (SP), pp. 315–334. IEEE (2018)
4. Cecchetti, E., Zhang, F., Ji, Y., Kosba, A., Juels, A., Shi, E.: Solidus: confidential distributed ledger transactions via PVORM. In: Proceedings of the 2017 ACM SIGSAC Conference on Computer and Communications Security, pp. 701–717 (2017)
5. Chaum, D., Pedersen, T.P.: Wallet databases with observers. In: Brickell, E.F. (ed.) CRYPTO 1992. LNCS, vol. 740, pp. 89–105. Springer, Heidelberg (1993). https://doi.org/10.1007/3-540-48071-4_7

6. Fiat, A., Shamir, A.: How to prove yourself: practical solutions to identification and signature problems. In: Odlyzko, A.M. (ed.) CRYPTO 1986. LNCS, vol. 263, pp. 186–194. Springer, Heidelberg (1987). https://doi.org/10.1007/3-540-47721-7_12

7. Gill, M., Taylor, G.: Preventing money laundering or obstructing business? financial companies' perspectives on 'know your customer'procedures. Br. J. Criminol. **44**(4), 582–594 (2004)

8. Gstrein, O.J., Kochenov, D.: Digital identity and distributed ledger technology: paving the way to a neo-feudal brave new world? Front. Blockchain **3**, 10 (2020)

9. Johnson, D., Menezes, A., Vanstone, S.: The elliptic curve digital signature algorithm (ECDSA). Int. J. Inf. Secur. **1**(1), 36–63 (2001)

10. Kang, H., Dai, T., Jean-Louis, N., Tao, S., Gu, X.: Fabzk: supporting privacy-preserving, auditable smart contracts in hyperledger fabric. In: 2019 49th Annual IEEE/IFIP International Conference on Dependable Systems and Networks (DSN), pp. 543–555. IEEE (2019)

11. Larina, T.V., Ozyumenko, V.I., Kurteš, S.: I-identity vs we-identity in language and discourse: Anglo-Slavonic perspectives. Lodz Papers Pragmat. **13**(1), 109–128 (2017)

12. Luo, X.: Suspicious transaction detection for anti-money laundering. Int. J. Secur. Its Appl. **8**(2), 157–166 (2014)

13. Mugarura, N.: Customer due diligence (CDD) mandate and the propensity of its application as a global AML paradigm. J. Money Laund. Control **17** (2014)

14. Nakamoto, S.: Bitcoin: A Peer-to-peer Electronic Cash System (2008)

15. Narula, N., Vasquez, W., Virza, M.: zkledger: Privacy-preserving auditing for distributed ledgers. In: 15th {USENIX} Symposium on Networked Systems Design and Implementation ({NSDI} 2018), pp. 65–80 (2018)

16. Panait, A.-E., Olimid, R.F., Stefanescu, A.: Analysis of uPort open, an identity management blockchain-based solution. In: Gritzalis, S., Weippl, E.R., Kotsis, G., Tjoa, A.M., Khalil, I. (eds.) TrustBus 2020. LNCS, vol. 12395, pp. 3–13. Springer, Cham (2020). https://doi.org/10.1007/978-3-030-58986-8_1

17. Pointcheval, D., Stern, J.: Security Proofs for signature schemes. In: Maurer, U. (ed.) EUROCRYPT 1996. LNCS, vol. 1070, pp. 387–398. Springer, Heidelberg (1996). https://doi.org/10.1007/3-540-68339-9_33

18. Sasson, E.B., et al.: Decentralized anonymous payments from bitcoin. In: 2014 IEEE Symposium on Security and Privacy, pp. 459–474. IEEE (2014)

19. Sullivan, K.: Anti-Money Laundering in a Nutshell. Apress, Berkeley (2015)

20. Sun, S.-F., Au, M.H., Liu, J.K., Yuen, T.H.: RingCT 2.0: a compact accumulator-based (linkable ring signature) protocol for blockchain cryptocurrency Monero. In: Foley, S.N., Gollmann, D., Snekkenes, E. (eds.) ESORICS 2017. LNCS, vol. 10493, pp. 456–474. Springer, Cham (2017). https://doi.org/10.1007/978-3-319-66399-9_25

21. Tsiounis, Y., Yung, M.: On the security of ElGamal based encryption. In: Imai, H., Zheng, Y. (eds.) PKC 1998. LNCS, vol. 1431, pp. 117–134. Springer, Heidelberg (1998). https://doi.org/10.1007/BFb0054019

22. Unger, B., Hertog, J.D.: Water always finds its way: identifying new forms of money laundering. Crime Law Soc. Change **57**(3), 287–304 (2012)

23. Wolfond, G.: A blockchain ecosystem for digital identity: improving service delivery in Canada's public and private sectors. Technol. Innov. Manag. Rev. 7(10), 35–40 (2017)

24. Yuen, T.H.: Pachain: private, authenticated & auditable consortium blockchain and its implementation. Fut. Gen. Comput. Syst. **112**, 913–929 (2020)

Granularity and Usability
in Authorization Policies

Boyun Zhang[1], Puneet Gill[1], Nelu Mihai[2], and Mahesh Tripunitara[1(✉)]

[1] University of Waterloo, Waterloo, Canada
{boyun.zhang,p24gill,tripunit}@uwaterloo.ca
[2] Cloud of Clouds Project, San Francisco, USA
nelumihai@icloud.com

Abstract. Emerging security systems need to carefully reconcile usability considerations in their design. In this context, we address authorization policies, which are used to limit the actions a principal may exercise on a resource. We compare two designs from the standpoint of the ease with which such policies can be devised and expressed. The two designs we consider are read-write-execute policies in UNIX, which was designed many decades ago, and identity-based policies in Amazon Web Services (AWS), which is a modern system. These can be seen, in the evolution of such designs, as two extremes—in the former, only the three actions read, write and execute are allowed in an authorization policy; in the latter, more than a thousand actions are allowed. While a richer set of actions lends to finer-grained authorization policies, the question we pose is: are such policies easier to formulate? Our question is important because a trend in the design of such policy languages in real systems over the years has been to enrich the set of actions. For a meaningful comparison between the two extremes, we design an overlay authorization policy syntax for AWS that allows the three actions read, write and execute only. We then describe our design of an ethics-approved, human participants study to assess whether a richer set of actions indeed results in better usability, and our results from carrying out the study. Using carefully chosen statistical methods that are appropriate for our study, we find that there is indeed evidence that allowing for a richer set of actions lends to better usability. Our work has significant implications to design in emerging security systems that seek to reconcile usability.

Keywords: Usability · Authorization · Policy

1 Introduction

Access control is widely, and rightfully, seen as an essential component of the security of a system. It deals with whether a principal, e.g., a user or role, is allowed to exercise an action, e.g., read or write, over a resource, e.g., a file in

Portions of this work were supported via grants from the Natural Sciences and Engineering Research Council of Canada (NSERC) and Mitacs, Canada.

© Springer Nature Switzerland AG 2022
W. Meng and S. K. Katsikas (Eds.): EISA 2021, CCIS 1403, pp. 68–86, 2022.
https://doi.org/10.1007/978-3-030-93956-4_5

the system. At the time a principal seeks to exercise an action over a resource, a trusted entity called a reference monitor checks whether that principal is indeed authorized to do so [11]. We address the setting in which the reference monitor bases its decision on an authorization policy that can change with the system or even over time within the same system, rather than, for example, a universally established set of rules. An authorization policy can be seen as a collection of triples, ⟨Principal, Action, Resource⟩, where such a triple authorizes the Principal to exercise the Action over the Resource.

```
$ stat --format=%A /etc/passwd
-rw-r--r--
```

Fig. 1. UNIX example.

Each system adopts a syntax for a language, and associated semantics, in which an authorization policy is specified. Two examples from designs for such a language which are the foci of this work are shown in Figs. 1 and 2.

In Fig. 1 we show the output of a command called stat in a version of the UNIX system [31]. The command shows us the so-called file permission bits for a file whose name we specify as the argument to the command, in this example, /etc/passwd. The file permission bits express an authorization policy over the particular file. In this example, a principal called the owner is allowed to both read and write the file, and the principals group and others are allowed to read the file only. Inherent to the design of the authorization policy syntax in the UNIX system and its variants is that only the three actions, read, write and execute are allowed to be specified in a policy. The semantics of the possession of one of those actions by a principal on a resource depends on the kind of resource it is. For example, what it means to possess the execute action over a directory is different from what it means to possess the execute action over a file.

In Fig. 2, we show an example of an authorization policy from Amazon Web Services (AWS) [7]. AWS allows for a few different kinds of authorization policies; we focus on so-called identity based policies, which are the most frequently used in AWS [8]. The figure shows an example of what AWS calls a statement, which specifies that a principal, which is a user or role, to whom this statement is bound is authorized the two actions dynamodb:DeleteItem and dynamodb:DeleteTable to the resource.

We recognize that AWS identity based policies may be seen more as capabilities each of which is bound to a principal, whereas UNIX file permission bits may be seen as Access Control Lists (ACLs) each of which is bound to a resource [11]. This distinction is relevant to our work only in that we really would be comparing across two rather different kinds of systems if we were to directly compare UNIX file permission bits with AWS identity based policies. Apart from that, our focus is only on the number of different actions each design permits to be specified in an authorization policy.

In comparing the two different designs for the possible actions in a policy, we ask: does one design choice lend to more usable authorization policies than the other? Usability in our context refers to the ease with which a policy can be specified in a particular syntax given goals for that policy. Prior work recognizes that it can be difficult for a human to specify authorization policies correctly, and with sufficient expediency (see, for example, [10,17,20,30]). And indeed, in such systems, it is a human, for example the owner of a file or a systems administrator, who specifies such policies.

```
{ "Statement": [{
        "Effect": "Allow",
        "Action": [ "dynamodb:DeleteItem",
                    "dynamodb:DeleteTable" ],
        "Resource": "arn:aws:dynamodb:::table/myTable"
}] }
```

Fig. 2. An example of an identity-based policy in AWS.

In this context, we observe that since the invention of the UNIX system and its file permission bits syntax for authorization, over time, the trend seems to be to increase the size of the set of actions in a design. For example, the Windows NT system allows for six actions [22]; in addition to **read**, **write** and **execute**, we have **delete**, **change permission** and **take ownership**. (These actions are, in turn, grouped into so-called "permissions" such as **full control**, which grants all the six actions, and **change**, which grants **read**, **write** and **delete** only.) More recently, in the Android system, we have about 250 app permissions, for example, ADD_VOICEMAIL and WRITE_CALL_LOG [14]. In AWS identity-based policies, the possible set of actions is of size more than a thousand.

It is then reasonable to ask: why has such an evolution occurred from a set of three actions only to a set of more than a thousand? We do not have a definitive answer to this question, as we are unable to find any prior work that reasons about these design choices in the corresponding systems. However, we observe that a richer set of actions lends to finer-grained authorization policies. In the example from AWS in Fig. 2, we observe that actions are bound to a particular service, **dynamodb** in the example. Thus, they seem more custom to the particular action that is being authorized, rather than the more generic **read**, for example. Thus, our work can be seen as relating the ability for such finer-grained specification of authorizations, to the ease with which authorization policies can be specified. Does one correlate with the other?

Our Work. Our hypothesis is that a system with a richer set of actions is more usable than one with **read**, **write** and **execute** only. Our work tests this hypothesis. We have done two things, which we discuss in sequence. First, for a meaningful comparison, we have devised a syntax for identity-based policies in AWS that allows the actions **read**, **write** and **execute** only. We discuss our design in

Sect. 2 for this. Our design leverages our observations regarding the similarity between the manner in which resources are referred to in the UNIX filesystem, and those in AWS. Then, we discuss our design of a human participants study entirely on AWS. Our study adopts a split participants design [21]—of all the human participants, a randomly chosen half are assigned to one of the two syntaxes, and the other half to the other syntax (see Sect. 3). We then discuss the manner in which we carried out the study, and our observations and inferences from the data we collected (see Sect. 4). We conclude by observing that there is indeed evidence to the better usability of an authorization syntax with a richer set of actions. We discuss related work in Sect. 5 and conclude with Sect. 6, with suggestions for future work.

2   A Read-Write-Execute Syntax for AWS Policies

As we discuss in Sect. 1, for us to be able to carry out an "apples to apples" comparison with a focus on the set of permitted actions only, we designed a syntax for AWS identity-based policies whose set of actions is `read`, `write` and `execute` only. In this section, we discuss our design. We begin with an example.

```
{ "Statement": [                          { "Statement": [
    {   "Effect": "Allow",                    {   "Effect": "Allow",
        "Actions": [                              "Actions": [ "read" ],
            "elastictranscoder:ReadPreset" ],    "Resources":[
        "Resources":[                                "arn:aws:elastictranscoder:::
            "arn:aws:elastictranscoder:::            preset/apple-mp4" ] },
            preset/apple-mp4" ]              {   "Effect": "Allow",
    } ] }                                        "Actions": [ "execute" ],
                                                 "Resources":[
                                                     "arn:aws:elastictranscoder:::
                                                     preset"
                                          ] } ] }
```

Fig. 3. A before and after example that helps explain our design for identity-based policies in AWS with `read`, `write` and `execute` actions only. To the left is an example identity-based policy in AWS, and to the right is the policy to the left under our design with those three actions only. As we explain in the prose, we need not only `read` to the resource `present/apple-mp4` that is mentioned in the policy on the left, but also `execute` on its "parent" resource, `preset`.

To the left of Fig. 3 is a policy in AWS's Elastic Transcoder service. It grants a user or role who is bound with that policy an action called `elastictranscoder:ReadPreset` on the resource `preset/apple-mp4`. The entire string that constitutes the name of the resource, `arn:aws:...`, is called an Amazon Resource Name (ARN), which is AWS's way of uniquely identifying a resource. We omit portions of the ARN such as partition and region as those are not relevant to our work. We can correctly refer to an ARN as the canonical identity of a resource and do not belabour AWS's choices in naming its resources as that is not a focus of our work.

Resource type	ARN
job	arn:...:job/${JobId}
pipeline	arn:...:pipeline/${PipelineId}
preset	arn:...:preset/${PresetId}

Fig. 4. The three types of resources in AWS's Elastic Transcoder service, and their corresponding ARNs, i.e., manner in which they are identified. We omit portions that are not relevant to our work using ellipses "..."

Our design of AWS identity-based policies with `read`, `write` and `execute` actions only is based on our observation that there is a natural and straightforward similarity between the naming scheme in the UNIX filesystem and resources in AWS. Before discussing this similarity, we overview the naming scheme of the UNIX filesystem, which has subsequently been adopted by its more modern variants, such as the `ext4` filesystem [12]. Figure 5 shows the naming scheme in UNIX and the naming scheme in AWS side-by-side to emphasize the similarity. They are both shown as trees because that is a natural way to represent the structure inherent to both naming schemes.

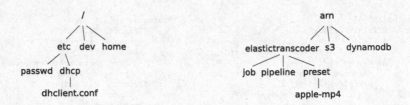

Fig. 5. The similarity between the naming scheme in the UNIX filesystem and in AWS. To the left is a portion of the directory and file structure in UNIX. To the right is a portion of AWS's services and resource types. We omit some portions of the names (ARNs) in AWS that are not relevant to our work.

In UNIX, there are two basic kinds of filesystem objects: directories and files. A directory contains other directories and files. A file contains data, or is a reference to some other information such as a device. The fully qualified name of a file starts with the symbol "/," which refers to the root directory, and is followed by one or more directory names separated by "/," with the file name at the end. For example, `/etc/dhcp/dhclient.conf` is the fully qualified name of a particular file. There are directories that are immediate sub-directories of the root level directory that have specific names and are associated with specific semantics. Examples of these are `/etc` and `/dev`.

We now discuss the manner in which resources in AWS are named. AWS classifies what it provides into services such as Elastic Transcoder, DynamoDB and S3. Each such service consolidates some common functionality that AWS provides. Elastic Transcoder, for example, is intended to provide functionality for converting media files into formats that can be played back on end-user devices [4]. Associated with every AWS service is a set of resource types [5]. Every resource which is mentioned in any identity-based policy is one of these types. The resource's name, i.e., ARN, includes the name of the service and the resource type within that service that the resource is. In the Elastic Transcoder service of AWS, for example, there are three resource types: job, pipeline and preset. We reproduce in Fig. 4 the table from the documentation for the Elastic Transcoder service which mentions these types and their corresponding ARNs [2].

Now that we have discussed the manner in which UNIX names its files and AWS names its resource, we now discuss the similarity we see between the two. Using the Elastic Transcoder service as an example again, we perceive the prefix `arn:...` up to one of the mnemonics `job`, `pipeline` or `preset` as the root-level directory in the UNIX filesystem "/." Each of the resource types `job`, `pipeline` and `preset` in the Elastic Transcoder service can be seen as a sub-directory of the root-level directory in UNIX, e.g., `/etc` and `/dev`, which must be named exactly as such and has specific semantics associated with what it contains.

Necessary and Sufficient Permissions in UNIX. Having observed the similarity between the naming schemes in UNIX and AWS, which in turn is a consequence of the manner in which resources are structured in the respective systems, we consider what necessary and sufficient permissions in the UNIX filesystem are for a user to be able to exercise an action on a resource. For example, consider that a user wants to read the file `/etc/dhcp/dhclient.conf`. Does it suffice that that user possess `read` over that file? The answer is no. In addition to possessing `read` over the file, the user needs to possess `execute` permission to each of the directories `/etc` and `/etc/dhcp`. This is the reason that in the example in Fig. 3, in translating the permission to exercise `elastictranscoder:ReadPreset`, we give the user both `read` to the resource `preset/apple-mp4` and `execute` to its "parent directory," `preset`.

More broadly, Fig. 6 shows a table that expresses the permissions that are necessary and sufficient to perform some actions in a UNIX directory and file structure that is `mydir/myfile`. That is, we have a directory named `mydir`, within which we have a file named `myfile`. For example, to be able to read `myfile`, the necessary permissions are `execute` on `mydir` and `read` on `myfile`.

In Fig. 6, we present a table of three actions in the Elastic Transcoder service in AWS, and our design of permissions from amongst `read`, `write` and `execute` only that are necessary and sufficient. The action ReadPipeline, given a pipeline ID, is similar to reading a "file" within the `pipeline` "directory." Therefore, as the table in Fig. 6 suggests for the UNIX filesystem, we need `execute` on the `pipeline` "directory," and `read` on the "file" that corresponds to pipeline ID that is part of the argument to the action. DeletePreset is similar to deleting a

Action	Permissions	
	mydir	myfile
read myfile	{x}	{r}
delete myfile	{w,x}	∅
create file in mydir	{w,x}	∅
write myfile	{x}	{w}

Action	Resource	Permissions
ReadPipeline	pipeline/ ${pipeline ID}	{x} to pipeline/ {r} to pipeline/ ${pipeline ID}
DeletePreset	preset/ ${preset ID}	{w,x} to preset/
CreateJob	job/ ${job ID}	{w,x} to job/ {w,x} to job/${job ID}

Fig. 6. To the left are necessary and sufficient permissions for some actions in a UNIX filesystem fragment that is `mydir/myfile`. We adopt `r` for `read`, `w` for `write` and `x` for `execute`. To the right are permissions that are necessary and sufficient for some actions in the Elastic Transcoder service of AWS in our design that allows `read (r)`, `write` (`w`) and `execute (x)` only.

"file" within the `preset` "directory," and therefore, as per the table in Fig. 6, requires `write` and `execute` on the `preset` "directory."

And as a final example, CreateJob given a job ID corresponds to creating a "file" within the `job` directory and also writing to that file, because the action of creating a job in Elastic Transcoder in AWS causes some data to the written to the "file" that corresponds to that job. Thus, this corresponds to both creating a file and write to that file from the table in Fig. 6 on UNIX permissions. That is, we require `write` and `execute` to both the "file" that corresponds to the job ID, and the "directory" `job` within which that "file" is contained.

Summary. In summary, we first observe the correspondence between the manner in which resources in AWS are organized and the manner in which files and directories in the UNIX filesystem are organized. We then adopt exactly the same permissions that would be necessary and sufficient in the UNIX filesystem, in our design of AWS policies that allow `read`, `write` and `execute` only. Thus, we anticipate that anyone who is familiar with UNIX file permissions and is informed of the correspondence between the two schemes, will be able to formulate `read`, `write` and `execute` permissions for resources in AWS. As we discuss in our next section, we exploit this in the design of our human participants study.

3   The Design of a Human Participants Study

The intent of our human participants study is to test the hypothesis that policies are easier to write with a richer set of actions than read-write-execute only. Towards this, each human participant was asked to formulate and write an identity-based policy in AWS in one of two syntaxes: the original syntax that AWS has designed for such policies that allows for a rich set of actions, or the syntax we designed for AWS that allows the actions `read`, `write` and `execute` only that we discuss in Sect. 2. In this section, we discuss details of the design of our study.

Nature of Human Participants. Our study follows a split participants design [21], wherein a human participant is randomly assigned to one of the two syntaxes,

```
response =                   dynamodb.CreateTable(        dynamodb.UpdateTable(
dynamodb.GetItem(              TableName="mynewcart")       ReadCapacityUnits=15,
    Item = "cart-item",     for item in items_in_cart:      TableName="mycart")
    TableName="mycart")       dynamodb.DeleteItem(       sqs.UpdateQueue(
                                Item = "cart-item",         QueueName="update-success")
                                TableName="myoldcart")    dynamodb.DeleteItem(
                                                            Item="cart-item",
                                                            TableName="mycart)
```

Fig. 7. The three snippets of code that we use in the three tasks in our human participants study. The snippet to the far left corresponds to Task 1: Get cart item. The snippet in the middle corresponds to Task 2: Change cart. And the snippet to the far right corresponds to Task 3: Edit cart.

such that each syntax has an equal number of participants. Each participant was scheduled for one hour. Of the hour, the first 15 min were dedicated to training, and the remainder to fulfill three tasks that each participant was assigned. For each syntax, every participant was assigned the same three tasks which we discuss below. On account of the pandemic, all interactions were via teleconferencing. The participants were provided with a consent letter at the time their appointment was made, which detailed various aspects of the study and assured their anonymity. Each participant was required to verbally consent to the study at the outset. Each participant was provided a feedback letter at the end. With the consent of each participant, we required the participant to share their screen so we could record the manner in which they worked. Part of the training was in thinking aloud. We recorded each participant's audio as well. All our materials were approved as part of our institution's ethics approval process. We remunerated each participant a small amount of money, again with the approval of our ethics board, for their participation.

As our study involves fairly sophisticated technical aspects, we wanted participants who most closely had the qualifications of a security or systems administrator. Consequently, all our participants were final- (fourth-) year undergraduate students, or first or second year graduate students in computer engineering and computer science. We required that all of our participants be (i) familiar with UNIX file permissions, and, (ii) not be familiar with identity-based policies in AWS, nor serverless applications in AWS. Our intent with (i) was that we wanted to "factor out" difficulties with what we wanted to consider baseline knowledge in our study, and, with (ii) was that we did not want such prior knowledge to give an advantage to a participant for which we could not compensate with our statistical methods.

Number of Human Participants. We recruited 20 participants in total, 10 each for each of the two syntaxes. Separately, we had three participants earlier who piloted our study, from whose observations we made improvements and fixes. A common concern in such studies is the number of participants: is 20 participants sufficient? There is no magic answer to this question. We observe that in studies of a technical nature as ours, around 10 participants appears to suffice. For instance, recent work that assesses the usability of static analysis tools for security [32] recruited 12 participants. Maxion and Reeder [19], whose work is related closely to ours, recruited 24 participants. Non-parametric tests, such as the Mann-Whitney U test on which we rely, have shown strong performance with small samples [25]. What is more important than a large number of participants is the nature of the participants, the design of and the manner in which we carry out our study, and appropriate choice and use of statistics on whose basis we make inferences. We have taken great care in these aspects.

An Application. We chose to focus on tasks that involve a single serverless cloud application that AWS provides as an example of such applications—a shopping cart [1]. Within that application, we specify tasks that involve two services: DynamoDB [3] and SQS [6]. The former is a database service and the latter, a queue service. DynamoDB supports a set of 81 actions across the entire service which can appear in an identity-based policy. SQS supports 20 actions. Of these, the ideal policies for our tasks require the specification of four actions from DynamoDB, and one from SQS. The only resource type from the six types DynamoDB specifies to which our tasks pertain is `table`, which is a database table. SQS has one resource type only, `queue`.

Tasks. We devised three tasks that a participant is to fulfill. Each involves formulating and writing an identity-based policy in the shopping cart application that we mention above [1]. For each task, we provide the human participant a snippet of the code in the python programming language, in which the backend of the application is written. Our code snippets are not fully faithful to the original application. Specifically: (i) We reproduce in our snippets only those pieces that pertain to our tasks so as not to burden a human participant with extraneous information. For example, in a call to get an item from a database table, we mention as arguments the table name and an identifier for the item only. (ii) We have changed the names of function calls to match exactly the names of actions that would appear in a policy. For example, rather than `get_item()`, which is the name of the corresponding method in AWS's python bindings, we use `GetItem()`, which exactly matches the action `dynamodb:GetItem` that would appear in an identity-based policy. (iii) We use keyword arguments that are allowed in python. That is, in python, if we have a subroutine that is defined as `def myfunc(name, id)`, then it can be invoked as `myfunc(id = 5, name = 'alice')`, which explicitly specifies which argument-value matches each parameter to the subroutine. (iv) We removed the "effect" field (see Figs. 2 and 3), with the assumption that we have a default deny, and any permissions that are specified are "allow." All participants were trained as such.

All of our adaptations (i)–(iv) are intended to not distract from the tasks on which we seek to focus. A human participant was scheduled for one hour. We could have scheduled each participant for longer; however, we would then have to account for fatigue.

The three snippets of code that correspond to the tasks are shown in Fig. 7. We call Task 1 "Get cart item." As the code snippet to the far left of Fig. 7 suggests, we retrieve a data item from a table using the `GetItem()` method. We call Task 2 "Change cart," and it corresponds to the code snippet to the middle of Fig. 7. In it, we create a new table that appears to correspond to a new cart, and delete items one-by-one from an existing table, which is another cart. We do not show more actions to keep the policy that is needed somewhat compact. We call Task 3 "Edit cart." It corresponds to the code snippet to the far right of Fig. 7. In it, we modify an attribute of the table that corresponds to the cart via a call to `UpdateTable()`. We then invoke the SQS service to report on the update, and then delete an item from the table that is the cart.

For both syntaxes, for each snippet of code, we had an 'ideal' solution against which we compared the results. For example, in Fig. 8, we show an ideal solution for the task to the far left of Fig. 7.

```
{ "Statement": [                          { "Statement": [
  { "Actions": [ "dynamodb:GetItem" ],      { "Actions": [ "execute" ],
    "Resources":[                             "Resources":[
      "dynamodb/mycart/cart-item" ]             "dynamodb",
  }] }                                          "dynamodb/mycart" ] },
                                            { "Actions": [ "read" ],
                                              "Resources":[
                                                "dynamodb/mycart/cart-item" ]
                                          }] }
```

Fig. 8. An ideal policy for the task to the far left of Fig. 7. To the left in this figure is an ideal policy for the AWS syntax with a rich set of actions, and to the right is an ideal policy in the syntax with read, write and execute actions only.

Training. Both sets of participants were trained for 15 min at the start of their session. For a participant who was assigned to the read-write-execute syntax, there were two components to the training, both of which were done via pre-recorded videos. The first component was a review of UNIX file permissions. The second was AWS identity-based policies, but using read, write and execute actions only. This component was driven by an example of a code snippet and a policy for it. For a participant who was assigned the AWS syntax with a rich set of actions, we provided training on identity-based policies in AWS, where to find information on the various actions that can appear in policies, and an example of a snippet of code, and a policy for it. During our training for both sets of users, we incorporated training on thinking aloud, so we could capture the participants' thought processes as they worked through their tasks.

Limitations. While we have been careful with our design, it certainly has a few limitations. One is an assumption that the participants we have chosen are representative of the population of human users who would author such policies. Another limitation is that the design our study addresses authoring policies from scratch only. It does not addresses changes to policies, which may be an event that occurs with more frequency than authoring a policy from scratch. We hypothesize that ease of authoring policies from scratch corresponds to ease of editing policies; however, this hypothesis itself needs to be validated. Yet another limitation lies in the choice of our tasks. We have chosen to focus on an application, which in turn is limited in the AWS services it exercises. It is possible that with a different set of services and/or a different set of possible actions, authoring policies in AWS's current syntax with a rich set of actions is harder than our study would suggest.

Notwithstanding these limitations, we argue that our study is novel, and has value, in that rejection of an appropriately posed null hypothesis with a sufficiently low p value based on our study is a valid indicator that the null hypothesis is indeed false in the broader population.

4   Results

Our study ran smoothly, and we were able to collect data as planned from all of our participants. None of the participants chose to withdraw upon commencement of their participation; this was an option they were allowed to exercise.

We consider the accuracy with which a participant fulfilled their task and their time-to-completion to be meaningful quantitative measures towards establishing or rejecting our hypothesis. That is, if a participant is able to achieve a task correctly, we credit the corresponding syntax as being usable, i.e., easy with regards to formulating a policy. Similarly, if the time to complete a task is short, this suggests that the syntax lends itself to usability. Of course with time, we need to consider whether a participant completed a task correctly as well. In addition to these quantitative results, an identification of the nature of errors our participants made is informative in that it tells us possible weak points from the standpoint of usability with a particular syntax.

Our raw observations for accuracy and time-to-completion are shown in Figs. 9 and 10. Not surprisingly, Task 1 was the easiest from the standpoint of accuracy for the participants—it is similar to example on which the participants were trained. Tasks 2 and 3 are more challenging to both sets of participants, however, it appears that the tasks were easier for the participants with the richer set of actions which is AWS's current design. It appears that across the board, participants who worked with the richer set of actions took less time. Also, there are cases that those who completed the tasks correctly took less time than those who did not, for example, Task 1 for read-write-execute, and Task 3 for the richer set. This is not necessarily surprising—it suggests to us that our participants were committed to the study.

Statistical Significance. We adopt a p value of 0.05 for every test at the outset. Thus, if the computed p value is < 0.05, then we deem the evidence strong enough to reject the null hypothesis. As a reminder, our null hypothesis is that authoring identity-based policies in AWS with the richer set of actions is no easier than authoring them when the set of actions is read, write and execute only.

As our statistical method, we adopt empirical bootstrap [26, 33] with the median as the central tendency. Empirical bootstrap works as follows. Given a set of observations $\{X_1, \ldots, X_n\}$ which has sample median M_n, suppose we

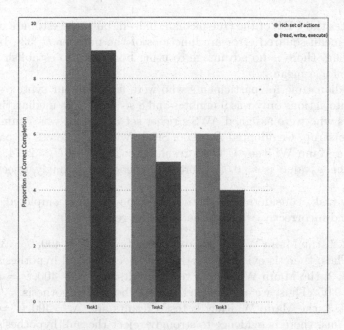

Fig. 9. The proportion of accurate responses per task.

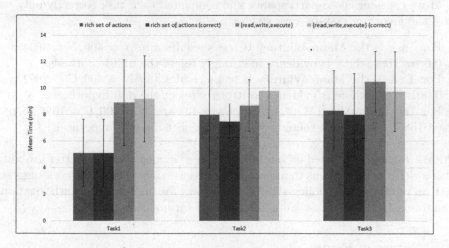

Fig. 10. The mean time-to-completion per task for both correct and all participants. The standard deviation is shown using error bars.

sample with replacement from the observations to get a "new" set of observations $X_1^{*(1)}, \ldots, X_n^{*(1)}$ with median $M_n^{*(1)}$. We repeat this, i.e., sample with replacement again with our original set of observations denote it B times. Thus, we have B sets of observations, each with a median $M_n^{*(i)}$ of its own. The key result is: the Cumulative Distribution Function (CDF) of a bootstrap median approximates the CDF of the true median. Indeed, both the estimate of variance and of the mean-squared error are functions of the number B [33]. In contrast to the median, there is no advantage to using bootstrap to establish statistical significance for a mean.

The median time for participants who were assigned our syntax with read-write-execute actions only was 9 minutes and 8 seconds. The median time for the participants who were assigned AWS's richer set of actions was 7 min and 10 s. For our bootstrap, we adopted $B = 200$. Study-wide, i.e., across all participants and tasks, a Mann Whitney U test's results are: $N = 400, U = 2674, p < 0.001$. Thus, as the p value is < 0.05, there is evidence to strongly reject the null hypothesis.

Task-by-task, considering both the participants who completed each task correctly and incorrectly, we have the following results.

- For Task 1, the Mann Whitney U test's results are: $N = 400, U = 3244.5, p < 0.001$. Thus, there is evidence to strongly reject the null hypothesis.
- For Task 2, the Mann Whitney U test's results are: $N = 400, U = 19804, p = 0.433 > 0.05$. Thus, we are unable to reject the null hypothesis.
- For Task 3, the Mann Whitney U test's results are: $N = 400, U = 7118, p < 0.001$. Thus, there is evidence to strongly reject the null hypothesis.

If we consider those participants who completed each task correctly only, we have the following task-by-task results.

- For Task 1, the Mann. Whitney U test's results are: $N = 400, U = 3604, p < 0.001$. Thus, there is evidence to strongly reject the null hypothesis.
- For Task 2, the Mann Whitney U test's results are: $N = 400, U = 2802, p < 0.001$. Thus, there is evidence to strongly reject the null hypothesis.
- For Task 3, the Mann Whitney U test's results are: $N = 400, U = 10988.5, p = 0.0158 < 0.05$. Thus, there is evidence to reject the null hypothesis.

Overall Inferences. Based on our study, there is evidence to the better usability with a richer set of actions than read-write-execute only. Thus, our work suggests that an authorization policy syntax that allows for finer-grained authorizations is more usable from the standpoint of ease of formulating policies.

4.1   Nature of Errors

In addition to our observations we report in the previous section, we have analyzed the errors that were made by those participants who were unable to complete a task correctly, across both sets of participants. In the following, for each set of participants, we first identify all the kinds of errors we observed, and then present the number of participants who made one of those errors. We discuss our overall observations from this part of our analysis at the end of this section.

For the set of participants who were assigned the set of actions read-write-execute only, we observed the following kinds of errors (Fig. 11).

(A) *Too few actions*: the policy does not award sufficient authorizations on account that some actions were not granted. In particular, an action to the "parent directory" was not granted.
(B) *Incorrect action granted*: the policy grants an incorrect action, for example, read instead of execute.
(C) *Redundant grants*: the policy grants unnecessary actions.
(D) *Incorrect naming of a resource*: a resource was not named correctly, likely on account of incorrect mapping of AWS resources to the UNIX filesystem scheme as we discuss under our design in Sect. 2.

Error	# instances	Tasks in which error occurred
(A)	5	1, 2, 3
(B)	3	2, 3
(C)	3	2, 3
(D)	2	3

Error	# instances	Tasks in which error occurred
(E)	4	2, 3
(F)	2	2, 3
(G)	2	3

Fig. 11. To the left are the kinds of errors made by participants whose set of actions was read-write-execute only, the number of instances of each error, and the tasks in which the error occurred. To the right are the kinds of errors made by participants who were assigned the rich set of actions, the number of instances of each error, and the tasks in which the error occurred.

For the set of participants who were assigned the rich set of actions, we observed the following kinds of errors.

(E) *Incorrect naming of a resource.* Note that even though we associate the same phrase as error (D) for the other set of participants, the kind of error is different, as for this set of participants, no mapping to the UNIX filesystem is needed.
(F) *Incorrect action granted*: the policy grants an incorrect action, perhaps on account of the inability of the participant to navigate the information we provided on the list of all actions in an AWS service. Even though we use the same phrase as error (B) from the other set of participants, the cause of the error is different, and so we associate it with a different letter, i.e., (F).
(G) *Redundant actions granted*: this error appears to have been caused by lack of recognition that two actions needed to be associated with the same resource. Again, even though we use the same phrase as error (C) for the other set of participants, we deem this error to be of a different nature than (C).

The most prevalent error for the participants who dealt with the read-write-execute set of actions was (A), too few actions. Based on our study of the instances of these errors, it appears that the participants were not entirely familiar with UNIX filesystem permissions, e.g., that a permission to a parent directory is necessary for access to a file. This is the case notwithstanding the fact that familiarity with UNIX file system permissions was a required qualification for all participants, and we included a review of those permissions for those participants who were assigned the read-write-execute set of actions. Thus, it appears that lack of adequate knowledge of UNIX permissions may have been coupled with over-confidence in one's knowledge.

Incorrect naming of resources, errors (D) and (E), come as a surprise to us. We take this as part of errors that occur with such textual specification of policies. We point out that AWS does provide a visual editor for specification of policies, which may mitigate both this kind of error, and error (F), incorrect action. We do not anticipate that a visual editor will mitigate the counterpart error (B) for the participants with the read-write-execute actions only, as the likelihood of making the same kind of error (F) is small, given the highly limited set of actions.

Finally, errors (C) and (G) suggest a dangerous consequence: over-privilege. Over-privilege is known to be a source of security issues in cloud applications [23]. Our study did not focus on this problem; but our discovery of such errors suggests that work in over-privilege in this context may be of interest and value.

5   Related Work

The usability issues that plague security systems, authorization systems in particular, from the standpoint of formulating and expressing policies is well documented in the literature. The work of Maxion and Reeder [19] is pioneering in this regard. It considers the file-permissions interface of the Windows XP operating system, and compares it against an alternative design that it calls Salmon. It adopts a split-participants design for its human participant study, and based on the accuracy, time to completion and elimination of a class of errors, it concludes that Salmon is a better interface. Reeder and Maxion have since followed up that work with work that focuses on a particular class of errors called goal errors [27] and prevention of defects in an interface through hesitation analysis [28], and Reeder et al. [30] have devised a novel interface for Windows XP file permissions called expandable grids and analysed it. Similarly, Brostoff et al. [13] have devised and analysed an interface for Role-Based Access Control (RBAC) policies. Krishnan et al. [17] have addressed the usability of file Access Control Lists (ACLs) in Linux systems, and proposed an alternative interface to the existing one and shown its benefits via a human participants study. Our work adopts a number of elements from those pieces of work with regards to the manner in which a human participants study is conducted, and the results are analyzed. However, unlike such prior work, we do not seek to tout a new design for an interface, but rather compare a design that has been of historical interest and influence, which is the UNIX file permissions, to a modern design, which is AWS identity-based policies, from the standpoint of the number of actions that are allowed in a policy.

Mazurek et al. [20] have addressed the aspect of the manner in which users think about access control in a home setting, and have interviewed 33 users across 15 households in this regard. One of their key findings is that the mental models that humans have for access control do not match well with the interface and mechanisms that access control systems provide to articulate policies. That work clearly establishes some of the challenges in formulating access control policies, even in the seemingly simpler setting, compared to, for example, an enterprise setting, of households. Our work does not directly address the challenges that work raises. Rather, our focus is on whether a richer, more fine-grained set of actions renders policy formulation easier.

Beznosov et al. [10] have posed and answered a number of interesting questions from the standpoint of usability challenges in access control. Some of the questions that they address are novel; for example, whether the articulation of policies should be "transparent," and the manner in which federated policies required by technologies such as grid and distributed computing can be articulated and managed. Our work does not address questions of the nature that that panel discussion addressed, but rather, focuses on the rather more specific question in the context of real-world systems that have seen heavy use over time: UNIX file permissions and AWS identity-based policies.

Inglesant et al. [16] have devised a natural language interface for the specification of RBAC policies in grid computing systems. They discuss the process by which they arrived at their design, which includes interviews with 45 practitioners. They observe that while their design does lend to better usability, iterative-refinement is still needed for users to converge to correct policies. In contrast to their work, we consider a much more controlled setting, and compare two real-world designs for articulating access control policies. While our policies are textual and not visual, they are not based on a natural language.

Reeder et al. [29] recognize that access control policies can be in conflict with one another, and observe that the manner in which conflicts are resolved can have a significant impact on usability from the standpoint of policy authoring. Our work is different from theirs in that while we do consider usability from the standpoint of policy authoring, we do not consider conflicts nor the impact of the approach to conflict-resolution on usability.

Bauer et al. [9] address access control in a physical setting, and in particular, compare physical access to office rooms using a smartphone instead of a physical key. A particular focus of that work is that it is with real users, in the sense that those are the users to whom the office rooms have been assigned. In contrast to that work, our work chooses human participants that we hypothesize are representative of the kinds of humans who will author policies in our setting. Also, we consider textually specified policies to protect digital assets rather than physical access control with keys and smartphones.

Gusmeroli et al. [15] have incorporated considerations of usability in their work on devising a capability-based access control model for an Internet of Things (IoT). In the context of their work, usability is a design consideration. However, unlike our work, they do not carry out a human participants study to validate their design. Also, our work is in the entirely different context of identity-based policies in AWS. Lipford et al. [18] and Paul et al. [24] have studied the usability problems in the Facebook social network with regards to specification of permissions, and have found a number of deficiencies. Our work is entirely different from theirs in that we consider AWS identity-based policies, with a focus on the richness of the set of actions.

6 Conclusion and Future Work

We have compared two designs from the standpoint of the richness of the set of actions for authoring access control policies. Both designs are for identity-based policies in AWS. One of the designs allows three actions only: read, write and execute, and is based on file system permissions in the UNIX operating system. The other is the design from AWS which, in total, supports a set of more than 1000 actions. We see these two designs as extremes, and also at two ends of the continuum in the design of such syntaxes for policy authoring. We designed a syntax for identity-based policies in AWS, which we have discussed in this work, to allow us to carry out an "apples-to-apples" comparison between the two designs. We have carried out an ethics-approved human participants study to test the hypothesis as to whether a richer set of actions lends to better usability from the standpoint of policy formulation and authoring. Our study establishes that there is indeed evidence that a richer set of actions lends to better usability.

There is considerable scope for future work. One is a more elaborate study that incorporates users who author such policies in AWS. It may be difficult to assemble such a set of users, however. Another is a study with more realistic serverless applications, at scale, and the challenge involved in formulating and authoring policies for such applications. Yet another topic for future work is a study of over-privilege. We have identified in this work that over-privilege can be related to how usable a policy authoring syntax is. And over-privilege is dangerous from the standpoint of security. Consequently, a study with a focus on the manner in which usability as characterized by ease of policy formulation and authoring, and the risk of over-privilege, would be interesting future work for emerging systems.

References

1. Amazon Web Services (AWS): Serverless shopping cart microservice, January 2021.https://github.com/aws-samples/aws-serverless-shopping-cart
2. Amazon Web Services (AWS): Actions, resources, and condition keys for amazon elastic transcoder. https://docs.aws.amazon.com/service-authorization/latest/reference/list_amazonelastictranscoder.html. Accessed 31 Jan 2021
3. Amazon Web Services (AWS): Amazon dynamodb, https://aws.amazon.com/dynamodb/. Accessed 31 Jan 2021
4. Amazon Web Services (AWS): Amazon elastic transcoder. https://aws.amazon.com/elastictranscoder/. Accessed 31 Jan 2021
5. Amazon Web Services (AWS): Amazon resource names (ARMS). https://docs.aws.amazon.com/general/latest/gr/aws-arns-and-namespaces.html. Accessed 31 Jan 2021

6. Amazon Web Services (AWS): Amazon simple queue service. https://aws.amazon.com/sqs/. Accessed 31 Jan 2021
7. Amazon Web Services (AWS): Amazon web services (AWS) - cloud computing services. https://aws.amazon.com. Accessed 31 Jan 2021
8. Amazon Web Services (AWS): Aws identity and access management – user guide – access management – policies and permissions in IAM. https://docs.aws.amazon.com/IAM/latest/UserGuide/access_policies.html. Accessed 31 Jan 2021
9. Bauer, L., Cranor, L.F., Reeder, R.W., Reiter, M.K., Vaniea, K.: A user study of policy creation in a flexible access-control system. In: Proceedings of the SIGCHI Conference on Human Factors in Computing Systems, CHI 2008, pp. 543–552. ACM, New York (2008)
10. Beznosov, K., Inglesant, P., Lobo, J., Reeder, R., Zurko, M.E.: Usability meets access control: challenges and research opportunities. In: Proceedings of the Symposium on Access Control Models and Technologies, SACMAT 2009, pp. 73–74. ACM, New York (2009)
11. Bishop, M.: Introduction to Computer Security, 1st edn. Addison-Wesley, Boston (2004)
12. Both, D.: An introduction to linux's ext4 filesystem. opensource.com, May 2017. https://opensource.com/article/17/5/introduction-ext4-filesystem
13. Brostoff, S., Sasse, M.A., Chadwick, D., Cunningham, J., Mbanaso, U., Otenko, S.: 'R-what?' development of a role-based access control policy-writing tool for e-scientists. Softw. Pract. Exp. **35**(9), 835–856 (2005)
14. Google Developers: Android API reference – android platform – manifest.permission, https://developer.android.com/reference/android/Manifest.permission. Accessed 31 Jan 2021
15. Gusmeroli, S., Piccione, S., Rotondi, D.: A capability-based security approach to manage access control in the internet of things. Math. Comput. Model. **58**(5), 1189–1205 (2013)
16. Inglesant, P., Sasse, A.M., Chadwick, D., Shi, L.L.: Expressions of expertness: the virtuous circle of natural language for access control policy specification. In: Proceedings of the Symposium on Usable Privacy and Security, SOUPS 2008, ACM, New York (2008)
17. Krishnan, V., Tripunitara, M.V., Chik, K., Bergstrom, T.: Relating declarative semantics and usability in access control. In: Proceedings of the Eighth Symposium on Usable Privacy and Security. SOUPS 2012, ACM, New York (2012)
18. Lipford, H.R., Besmer, A., Watson, J.: Understanding privacy settings in facebook with an audience view. In: Proceedings of the 1st Conference on Usability, Psychology, and Security. UPSEC2008, USENIX Association (2008)
19. Maxion, R.A., Reeder, R.W.: Improving user-interface dependability through mitigation of human error. Int. J. Hum.-Comput. Stud. **63**(1), 25–50 (2005)
20. Mazurek, M.L., et al.: Access control for home data sharing: attitudes, needs and practices. In: Proceedings of the SIGCHI Conference on Human Factors in Computing Systems, pp. 645–654. ACM, New York (2010)
21. McLeod, S.A.: Experimental design. Simply Psychology, January 2017. https://www.simplypsychology.org/experimental-designs.html
22. Network Encyclopedia: NTFS permissions (windows NT). https://networkencyclopedia.com/ntfs-permissions-windows-nt/. Accessed 31 Jan 2021
23. Osborne, C.: The top 10 security challenges of serverless architectures. Zero Day, January 2017. https://www.zdnet.com/article/the-top-10-risks-for-apps-on-serverless-architectures/

24. Paul, T., Puscher, D., Strufe, T.: Improving the usability of privacy settings in Facebook. arXiv e-prints arXiv:1109.6046, September 2011
25. Pero-Cebollero, M., Guardia-Olmos, J.: The adequacy of different robust statistical tests in comparing two independent groups. Psicologica **34**, 407–424 (2013)
26. Ramesh Johari: MS & E 226: "Small" Data, Lecture 13: The bootstrap (v3). September 2020.http://web.stanford.edu/~rjohari/teaching/notes/226_lecture13_inference.pdf
27. Reeder, R.W., Maxion, R.A.: User interface dependability through goal-error prevention. In: 2005 International Conference on Dependable Systems and Networks (DSN 2005), pp. 60–69 (2005)
28. Reeder, R.W., Maxion, R.A.: User interface defect detection by hesitation analysis. In: International Conference on Dependable Systems and Networks (DSN 2006), pp. 61–72 (2006)
29. Reeder, R.W., Bauer, L., Cranor, L.F., Reiter, M.K., Vaniea, K.: More than skin deep: measuring effects of the underlying model on access-control system usability. In: Proceedings of the SIGCHI Conference on Human Factors in Computing Systems, CHI 2011, pp. 2065–2074. ACM, New York (2011)
30. Reeder, R.W., et al.:Expandable grids for visualizing and authoring computer security policies. In: Proceedings of the SIGCHI Conference on Human Factors in Computing Systems, CHI 2008, pp. 1473–1482. ACM, New York (2008)
31. Ritchie, D.M., Thompson, K.: The Unix time sharing system. Commun. ACM **17**, 365–375 (1974)
32. Smith, J., Nguyen Quang Do, L., Murphy-Hill, E.: Why can't johnny fix vulnerabilities: a usability evaluation of static analysis tools for security. In: Proceedings of the Symposium on Usable Privacy and Security. SOUPS2020, Usenix, Aug 2020
33. Chen,Y.-C.: STAT/Q SCI 403: introduction to resampling methods, Lecture 5: Bootstrap, April 2017. http://faculty.washington.edu/yenchic/17Sp_403/Lec5-bootstrap.pdf,

A Two-Fold Study to Investigate Users' Perception of IoT Information Sensitivity Levels and Their Willingness to Share the Information

Sanonda Datta Gupta[✉], Stephen Kaplan, Aubree Nygaard, and Sepideh Ghanavati

School of Computing and Information Science, University of Maine, Orono, ME, USA
{sanonda.gupta,stephen.kaplan,aubree.nygaard,sepideh.ghanavati}@maine.edu

Abstract. The increase in the usage of the Internet of Things (IoT) raises privacy concerns for users. Depending on the types of information collected by IoT devices and shared with third-parties, users' privacy concerns may vary. In this paper, we describe our detailed analysis of a two-fold user study with (1) 70 students from our institution and (2) 164 Amazon Mechanical Turk workers to understand how users perceive sensitivity level of different information types and to examine their attitude towards sharing their personal information with third-parties. We developed a taxonomy of IoT data practices to use for the study. In both of our studies, we noticed that users' understanding of sensitivity levels differs based on their gender. We also identified users' willingness to share an information with a third-party strongly depends on the sensitivity levels of the information type and the third-party categories. Based on our findings, we provide suggestions for privacy regulators, policymakers, companies, and researchers to mitigate and resolve IoT privacy risks.

1 Introduction

The Internet of Things (IoT) is composed of interconnected smart devices that can collect and share a wide and diverse range of data, such as health and environmental information, from the physical world. With access to such a variety of information types, IoT devices present three major privacy risks: (1) *collecting additional data:* An IoT device may collect data unrelated to its core functionalities [8]; (2) *inconsistency between an IoT device and its privacy policy:* An IoT device may collect data beyond the types mentioned in its privacy policy [8,11]; and (3) *inference of personal information:* if two or more IoT devices share data with the same third-party, the third-party may infer users' personally identifiable information (PII) without the their knowledge [11,28,32,34,36]. It is estimated that, by 2025, over 40 billion IoT devices will be deployed worldwide, generating over 79.4 zettabytes of data annually [2]. This rapid growth in deployment of IoT devices may increase the risk of exploitation of a larger number of users' PII [21]. Prior research has shown that users want to be better informed about privacy

© Springer Nature Switzerland AG 2022
W. Meng and S. K. Katsikas (Eds.): EISA 2021, CCIS 1403, pp. 87–107, 2022.
https://doi.org/10.1007/978-3-030-93956-4_6

risks of IoT devices before purchasing or using them [12,30]. Much research has been done to evaluate privacy risks of IoT devices, such as analyzing inference of PII [11,28,32,36], identifying discrepancies between IoT devices and their privacy policies [11,13,14,29,35,37], and informing users about privacy and security practices of IoT devices before their deployment [11,24].

Although previous research attempt to identify privacy risks, they do not consider the sensitivity level of the collected information in their analysis and they recognize privacy risks related to all types of information equal. Privacy regulations such as the General Data Protection Regulation (GDPR) [6] and California Consumers Privacy Act (CCPA) [1], and agencies such as the National Institute of Standards and Technology (NIST) [22] define a baseline for sensitivity level of PII. GDPR defines a list of *special category* data, often considered the most sensitive categories, which includes, for example, health and biometric information [6]. The CCPA [1] defines "sensitive personal information" as the type of information that is not publicly available, such as social security and driver's license numbers. However, these categories are broad and include a large spectrum of PII which users may not consider as equally sensitive and thus, their perceived privacy risks may vary. In this work, we define the *sensitivity* of an information as an individual's comfort level in collecting or sharing that information by or with the IoT device. For example, users might be less comfortable to share their biometric information (such as thumbprint) with an IoT device than other types of information (such as environmental temperature). Prior studies explore users' perceptions of privacy risk [17] and how this perception affects their willingness to purchase a device [25]. However, none of them focus on understanding users' privacy risk perception of the information *specifically* collected by IoT devices. IoT devices have diverse functionalities and continuously collect or generate a wide range of data such as fingerprint, heart-rate, and environmental temperature which are unique to them and not generally collected by other types of devices. Thus, the degree of sensitivity of IoT's collected information may vary in compare to other types of devices or applications.

To address these research gaps, in this paper, we aim to investigate (a) how users perceive the sensitivity level of different information collected by IoT devices and (b) their attitudes toward sharing their collected information with third-parties. We developed a taxonomy and a mapping schema for IoT data practices, to help categorize information types collected or generated by IoT devices. We identified 79 PII which we categorized into eight categories for our studies. We, then, conducted a two-fold user study with (1) 70 students from our institution and (2) a larger and more general audience, 164 Amazon Mechanical Turk (MTurk) workers. In our two-fold user study, we provided the participants with scenarios where an IoT device collects an information from one of the eight categories and then, asked them to report their perceived sensitivity level and willingness to share the information. Responses from this two-fold survey seek to answer the five research questions as follows:

- **RQ1.** How does users' perception of the degree of sensitivity of an information vary by the types of information?
- **RQ2.** How does information types influence users' concerns about a potential privacy violation when an information is shared with third-parties?
- **RQ3.** How does gender influence users' perception of the degree of sensitivity of an information?
- **RQ4.** How does sensitivity level of an information correlate with users' attitudes towards sharing that information with various third-party categories?
- **RQ5.** How does users' willingness to share different types of information vary according to third-party categories?

Our study shows that, both participant groups consider biometric information more sensitive than health information. We notice occupation plays a role in perception of information sensitivity and their privacy perception for sharing that information with a third-party. We also observe a positive correlation between information sensitivity level and users' privacy attitude towards sharing the information with third-parties. We also notice that, in both studies, female participants perceive more sensitivity towards different information types than male. Moreover, our study shows that users' willingness to share an information with third-parties depends on both the information type and third-party categories. For example, users are most comfortable sharing their health information with third-parties in the legal or insurance category whereas they are less comfortable sharing it with third-parties in the search engine category.

2 Related Work

Much work has been done to understand users' perception of privacy risks regarding social networking platforms and the internet [17,33,39,40], sharing their information [15,38], and privacy risks of IoT devices [25–27,43].

Xu et al. [40] propose a model based on the theory of panel behavior (TPB) and privacy calculus model [23] to evaluate users' perception of privacy concerns surrounding social networking platforms. They show that users are more concerned about privacy risks caused by the misuse of PII than unauthorized disclosure of them. Bhatia et al. [17] propose a framework that consists of factorial vignette to measure users' viewpoint about privacy risks with regard to six factors: data type, computer type, data purpose, privacy harm, harm likelihood, and individual demographic factors, such as education level. They show that users' willingness to share their PII is influenced by their views about the benefits of such sharing. Milne et al. [33] propose an information sensitivity typology by evaluating 52 information types with 310 users. They report that users associate higher risks to identifiable information such as social security numbers, and are less concerned about their basic demographic information, such as age. Their work has two limitations: (1) these 52 information types do not include the specific types information collected by IoT devices. (2) the information typology does not provide a complete sensitivity level for those information types.

Other work attempt to study users' attitudes towards sharing their personal information [12,15,38,42]. An interview of 33 users shows that they have minimal concerns about their privacy while sharing thèir fitness data [15]. Zeng et al. [42] surveyed 15 users and observed that their primarily concern is about unauthorized access to their data by third-parties. Mare et al. [12] interviewed 82 hosts and 554 guests to identify their privacy and security concerns with regard to IoT devices in AirBnBs and showed that they are mainly concerned about collection of their information without their knowledge or consent. To evaluate the trade-off of privacy risks and benefits of providing information, Kim et al. [27] surveyed 154 IoT device users, and show that their view of privacy risks is minimal when the benefit of sharing such information is high. Emami et al. [25] surveyed 1,371 Amazon MTurk workers to understand the effectiveness of privacy labels proposed in [24]. Their findings indicate that participants are more reluctant to purchase an IoT device if companies sell their data to third-parties.

While the above mentioned research focus on understanding users' viewpoint on privacy risks [15,17,25–27,31,33,38–40], most of them are limited to non-IoT domain [17,31,33,38,40]. Research that focuses on IoT also does not examine sensitivity levels of PII collected by IoT devices and users' attitude towards sharing their PII with third-parties, which are the focus of this paper.

3   Methods

In this section, we discuss the steps for identifying 79 information types and 15 third-party categories, the details of the two participant groups, and the design of our two-fold user study. We selected university students and Amazon MTurk workers as our audience to compare the results with both academic and general public. Our two-fold user study has been approved by the University of Maine institutional review board (IRB Application Number: 2021-03-20). Before the data collection, participants were informed about the purpose of these studies and how their responses will be protected. Responses are recorded without any personally identifiable data and are kept in a password protected folder.

3.1   IoT Privacy Policies Analysis

Our two-fold study focuses on investigating users' perception of sensitivity levels of the information that are *specifically* collected by IoT devices. For this, we collected privacy policies from the 100 most popular IoT devices listed on IoT Line Up website [3]. We noticed that several IoT devices with distinct functionalities have the same privacy policy. For example, Amazon Alexa and Echo bud have one privacy policy. As a result, the total number of privacy policies reduced to 75. We divided these privacy policies among the first three authors and each of them analyzed 25 of them to extract information types. If two out of three agreed on the information type, they accepted it as one. We followed the guideline provided by Nickerson et al. [9] and developed a taxonomy **IoT-Data Practice Analyzer (IoT-DPA) [11]. We defined our *meta-characteristics* as *data practices that exist in IoT privacy policies.* We performed two empirical to conceptual and three conceptual to empirical iterations on the 75 IoT privacy policies and considered both subjective and objective end conditions specified in the methodology [9].

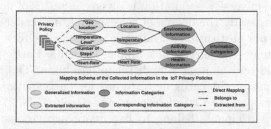

Fig. 1. An overview of the mapping schema for information categories [11]

During the analysis, we observed that terminologies for information types vary among privacy policies. For example, some policies use "location", whereas others mention "geo-location" instead. However, "location" and "geo-location" refer to the same type of information in this context. To resolve this inconsistency, we extended the approach provided by Bokaei [18]. We created a mapping schema as follows: we map both "location" and "geo-location" to their general form "location". Such mapping helps us handle cases such as synonyms and hypo-/hypernyms. We identified 67 such general forms, in total. Figure 1 shows an example of our mapping schema. Using this mapping schema, we extracted 79 types of information[1]. Since IoT devices collect different information types based on their functionalities, we decided to classify these 79 information types into eight information categories suggested by regulations such as GDPR [6] and CCPA [1]: Demographic (D), Identity (I), Technical (T), Environmental (E), Internet-Based (I-B), Health (H), Activity (A), and Biometric (B) Information. We selected the category, if at least two authors identified the information under the same category. As shown in Fig. 1, "location" and "temperature" are mapped to the information category "environmental information" [11].

We also examine if users' comfort level for sharing their information with certain third-parties varies depending on the sensitivity level of the information and the types of third-party with whom the information is shared. Thus, we identified 14 third-party categories listed on Privacy Grade website [4]. While analyzing the 75 privacy policies, we found that IoT devices are likely to share an information with "Legal or Insurance" category, as well. Hence, we added "Legal or Insurance" as the 15th third-party category. In our analysis, we also found that 78% of privacy policies mention generic categories of third-parties (e.g., Payment) while 22% of them provide specific names of a third-party (e.g., Paypal). Thus, we only consider third-party categories rather than each individual one.

---

[1] List of 79 information types: https://tinyurl.com/3vpk6evr.

3.2 Participant Recruitment and Demographics

We conducted our user studies with two groups of participants: i) students from our institution and ii) Amazon MTurk workers.

University Students. We consider university students as one of the targeted populations since the university population is diverse in terms of fields of study and age and it helps us study the degree of sensitivity from academic's perspective. We worked with our institution's graduate school and Office of International Programs to circulate the survey link among students. Participants were minimum 18 years old and at least a high school graduate. The first 30 students were given $5 Amazon gift cards as a reward for participation. We received a total of 70 responses where 72% of respondents were female, 27% male, and 1% non-binary. The participants belong to five major age groups: 18–24 ($\sim$26%), 25–31 ($\sim$44%), 32–38 ($\sim$17%), 39–45 ($\sim$10%), and 46 and above ($\sim$3%).

Amazon Mechanical Turk Workers. We chose Amazon MTurk workers as another targeted populations, since Amazon MTurk is a large cloud platform that enables us to have participants from diverse culture, education level, occupations, and location. Thus, it helps us evaluate the degree of sensitivity from generic public's perspective. To be eligible for this study, participants had to be at least 18 years old. We hired participants who had completed at least 1000 Human Intelligence Tasks (HITs) and had a 95% or greater HIT approval rate. All participants were rewarded with $1.5 upon successful completion of the survey. We received a total of 237 responses where 39 of them were incomplete, and thus excluded. To filter out responses with randomized answers, we evaluated the remaining 198 responses by checking the time each participant took to answer each question. If the duration between answering two questions was less than 20 s, we excluded that response on the basis that their answers appeared to be randomly given. We excluded an additional 34 responses and were left with 164 responses. Of the remaining 164 participants, $\sim$35% were female and 65% were male. The age distribution of these 164 participants is: 18–24 (7%), 25–31 (39%), 32–38 ($\sim$27%), 39–45 ($\sim$11%), and 46 and above (16%).

3.3 Survey Design

Our survey questions[2] focus on understanding participants' perception of IoT information sensitivity levels and their willingness to share the information with third-parties. We, first, asked participants to rate the sensitivity level of information categories on a five-point likert scale from "*Not At All Sensitive*" to "*Extremely Sensitive*" and to rate if they think sharing the data from an information category with third-parties may violate their privacy, again on a five-point likert scale from "*Strongly Disagree*" to "*Strongly Agree*". Second, we randomly selected two types of information from each information category and provided a scenario that describes how an IoT device collects the information. These scenarios help participants to imagine the context of information collection. One example of a scenario

---

[2] Survey Questionnaires: https://tinyurl.com/wcxw5tfk.

is: "*Consider an application which records the air temperature of a user's garden.*", where *air temperature* is one of the information from environmental information category. With each scenario, we asked participants to rate the information's sensitivity level and their privacy perception for sharing that information type with a third-party, using the same five-point likert scale as before. Lastly, we asked them to select which, if any, third-party categories they are comfortable to share that information type with. Finally, they were asked to rank the eight information categories based on their perceived sensitivity level for two reasons. First, we can match these ranks against the sensitivity levels rated by the participants in the first question. Second, responses to these questions provide us with a comparative sensitivity ranking of all the eight information categories and help us understand which information type users perceive as more sensitive and which one as less sensitive.

4 Results

In this section, we answer our five research questions and provide a brief comparison of the findings from the first-fold and second-fold studies for each question.

4.1 Sensitivity Level vs. Information Types

Our RQ1 focuses on understanding how sensitivity of information types varies based on the user's point of view. To answer this, participants were asked, *"What level of sensitivity would you assign to the I information category in general?"* where I represents one of the eight information types described in Subsect. 3.1. The response options for the sensitivity level followed a five-point likert scale (i.e. Extremely Sensitive, Very Sensitive, Moderately Sensitive, Slightly Sensitive, and Not At All Sensitive). Figure 2 and Fig. 3 show the frequency of the sensitivity levels reported by students and MTurk workers respectively.

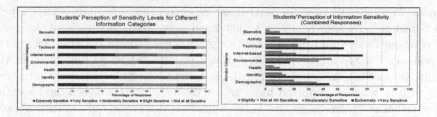

Fig. 2. Left: frequency of responses for all five sensitivity levels and Right: frequency of responses for combined levels from First-Fold study.

First-Fold Study - University Students. In our first-fold study, about 72% of students consider biometric information as "Extremely Sensitive" and among them, ~76% reported health information as "Extremely Sensitive". These data show that users are very concerned about the collection of their biometric and health information by IoT devices. No students reported biometric information type as "Not At All Sensitive". As shown in Fig. 2 (left-hand side), at least 14% of students consider all the eight information types as "Very Sensitive". Environmental information type received the highest response (>21%) as "Not At All Sensitive", which shows that users are less concerned about the collection of this information. Students may perceive 'Extremely" and "Very" sensitive level similarly and 'Slightly" and "Not At All" sensitive, on the same scale. Hence, as shown in Fig. 2 (right-hand side), we decided to merge the responses of "Extremely" and "Very" sensitive, and "Slightly" and "Not At All" sensitive together for more analysis. We noticed that over 80% of students reported biometric and health information types as "Extremely" or "Very" sensitive. More than 60% of students consider activity, identity, and internet-based information as "Extremely" or "Very" sensitive. About 50% of them consider environmental information as "Slightly" or "Not At All" sensitive.

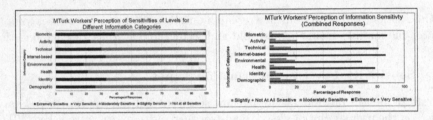

Fig. 3. Left: frequency of responses for all five sensitivity levels and Right: frequency of responses for combined levels from Second-Fold study.

Second-Fold Study - Amazon Mechanical Turk Workers. In our second-fold study, we observed that 39% of MTurk workers believe that biometric information is "Extremely Sensitive" and among them over 42% consider health information as "Extremely Sensitive". About 48% of the workers consider biometric information as "Very Sensitive". No participant reported this information as "Not At All Sensitive". As shown in Fig. 3, (left-hand side), only about 1% of the workers consider health information as "Not At All Sensitive". We also merged the responses on "Extremely" and "Very" sensitive, and "Slightly" and "Not At All" sensitive together. As shown in Fig. 3, (right-hand side), we noticed that about 80% MTurk workers reported biometric, technical, internet-based, and identity information as "Extremely" or "Very" sensitive. More than 60% MTurk workers reported activity, demographic, health, and environmental information types as "Extremely" or "Very" sensitive. About 15% of workers consider environmental information type as "Slightly" or "Not At All Sensitive".

Comparison Between First-Fold and Second-Fold Responses. We observed a clear difference in responses between students and MTurk workers for health and identity information. In our first-fold study, about 58% of students believe health information as "Extremely Sensitive" while about 21% of MTurk workers consider them as such. On the other hand, about 32% of MTurk workers report identity information as the second most "Extremely Sensitive" information type whereas 41% of students consider this information as the third most "Extremely Sensitive" one. As discussed earlier, participants may perceive "Extremely Sensitive" and "Very Sensitive" similarly. Figure 2 (right-hand side) and 3 (right-hand side) show that, the responses from students and MTurk workers are very similar for biometric, health, and identity information, which indicates that participants perceive these three information types more sensitive than the other information types. We also noticed students consider demographic and environmental information less sensitive than Mturk workers.

Table 1. Results of the Chi Square Test of Independence

Value	D	I	H	E	I-B	T	A	B
Result 1. Users' Perceived Sensitivity Level and Their Occupation Category of the Second-Fold Study								
χ^2	9.1	10.29*	12.52*	6.02	4.99	2.17	7.15	10.57*
p	0.058	0.038*	0.013*	0.19	0.28	0.7	0.97	0.03*
Result 2. Attitude towards Potential Privacy Violations and Their Occupation Category of the Second-Fold Study								
χ^2	7.08	9.08	3.12	1.5	8.33	6.77	2.06	11.2*
p	0.13	0.05	0.53	0.82	0.08	0.2	0.72	0.02*
Result 3. Users' Gender and Their Perceived Information Sensitivity Levels (First-Fold and Second-Fold Study)								
1st-Fold (χ^2)	3.76	1.07	3.87	3.45	21.76*	7.23	10.47*	2.09
1st-Fold (p)	0.43	0.89	0.46	0.484	0.0002*	0.12	0.04*	0.71
2nd-Fold (χ^2)	10.80*	10.27*	3.67	10.95*	6.43	6.73	2.11	3.76
2nd-Fold (p)	0.028*	0.035*	0.45	0.027*	0.168	0.15	0.71	0.439

Since MTurk workers are from a wider range of occupations compared to students, we also divided the responses from MTurk workers into academic (28%) and non-academic (72%) categories. Workers who stated their occupation as "student", "teacher", "faculty", or "professor" are considered as academic, and the rest of occupations such as "sale manager" and "IT" are categorized as non-academic. We conducted a Chi-Square Test of Independence to evaluate if the sensitivity level is dependent on users' occupation. Table 1 (Result 1) shows the result of the Chi-Square Test (χ^2) and statistical significance (p).[3] The result shows that sensitivity level for health, biometric, and identity information depends ($p < 0.05$) on the occupation (0.013, 0.03, 0.038 respectively).

Participants were also asked to rank the eight information types based on their sensitivity where 1 is the most sensitive and 8 is the least sensitive. Figure 4

---

[3] χ^2 Critical Value is 9.48 at 4° of freedom (df) and 5% level of significance.

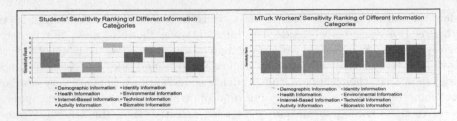

Fig. 4. Sensitivity ranking of different information types. Left: responses received from the students. Right: responses received from the MTurk workers.

shows this ranking by students (left-hand side) and the MTurk workers (right-hand side). In both whisker box plots, the mean and median of environmental information is higher than any other information types which indicates both groups consider environmental information the least sensitive. The median of health information is higher than of biometric in both studies which shows that both groups perceive biometric more sensitive than health information.

4.2   Privacy Concerns vs. Information Types

In RQ2, we investigate how users' attitude towards sharing their information with third-parties varies based on the information type. To answer this, participants were asked to respond to the following statement, *"Sharing I information will violate your privacy"*, where I represents one of the eight information types described in Subsect. 3.1. The response options are: Strongly Agree, Somewhat Agree, Neither Agree nor Disagree, Somewhat Disagree, and Strongly Disagree. Figure 5 and 6 show responses by students and MTurk workers.

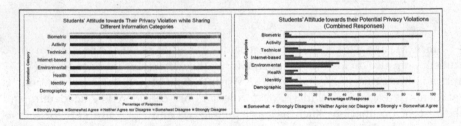

Fig. 5. Left: frequency of responses for all the five scales, Right: frequency of responses for combined responses from First-Fold study.

First-Fold Study - University Student. As shown in Fig. 5 (left-hand side), over 77% of students "Strongly Agree" that sharing a biometric information violates their privacy regardless of their consent. About 57% and 50% of them believe that sharing health and identity information may violate their privacy.

About 32% of them reported that they "Neither Agree nor Disagree" that sharing environmental information may violate their privacy. We also observed that at least 1% of students reported that sharing their biometric, technical, internet-based, demographic, or environmental information may violate their privacy. We also examined how many students *at least* agree or disagree that sharing one of the eight information types with a third-party may violate their privacy. For this, we combined "Strongly" and "Somewhat" agree responses (i.e. *at least* agree), and "Strongly" and "Somewhat" disagree responses (*at least* disagree). As shown in Fig. 5, (right-hand side), we observe that more than 80% of students *at least* agree that sharing biometric, activity, internet-based, health, and identity information with third-parties may violate their privacy. More than 50% of students *at least* agree that sharing technical and demographic information may violate their privacy. About 38% of students at least disagree, and more than 35% of them neither agree nor disagree that sharing environmental information may violate their privacy, which indicates, students are less concerned about privacy violations regarding to environmental information.

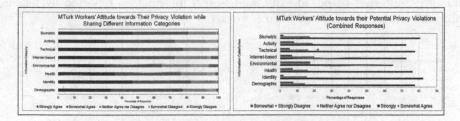

Fig. 6. Left: frequency of responses for all the five scales, Right: frequency of responses for combined responses from Second-Fold study.

Second-Fold Study - Amazon Mechanical Turk. As shown in Fig. 6, (left-hand side), about 45% of MTurk workers "Strongly Agree" that sharing biometric information with third-party may violate their privacy while for health information, this is about 35%. At least 1% of workers "Strongly Disagree" that sharing any of the eight information types may violate their privacy. We also merged MTurk workers' responses for "Strongly" and "Somewhat" agree (i.e. *at least* agree), and "Strongly" and "Somewhat" disagree responses (i.e. *at least* disagree). As shown in Fig. 6 (right-hand side), about 80% of them *at least* agree that sharing biometric and identity information may violate their privacy while for health information, this is about 75%. About 60% of the workers consider sharing information from any of the eight categories may violate their privacy. About 15% of workers *at least* disagree that sharing environmental information types with third-parties may violate their privacy.

Comparison Between First-Fold and Second-Fold Responses. We observed a clear difference in responses between students and MTurk workers for biometric and identity information. For example, as shown in Fig. 5 and 6, 77% of students in comparison to 45% of workers "Strongly Agree" that sharing biometric information may violate their privacy. Similar to Subsect. 4.1, we conducted a Chi-Square Test of Independence to observe if users' attitude towards sharing their information with third-parties depends on their occupation: academic vs. non-academic. Table 1 (Result 2) shows the result of the Chi-Square Test of Independence (χ^2) and statistical significance (p) for the second-fold study which demonstrate that MTurk workers' attitude towards sharing biometric information with third-parties is dependent on ($p < 0.05$) their occupation ($p = 0.02$). Although the result is not statistically significant, the occupation category is slightly associated with identity information ($p = 0.05$).

4.3 Information Sensitivity vs. User's Gender

In our RQ3, we investigate if users' gender play a role in finding an information type sensitive. To answer this, we analyzed the frequency of sensitivity levels reported for each of the eight information types based on the gender of both participant groups. Figure 7 shows the frequency of the sensitivity levels for biometric, internet-based, identity, and health information reported by female and male students (top) and MTurk workers (bottom).

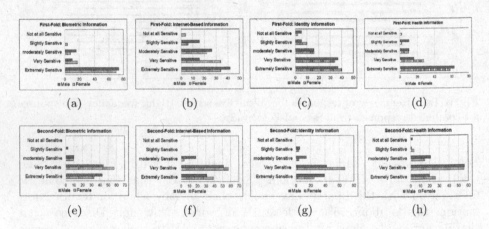

Fig. 7. Frequency of sensitivity levels for Biometric, Internet-Based, Identity, and Health based on Gender. (Top) Students and (Bottom) MTurk workers.

First-Fold Study - University Students. As shown in Fig. 7(a), about 73% of male students report biometric information as "Extremely Sensitive" whereas 70% of female students vote the same. About 58% of female students consider health information as "Extremely Sensitive" in comparison to about 63% of male students (Fig. 7(d)). For the internet-based information (Fig. 7(b)), about 28% of male students reported it as "Moderately Sensitive" compared to female participants (~22%) while ~34% of female students reported internet-based information as "Very Sensitive" compared to males (~15%).

Second-Fold Study - Amazon Mechanical Turk. Figure 7(e) shows that about 33% of female consider biometric information as "Extremely Sensitive" compared to 43% of male. For internet-based information, (Fig. 7(f)), about 57% of female and 51% of male workers reported it as "Very Sensitive". No male or female vote internet-based information as "Slightly Sensitive" or "Not At All Sensitive". As shown in Fig. 7(g), about 70% of female workers report identity information as "Very Sensitive" compared to 42% of male.

Comparison Between First-Fold and Second-Fold Responses. In both studies, we noticed a clear difference in female and male participants' responses between "Extremely" and "Very" sensitive. We decided to combine the answers for "Extremely" and "Very" sensitive for female and male participants in both studies. In the first-fold study, (Fig. 8 (left-hand side)), female students answered five out of eight information types more sensitive than male. For instance, about 85% of female students voted health information more sensitive than male ($\sim$80%). Both female and male students perceived identity and environmental information as equally sensitive. For demographic and technical information types, male students ($\sim$50%, $\sim$58% respectively) perceived them more sensitive compared to female students ($\sim$40%, $\sim$50% respectively). In the second-fold study, as shown in Fig. 8 (right-hand side), female MTurk workers reported all the eight information types more sensitive compared to male workers. For instance, >95% of female workers considered identity and internet-based information sensitive than male workers($\sim$80%).

We also conducted a Chi-Square Test of Independence to evaluate if the users' gender play a role in perceived sensitivity. Table 1 (Result 3) shows the result for both study. In both of our studies, we found users' understanding of sensitivity levels differs based on their gender. For instance, the first-fold study, students' perception of information sensitivity for internet-based and activity depends on ($p < 0.05$) their gender ($p = 0.0002$ and 0.04). For the second-fold study, MTurk workers' perceived information sensitivity for demographic, identity, and environmental information is dependent on their gender ($p = 0.028$, 0.035, and 0.027 respectively).

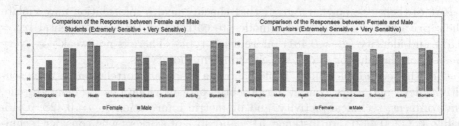

Fig. 8. Combined responses of extremely sensitive and very sensitive from female and male students (left-hand side) and MTurk workers (right-hand side).

4.4 Information Sensitivity vs. Users' Attitude Towards Sharing the Information with Third-Parties

Our RQ4 focuses on analyzing the correlation between users' perception of sensitivity level and their attitude towards sharing their information with third-parties. We conducted Spearman's correlation test for both first-fold and second-fold studies. Spearman's correlation coefficient (r_s) determines the degree to which a relationship between two ordinal variables is monotonic. The strength of the correlation can be determined from the value of r_s as follows: *very weak* (0.00–0.19), *weak* (0.20–0.39), *moderate* (0.40–0.59), *strong* (0.60–0.79), and *very strong*(0.80–1.0) [5]. In our study, the two variables are: sensitivity level of different information types and users' attitude towards sharing their information with a third-party. Table 2 shows the result of Spearman's correlation coefficient (r_s) and statistical significant values (p) of both studies.

Table 2. Results of the Spearman's correlation coefficient test.

Value	D	I	H	E	I-B	T	A	B
1st-Fold (r_s)	0.658	0.489	0.687	0.51	0.835	0.826	0.775	0.824
2nd-Fold (r_s)	0.428	0.342	0.382	0.415	0.354	0.452	0.442	0.442

For the first-fold study, Table 2 shows that there is a very strong correlation between sensitivity level and users' attitude towards sharing three information types: internet-based, technical, and biometric $(r_s = 0.835, 0.826, 0.824)$. This result states that the students who believe any of these three information types is 'Extremely Sensitive", they "Strongly Agree" that sharing them may violate their privacy. For instance, among "Extremely Sensitive" responses for biometric and internet-based information types, ~99% and 100% of students, respectively, "Strongly Agree" that sharing any of these two with third-party may violate their privacy. Activity, health, and demographic information demonstrate a strong correlation as well $(r_s = 0.775, 0.687, 0.658)$. For instance, 86% of students, who consider health information as "Extremely Sensitive", "Strongly Agree" and ~10% of them "Somewhat Agree" that sharing health information may violate their privacy. We also noticed a moderate correlation for environmental $(r_s = 0.51)$ and identity $(r_s = 0.481)$ information types. There is no "weak" or "very weak" correlations for any of the eight information types.

For the second-fold study, Table 2 shows a moderate correlation between sensitivity level and users' concern for potential privacy violations for: demographic, environment, technical, activity, and biometric information $(r_s = 0.428, 0.415, 0.452, 0.442, 0.442)$. For instance, 51% and 46% of workers who consider technical or biometric information as "Extremely Sensitive", "Somehow Agree" that sharing either of them with a third-party may violate their privacy. We also noticed a weak correlation for identity and health information $(r_s = 0.342$ and 0.382). There is no strong or very strong correlation for any of the types of information.

4.5   Information Types vs. Third-Party Categories

In our RQ5, our goal is to examine how users' comfort level for sharing certain information varies with different third-party categories. We randomly selected two information types from the eight information categories and asked participants to select the third-party categories with whom they are comfortable sharing the information. In addition to 15 third-party categories, we added two options: (i) "None": if users do not want to share their information with any of the third-party categories and (ii) "Not Sure": if users are not sure with whom they are comfortable to share their information. Figure 9 shows frequency of the responses from first (left-hand side) and second-fold (right-hand side) of the study.

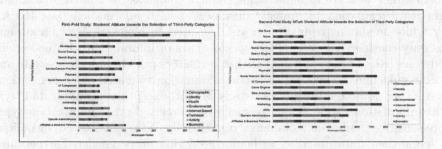

Fig. 9. Frequency of the selection of Third-Party categories. Left: university students. Right: amazon MTurk workers.

For the first-fold of the study (see Fig. 9 (left-hand side)), "None" was selected by students, more than other options (~410), which states that students are not comfortable sharing their information with any third-party. Among all third-party categories, students most frequently select the "Legal or Insurance" (8.2%) category to share their information with. They least frequently consider the "Advertisement" category and are not comfortable sharing their biometric information with this category at all. For health information, around 11% selected "Legal or Insurance" and 6.41% selected "Data Analytics". For the second-fold, as shown in Fig. 9 (right-hand side), we noticed that MTurk workers are most comfortable sharing their information with "Marketing" category. Similar to the first-fold, they least frequently selected the "Advertisement" category.

We also investigated how users' willingness to share their information varies according to third-party categories. Table 3 shows the top third-party category with whom participants are most comfortable sharing their information, for each information category. Our results show that students are more comfortable sharing their more sensitive information such as identity, health, and biometric with "Legal or Insurance" while MTurk workers are comfortable sharing their more sensitive information with "Marketing". We also observed that users' comfort level of sharing their information with third-parties depends on the information categories[4].

5   Discussion

A key learning from this study is that users' perception of information sensitivity level highly depends on the information types. As detailed in Sect. 4, most participants consider health and biometric information at least very sensitive. These results indicate that companies and regulatory bodies that traditionally emphasize solely on health-related data as their main priority may undervalue users' perception of sensitivity for biometric information. In general, privacy regulations place a greater emphasis on protecting health information than other information types. For example, some countries, such as the United States, have a separate regulation to protect consumers' health information (i.e., HIPAA [7]), while no similar regulation exists dedicated to biometric information and it is only considered as *one* of the special types of information with no-specific guidelines [1,6]. Our results suggest that regulators need to provide separate and specific guidelines to protect biometric information to match users' perception.

Another notable finding of our study is that, except demographic and technical information types, female participants perceived other information types more sensitive than male. Companies traditionally create generic privacy policies to define their data practices without considering users' gender. Furthermore, IoT devices that are primarily dedicated to provide services to female users, such as smart wrist band for women's safety, also define generic privacy practices. In such cases, results from our analysis can help companies create privacy policies according to female privacy perceptions.

In Table 2, we notice a clear difference between the first-fold and second-fold of our study with respect to correlation between users' perceived information sensitivity level and their attitude towards sharing the information with third-parties. One reason for this difference is the location of the MTurk workers. Previous research shows that the US MTurk workers are more likely to worry about their privacy than Indian workers [10]. In the first-fold of the study, all the 70 students are the US residents whereas, the 164 MTurk workers are from various locations such as US, India, and Italy. Users' views of privacy can be different based on their culture and geographical location. Hence, the diverse locations and culture of the MTurk workers is one possible reason for the difference in our results.

Sensitivity Levels	Information Types
Level A ($\geq$ 75%)	B, H, &I
Level B ($\geq$ 60%)	A, & I-B
Level C ($<$ 60%)	T, D, & E

Fig. 10. Sensitivity levels of the information types.

Another significant finding from this study is that the users' attitude towards sharing information with third-parties vary with the types of information. As detailed in Sect. 4, the users strongly agree that sharing biometric information may violate their privacy. Similar to the result in Subsect. 4.1, users believe that

---

[4] The detailed results can be found: https://tinyurl.com/yhschu2o.

sharing environmental information will less likely violate their privacy. Since IoT devices are complex and can collect diverse information types, providing a detailed privacy policy describing all types of data can be challenging. Hence, understanding users' perception of information sensitivity and their attitude towards sharing certain information with third-parties can help organizations and policymakers to create privacy policies according to users' perceptions.

Much research attempt to identify inconsistencies between an application and its privacy policy [13,14,16,19,20,29,41]. However, none of them focus on evaluating the *magnitude* of those inconsistencies. For example, if an application collects health information without mentioning such collection in its privacy policy, the extent of violation is different than when the information in question belong to a different, less sensitive information type such as environmental information. As mentioned in Sect. 4, our study shows that users' perception of privacy violation strongly correlates with the sensitivity of information types. We also noticed that users' comfort level of sharing their information with third-party depends on the information types. Based on our findings and to better evaluate the extent of inconsistencies, we divide the eight information types into three sensitivity levels by quantifying frequency of users' perceived information sensitivity (see Fig. 10). We consider biometric, health, and identity information as the most sensitive information types (Level A) since they received $\geq 75\%$ "Extremely" and "Very" sensitive responses from both studies. Internet-based and activity information types received $\geq 60\%$ "Extremely" and "Very" sensitive responses and thus, we assign them to Level B. We assign the remaining three information types, technical, demographic and environmental to Level C. The sensitivity levels, users' attitude towards sharing an information with third-parties, and lists of third-party categories with whom users are comfortable to share the information with help create a roadmap towards identifying the *magnitude* of inconsistencies between applications and their privacy policies.

6   Threats to Validity

Internal Validity. Internal validity involves the study procedures restricting analyzing correct inferences from the collected data [44]. One threat to internal validity is that both groups of participants may have different attitudes while responding to the survey questions. For instance, participants' responses might reflect differently than what they perceive. Additionally, participants may not understand the meaning of the eight information types. To mitigate this threat, we provided participants with detailed definitions and scenarios of collecting data for each information type. Although we provided definitions and scenarios, we cannot guarantee that participants read them before answering the survey questions.

Table 3. Top Third-Party categories with whom users are most comfortable to share their information.

Information	First-Fold study	Second-Fold study
Demographic	Insurance or Legal 11.62%	Marketing 8.98%
Identity	Insurance or Legal 15.47%	Marketing 8.4%
Health	Insurance or Legal 11.84%	Insurance or Legal 9.20%
Environmental	Data Analytics 9.15%	Data Analytics 8.80%
Internet-Based	Social Engine 6.51%	Utility 1.39%
Technical	Service/Content Provider 7.14%	Marketing 8.15%
Activity	Data Analytics 8.19%	Marketing 9.60%
Biometric	Insurance or Legal 8.20%	Service/Content Provider 7.83%

External Validity. External validity concerns how we can generalize the results to other situations [44]. In this study, we focus on studying IoT information sensitivity levels from two different perspectives as follows: i) academic's perspective (university students) and ii) general public's perspective (Amazon MTurk workers). However, among the participants from both groups, most of them are the United States residents. Thus, results drawn from this study cannot be generalized in other geographical locations and cultures. Additionally, we have a larger number of younger participants than older ones. Since older people might be less tech-savvy, their perception of information sensitivity may differ from younger IoT users. Furthermore, we focused on one demographic factor, gender, in evaluating sensitivity levels. Other factors, such as age and fields of study, may also influence users' perception of information sensitivity level [10]. Thus, results drawing from our analysis cannot be generalized to other cultures, locations or fields of study.

7   Conclusion and Future Work

In this paper, we presented the results of our user studies to examine users' perception of sensitivity level of different information types and their attitude towards potential privacy violations by sharing the information with third-parties. We developed a taxonomy to classify information types and third-party categories related to IoT devices. We conducted a two-fold study, one with 70 university students and the other with 164 Amazon Mturk workers. The result of our study shows that users' perception of information sensitivity levels and their attitude towards sharing the information with third-parties vary based on different information types. We also noticed, potential privacy violations statistically significantly correlates with the information's sensitivity level. In both studies, we found participants' perceived information sensitivity depends on their gender and their willingness to share their information with third-parties varies based on both third-party and information categories.

In future, we plan to examine how users' viewpoints with respect to protecting their collected information vary with different information categories. Our goal is to ask the following open end question with regard to 79 information types: *what should be done to protect this information?* Response from this question will help us understand what is the user's point of view regarding the protection of different information types and if it correlates with the sensitivity level of the information. IoT devices are multi-functional, and one device may collect different types of information such as biometric and environmental information. A third-party associated with this device might infer personally identifiable information by combining the data from these two different types. In future, we plan to study how users perceive sensitivity when information types are combined.

References

1. California Consumers' Privacy Act. https://oag.ca.gov/privacy/ccpa
2. International Data Corporation Forecast. https://tinyurl.com/y694wg2v
3. IoT Line Up. http://iotlineup.com/
4. Privacy Grade Website. http://privacygrade.org/third_party_libraries
5. Spearman Coefficient. https://tinyurl.com/nctpfudu
6. The EU GDPR - Article 14. https://eugdpr.org. Accessed 01 May 2020
7. The Health Insurance Portability and Accountability Act of 1996 (HIPAA)
8. Nobakht, M., et al.: PGFit: static permission analysis of health and fitness apps in IoT programming frameworks. J. Network Comput. Appl. **152**, 102509 (2020)
9. Nickerson, R.C., et al.: A method for taxonomy development and its application in information systems. Eur. J. Inf. Syst. **22**(3), 336–359 (2013). https://doi.org/10.1057/ejis.2012.26
10. Kang, R., et al.: Privacy attitudes of mechanical Turk workers and the US public. In: 10th Symposium on Usable Privacy and Security ({SOUPS} 2014) (2014)
11. Gupta, S.D., Nygaard, A., Kaplan, S., Jain, V., Ghanavati, S.: PHIN: a privacy protected heterogeneous IoT network. In: Cherfi, S., Perini, A., Nurcan, S. (eds.) RCIS 2021. LNBIP, vol. 415, pp. 124–141. Springer, Cham (2021). https://doi.org/10.1007/978-3-030-75018-3_8
12. Mare, S., et al.: Smart devices in AirBnBs: considering privacy and security for both guests and hosts. In: Proceedings on Privacy Enhancing Technologies
13. Slavin, R., et al.: PVDetector: a detector of privacy-policy violations for android apps. In: IEEE/ACM International Conference on Mobile Software Engineering and Systems, pp. 299–300 (2016)
14. Zimmeck, S., et al.: Maps: scaling privacy compliance analysis to a million apps. Proc. Priv. Enhancing Technol. **2019**(3), 66–86 (2019)
15. Zimmer, M., et al.: 'There's nothing really they can do with this information': unpacking how users manage privacy boundaries for personal fitness information. Inf. Commun. Soc. **23**(7), 1020–1037 (2020)
16. Bhatia, J., Breaux, T.D.: Privacy risk in cybersecurity data sharing. In: ISCS 2016 (2016)
17. Bhatia, J., Breaux, T.D.: Empirical measurement of perceived privacy risk. ACM Trans. Comput. Hum. Interact. (TOCHI) **25**(6), 1–47 (2018)

18. Bokaie, H.M.: Information Retrieval and Semantic Inference from Natural Language Privacy Policies. Ph.D. thesis, The University of Texas at San Antonio (2019)
19. Breaux, T., Hibshi, H.: Eddy, a formal language for specifying and analyzing data flow specifications for conflicting privacy requirements. REJ **19**(3), 281–307 (2014)
20. Breaux, T.D., Smullen, D., Hibshi, H.: Detecting repurposing and over-collection in multi-party privacy requirements specifications. In: 2015 IEEE 23rd International Requirements Engineering Conference (RE). IEEE (2015)
21. Checkit, G.: Smart home device adoption. Article. https://tinyurl.com/yba69fcp
22. Cyber Physical Systems Public Working Group: PRELIMINARY DISCUSSION DRAFT - Framework for Cyber-Physical Systems - Release 0.7 (2015)
23. Dinev, T., Hart, P.: An extended privacy calculus model for e-commerce transactions. Inf. Syst. Res. **17**(1), 61–80 (2006)
24. Emami-Naeini, P., Agarwal, Y., Cranor, L.F., Hibshi, H.: Ask the experts: what should be on an IoT privacy and security label? In: 2020 IEEE S&P (2020)
25. Emami-Naeini, P., Dheenadhayalan, J., Agarwal, Y., Cranor, L.F.: Which privacy and security attributes most impact consumers' risk perception and willingness to purchase IoT devices?
26. Haney, J., Acar, Y., Furman, S.: "It's the company, the government, you and i": user perceptions of responsibility for smart home privacy and security. In: 30th {USENIX} Security Symposium ({USENIX} Security 21) (2021)
27. Kim, D., Park, K., Park, Y., Ahn, J.H.: Willingness to provide personal information: Perspective of privacy calculus in IoT services. Comput. Hum. Behav. **92**, 273–281 (2019)
28. Liu, L., Karatas, C., et al.: Toward detection of unsafe driving with wearables. In: Proceedings of the 2015 Workshop on WSA, pp. 27–32. ACM (2015)
29. Maitra, S., Suh, B., Ghanavati, S.: Privacy consistency analyzer for android applications. In: 5th International Workshop (ESPRE), pp. 28–33 (2018)
30. Markos, E.C.: Consumer privacy: A two essay dissertation examining perceptions of information sensitivity. University of Massachusetts Amherst (2010)
31. Mekovec, R.: Factors that influence internet users' privacy perception. In: ITI 2011, pp. 227–232. IEEE (2011)
32. Michalevsky, Y., Schulman, A.: Powerspy: location tracking using mobile device power analysis. In: 24th {USENIX} Security Symposium, pp. 785–800 (2015)
33. Milne, G.R., Pettinico, G., Hajjat, F.M., Markos, E.: Information sensitivity typology: mapping the degree and type of risk consumers perceive in personal data sharing. J. Consum. Affairs **51**(1), 133–161 (2017)
34. National Science and Technology Council: National Privacy Research Strategy (2016). https://www.nitrd.gov/PUBS/NationalPrivacyResearchStrategy.pdf
35. Okoyomon, E., Samarin, N., et al.: On the ridiculousness of notice and consent: contradictions in app privacy policies (2019)
36. Safi, M., Reyes, I., Egelman, S.: Inference of user demographics and habits from seemingly benign smartphone sensors
37. Smullen, D.: Modeling, analyzing, and consistency checking privacy requirements using eddy. In: Proceedings of the Symposium and Bootcamp on the Science of Security
38. Torabi, S.: Understanding users' perception toward sharing personal health information
39. Weible, R.J.: Privacy and data: An empirical study of the influence of types of data and situational context upon privacy perceptions. Ph.D. thesis, MSU (1993)
40. Xu, F., Michael, K., Chen, X.: Factors affecting privacy disclosure on social network sites: an integrated model. Electron. Comm. Res. **13**(2), 151–168 (2013)

41. Yu, L., Lou, X.: Can we trust the privacy policies of android apps? IEEE (2016)
42. Zeng, E.: End user security and privacy concerns with smart homes. In: SOUPS
43. Zheng, S., Apthorpe, N., Chetty, M., Feamster, N.: User perceptions of smart home IoT privacy. In: Proceedings of the ACM on Human-Computer Interaction (CSCW), vol. 2
44. Creswell, J.W., Creswell, J.D.: Research Design: Qualitative, Quantitative, and Mixed Methods Approaches. Sage publications (2017)

SoK: A Systematic Literature Review of Bluetooth Security Threats and Mitigation Measures

Sunny Shrestha, Esa Irby, Raghav Thapa, and Sanchari Das[(⊠)]

University of Denver, Denver, CO 80208, USA
{sunny.shrestha,esa.irby,raghav.thapa,sanchari.das}@du.edu

Abstract. Bluetooth devices have integrated into our everyday lives such that we see an increase in wearable technologies. Users of these devices are often unaware of the security vulnerabilities that come with the use of Bluetooth. To this aid, we provide a comprehensive analysis of the security attacks and ways for users to mitigate these attacks focusing on Bluetooth technologies by reviewing prior literature. Here we analyze $N = 48$ peer-reviewed academic articles published in ACM and IEEE Digital Libraries. We investigate Bluetooth-specific attacks such as BlueSnarfing, Man-in-the-Middle for wearable technologies, MAC Address Spoofing, BLE-specific attacks, and others. Additionally, we analyze the papers detailing the malware targeting Bluetooth devices and compare our results with previous 15 prior systematization of knowledge (SoK) papers on Bluetooth attacks and mitigation measures. Additionally, in our review, we also provide a detailed analysis of the suggested mitigating measures, which include removing, repairing, or deleting access to devices that are no longer in use, utilizing Personal Identification Number (PIN) for user authentication, and other solutions. Thereafter, we conclude by providing actionable recommendations focused on wearable technology users.

Keywords: Bluetooth · Literature review · Security threats · Attack mitigation · Wearable devices

1 Introduction

First introduced in 1994 by Ericsson, Bluetooth is a short-range wireless communication technology that relies on radio waves to connect devices. Being an inexpensive and efficient technology, it allows users to create ad-hoc wireless networks, also known as piconets, constituting a pervasive technology that has seamlessly assimilated with our everyday lives [48]. Thus, Bluetooth security has become an increasing concern for many users and researchers alike. Thus, it is important to understand how information can be intercepted with the use of a Bluetooth-enabled device that is active within a network of connected devices [9].

Esa Irby and Raghav Thapa contributed equally in the project, thus they are joint second authors of this paper.

© Springer Nature Switzerland AG 2022
W. Meng and S. K. Katsikas (Eds.): EISA 2021, CCIS 1403, pp. 108–127, 2022.
https://doi.org/10.1007/978-3-030-93956-4_7

Bluetooth security is even more concerning as users keep personal information on their Bluetooth-connected devices such as banking information (credit card numbers, bank account numbers, etc.), personal photos or videos, text messages, health-related information, calendar schedules, emails, messages, and contact information [11,51]. Given the data we transmit over Bluetooth, attackers can cause financial loss, eavesdrop on communications, gain full control of a device, track or manipulate activities of the victim, and even propagate malware to a network of devices [28]. In addition to the security threats, it is important to understand users' knowledge of the mitigation tactics that can be adopted to defend against such vulnerabilities at the user level. Along these lines, a survey of 400 undergraduates by Tan and Masagca found that 61.08% of the students knew of at least one possible threat and yet only 32.93% took any preventive actions [65]. Thus, to understand further, we conducted a literature review by collecting papers from the ACM and the IEEEXplore digital libraries to understand the vulnerabilities in Bluetooth technology which users can be susceptible to and the best way to mitigate these risks. We analyzed 48 papers in total that discussed these vulnerabilities in a variety of different ways. These papers talked about attacks these Bluetooth devices are susceptible to, available software to prevent such attacks, and other ways to mitigate these threats. Our research focuses on analyzing these types of articles and provides a detailed synthesized result from them.

This paper is organized in following sections. First, we describe the review methodology in the Sect. 3. Thereafter we detail our analysis and the results on the types of threats that Bluetooth devices are susceptible to and ways for users to mitigate the risks in Sect. 4. Despite our best efforts to outline the solutions we understand there are limitations to a systematic literature review which we will mention in the following Sect. 7 and also provide suggestion on future research that can address these limitations. Finally, we provide a conclusion to our work in the Sect. 8.

2 Related Works

Bluetooth technology has been around for a while and so there have been many studies that have described various vulnerabilities and attack vectors related to Bluetooth-enabled devices. In his paper published in 2010, John Dunning examines and describes all the threats and vulnerabilities associated with Bluetooth technology [17]. Many authors have studied the Bluetooth related Man-In-The-Middle (MITM) attack landscape over the time, that has resulted into a deeper understanding of such attacks. Along these lines, these authors have provided many risk mitigation tactics that can be employed in a personal as well as organizational level [2,23,56,64,74].

Other papers provide a good, detailed overview of different types of attack vectors like MITM attacks, DDos attacks, worms and Trojans associated with Bluetooth technology in their paper [24,28,42,49,54,65]. Additionally, in recent years new literature reviews have been published that focus on security threats related to Bluetooth Low Energy (BLE) technology as well [8,20,45]. All the prior literature reviews that has been helpful in guiding this paper is listed out in Table 1. Here, we have provided an account of the papers which primarily focus on generic Bluetooth attacks, whereas, our paper provides a consolidated information on Bluetooth vulnerabilities, mitigation measures, and details BLE-specific attacks.

3   Method

As mentioned above, we conducted detailed literature review on the papers focused on analyzing the digital threats associated with Bluetooth-enabled wearable devices and also detail the mitigation measures to avoid these security vulnerabilities. Overall, through the systematic literature review we aimed at answering the following research questions:

- **RQ1: What types of cybersecurity attacks are Bluetooth devices vulnerable to and what are the user perception towards these threats?**
- **RQ2: What are the mitigation methods to protect data against Bluetooth attacks and which preventive measures can be adapted by the users?**

To obtain the relevant resources needed to conduct our analysis we first started with a keyword-based database search which followed with an abstract and full-text screening, and finally concluded with a detailed thematic analysis of the collected articles. To start our review, we conducted a keyword-based search using the following keywords: (1) 'Bluetooth Security', (2) 'Bluetooth Vulnerabilities', (3) 'Bluetooth Attacks', (4) 'Bluetooth Mitigation', (5) 'Bluetooth Security Attacks'. The keyword list was generated by going over 30 Google Scholar articles to extract these keywords as mentioned by the articles. After shortlisting the keyword list, we used different combinations of the keywords in our query using AND, OR and NOT logical operators as adapted by prior literature review by Stowell et al. [61], Noah and Das [43], Jones et al. [39], Majumdar and Das [40], and by Das et al. [14,15].

3.1   Database Search

We conducted the database search for the literature review by conducting our search through the ACM Digital Library (ACM DL) and the Institute of Electrical and Electronics Engineers (IEEE) Xplore. Our keyword-based search in the above-mentioned digital libraries resulted in 77 articles from the ACM DL and 104 articles from the IEEEXplore database.

3.2   Abstract and Full-Text Screening

For the next step, we conducted a thorough review of the 181 articles by screening the abstract and full text manually. This was primarily done to ensure the quality

Table 1. Summarization of prior research papers focused on literature reviews in bluetooth security threats

Author-Year	Title	Themes discussed
Haataja et al. (2008)	Man-In-The-Middle attacks on Bluetooth: a comparative analysis, a novel attack, and countermeasures	Bluetooth MITM Attacks Mitigation Framework
Dunning et al. (2010)	Taming the Blue Beast: A Survey of Bluetooth Based Threats	Bluetooth Threats and Mitigation
Haataja et al. (2011)	Ten years of Bluetooth security attacks: Lessons learned	Literature Review of Bluetooth Security Threats (2001–2011)
Margaret Tan and K. A. Masagca (2011)	An Investigation of Bluetooth Security Threats	Survey on Students' Perception of Bluetooth Security Threats
Sandhya et al. (2012)	Contention for Man-in-the-Middle Attacks in Bluetooth Networks	Literature review on Bluetooth MITM Attacks
N. B. I Minar and M. Tarique (2012)	Bluetooth security threats and solutions: a survey	Overview of Bluetooth Security Vulnerabilities and Mitigation
T. Panse and P. Panse (2013)	A survey on security threats and vulnerability attacks on Bluetooth communication	Overview of Bluetooth Security Vulnerabilities and Mitigation
Albahar et al. (2016)	Bluetooth MITM vulnerabilities: a literature review, novel attack scenarios, novel countermeasures, and lessons learned	Literature Review on Bluetooth MITM Vulnerabilities
Rijah et al. (2016)	Bluetooth security analysis and solution	Literature Review on Bluetooth Related Security Risk and Mitigation
Sun et al. (2017)	Man-in-the-middle attacks on Secure Simple Pairing in Bluetooth standard V5.0 and its countermeasure	Bluetooth MITM Attacks and countermeasures
Hassan et al. (2018)	Security threats in Bluetooth technology	Survey on Bluetooth Security Threats
T. O. Arney (2018)	A Literature Review on the Current State of Security and Privacy of Medical Devices and Sensors with Bluetooth Low Energy	Literature Review on BLE Security Threats
Ghori et al. (2019)	Review on Security in Bluetooth Low Energy Mesh Network in Correlation with Wireless Mesh Network Security	BLE Mesh Networks and Related Security Vulnerabilities
Oliff et al. (2019)	Review on Security in Bluetooth Low Energy Mesh Network in Correlation with Wireless Mesh Network Security	Spoofing Attack on BLE Occupancy Detection
Yaseen et al. (2019)	MARC: A Novel Framework for Detecting MITM Attacks in eHealthcare BLE Systems	Bluetooth MITM Attack Mitigation Framework

of the articles collected and its relevance to the topic of the research, which was on Bluetooth security and mitigation measures. Two researchers of the project who were trained in qualitative data analysis went through the abstract and full text to verify if the papers discussed the vulnerabilities and mitigation solutions of the

Bluetooth technologies. From the initial review if there were any discrepancies then that was resolved by a third researcher (last author of the paper) as the decision maker in terms of keeping the paper for the literature review. The abstract and full-text screening resulted in a final dataset consisting of 28 articles from the ACM DL and 20 articles from the IEEEXplore database resulting in 48 articles in total.

3.3   Thematic Analysis

Our analysis focused on deciphering papers that discussed any aspects of Bluetooth security vulnerabilities and mitigation measures to resolve those issues. We performed open coding to detail those aspects from the studies. For this, we went over all of the papers to create our codebook for the analysis. Thereafter, for the collected papers, we performed an in-depth thematic analysis from the code book generated as detailed in the results section below. For the analysis of the 48 papers, three independent researchers (first and second authors of the paper) coded the initial set of papers with an inter-coder reliability score of 85.9%. During the course of our analysis, we sought to examine the trends and practices across of the articles published in the vulnerabilities and mitigation aspects. For any discrepancies in the inter-coder agreement, the last author of the paper resolved the discrepancies. We report below on the threats and mitigation measures, which were mentioned in these articles. This process is similar to thematic analysis protocols by prior researchers [14,39,43].

4   Analysis and Results: Threats

4.1   Bluetooth-Specific Attacks

Researchers identified attacks as attempts to gain unauthorized access to a victim's device without the knowledge of the victim [4,18,50,69]. Attacks can be used to destroy, alter, disable, or steal data from a user.

Blue-Bugging. From our analysis, 18.75% of the articles pertained relevant information relating to Blue-Bugging. In a Blue-Bugging attack, the attacker connects to the target device without the knowledge of the owner and is able to take full control of the device at their leisure [30,75]. Prior researchers identify potential malicious activity to implement this type of attack which included making phone calls, sending texts, accessing files and applications, and inserting malware [5,16,36,44,48,52]. Along these lines, Bouhenguel et al. mentions that Blue-Bugging allows hacker to use victim's device to access phone's commands making it easier for the hacker to access data stored in the phone and even, eavesdrop in the conversations [10].

Denial of Service Attack. In a Denial of Service (DoS) attack the victim's device and/or network is impacted by unmanageable service requests thus depleting the network of its resources. The user becomes unable to access anything on the device as the resource usage is hampered. For this paper we will detail some of the primary attacks discussed in the analyzed papers, including, BlueSmack, BlueChop, and MAC Address Spoofing.

– **BlueSmack:** Our analysis resulted in 10.41% of the articles containing relevant information relating to BlueSmack [36,52]. Hunt and Zubair et al. expressed that a BlueSmack attack, similar to the 'Ping of Death Attack', is when the attacker's device repeatedly sends an L2CAP request to a victim's Bluetooth device through an L2CAP ping [30,75]. The victim's device then receives multiple L2CAP echo requests that push ping packets in response, which according to Zubair et al. can be around 600 bytes in size. In the similar research area, Carettoni et al. found that these echo requests could overload the victim's device, resulting in a crash where malicious code can be inserted [11].
– **BlueChop:** Out of our 48 articles, 6.25% of the articles we analyzed discussed information relating to BlueChop. Carettoni et al. describe a BlueChop attack as when the attacker's device disrupts an established piconet [11]. However, according to Hunt, in order for this attack to be carried out, the master of the piconet must allow for multiple connections to be made. This attack is carried out by having a device that is not part of the existing piconet spoof a slave device and attempt to contact the master. If successful, it will cause the master device's internal state to become confused and ultimately disrupt the piconet slowing down the regular communication flow [30]. According to Kennedy et al., traditionally these types of attacks have to be conducted within a 10 m bubble and are easy to detect [36].
– **MAC Address Spoofing Attack:** From our analysis, 8.33% of the articles we analyzed relayed information relating to MAC Address Spoofing Attack [57,68]. The attacker attempts to steal the MAC address of the victim's device, clone it, and use it to trick other devices to think it is the victim's device. Kaur and Satwant note that this is usually carried out during the link key generation before a successful pairing of devices occurs and before the encryption is even established [35]. Once the attacker has cloned the victim's device, Zubair et al. describe the attacker performing a man in the middle attack [75].

PIN Theft Attacks. Our findings resulted in 4.16% of the articles with significant information relating to PIN Theft Attacks. PIN theft attacks can come in two different forms, PIN cracking and Offline PIN recovery. Hager and Midkiff define PIN cracking attacks as when the attacker cracks the victim's PIN by first having a trusted relationship with the device [26]. Shaked and Wool explain how the nature of this trusted relationship takes place via the standard Bluetooth pairing method. To pair, the attacker's device must first create an initialization key, then a link key, and finally successfully enter the authorization process.

Once these three steps of pairing have been achieved there is an optional fourth step, where the attacker can choose to create an encryption key allowing them to hide any future communications from the victim [58].

Man in the Middle Attack. From our analysis, 14.58% of the articles has pertinent information relating to Man in the Middle attacks [7,12]. An attacker poses as a fake access point by disconnecting the connection of two Bluetooth devices connected on the piconet [6,75]. If there is no encryption between the devices, the attacker can form a new connection with each device without their knowledge. From there, the attacker attempts to access the data that is transmitted between two Bluetooth devices by intercepting the submission. The victims here often believe that they are sending information on a private connection, however, the attacker is in control of the connection the whole time [48]. They can pick and choose what data gets sent over as well as read all the personal data sent over, which could be photos, emails, texts, and more. Sun et al. identifies that the attack often occurs due to flaws in the pairing process, such as the passkey that pairing devices display on the screen [64]. According to Wang et al., a MITM attack can only be performed on non-BLE devices, unless the attacker knows the encryption and authentication key [68].

Blue Snarfing. Out of our 48 articles, 16.66% of the articles we analyzed pertained relevant information relating to the BlueSnarfing attack. A BlueSnarf attack is an Object Exchange (OBEX) Push Service pairing protocol in which the attacker hacks into and gains unauthorized access to the victim's device [10,36, 48,52,66,75]. An attacker is able to steal any data that is stored in the memory of the device without leaving a trace, including contacts, images, emails, calendar, and more [31]. They can also divert calls and texts to other devices. Alfaiate and Fonseca discuss an advanced form of Blue-Snarfing, where attackers can gain full read and write access to the victim's device's file system [5]. By acquiring such data, they can exploit the victim or gain financial information that would be detrimental to that user. Hunt also notes that a BlueSnarf attack was performed at a distance of 1.08 miles by simply modifying the Bluetooth antenna of a Bluetooth device that normally has a range of around 0.006 miles [30].

Fuzzing. Our findings resulted in 8.33% of the articles pertaining relevant information relating to Fuzzing attacks. Ray et al. describes fuzzing as rewriting data fields that leads to abnormal behavior and server crash. According to the paper, one of the many ways this can be done is by intercepting communication between server and client. In this process, the hacker gets hold of the data packets that are in-transit between server and client, modifies it to include invalid data and sending it back to the server [53]. Karim et al. and Lee et al. note that this attack is popular in smart phones and cars as they can send the packages via Bluetooth [33,37]. Once the attacker has slowed the device, they are able to send AT commands (high-level commands that are used on the baseband processor [34]) to the device that allow them to gain access to sensitive information.

They can steal the victim's IMSI (International Mobile Subscriber Identity) or the IMEI (International Mobile Equipment Identity) (both of which are unique to the device), downgrade the cellular protocol version, halt internet connection, gain access to media and phone calls, and paralyze the anti-theft module.

CarWhisperer. In our analysis, 10.41% of the articles we analyzed had relevant information to CarWhisperer attacks. CarWhisperer is a software that exploits default passkeys of hands-free Bluetooth connected vehicles [10,11,51]. Once the unauthorized connection is made, the hacker is able to listen-in to audio from the Bluetooth-enabled car stereo [48]. Podhradsky et al. mentions that CarWhisperer even enables the hackers to broadcast malicious audio by opening a RFCOMM connection [51].

BlueJacking. Out of our 48 articles 18.75% of the articles we analyzed had relevant information relating to BlueJacking. A BlueJacking attack is a social engineering-based attack where the attacker must be authorized to pair with the victim's device [5,32,48,75]. To be authorized the attacker needs to attain the access code, and according to Su et al., the attacker will often choose an intriguing device name such as "Your Friend" or "Secret Admirer" to entice the victim to accept the connection. Once the victim authorizes the pairing the attacker is able to send uninvited messages to their device [63]. The messages are often promotional purposes such as sending texts, images, or sound clips. However, Carettoni et al. and Jamaluddin et al. explain that some attackers could use this attack to access the data on the victim's device such as their text messages, contacts, files, and more [11,31,52]. Bouhenguel et al. claim that Bluejacking can cause harm to the victim should they respond to the message sent, as it can be used as a phishing attack to get more information out of them [10].

BluePrinting. Our findings resulted in 8.33% of the articles with pertinent information relating to BluePrinting. Zubair et al., Carettoni et al., and Dell and Khwaja note a BluePrint attack is when the attacker tries to gain the details of the device, such as the IMEI, the manufacturer name and details, the device model, or the firmware version [11,16,75]. The attacker doesn't steal anything in this attack, but the information that they gain can be used for future attacks [52].

4.2   Malware Threats

Malware is malicious software that is programmed with an intention to do harm to the user and the device. Carettoni et al. demonstrate that Bluetooth-enabled devices are especially vulnerable to malware attacks as these devices can be a good medium of propagation for such software [11]. There are two types of malware threats, worms and Trojans. However, because the literature reviewed do not contain much information on Trojans, here we will focus on different malware worms that can pose harm to Bluetooth devices.

Worms. Out of our 48 articles, 12.5% of the articles we analyzed pertained relevant information relating to Worms. As described by Ghallali et al., Su et al., and Haataja, worms are designed to spread quickly and aggressively, attempting to infect as many victims as they can, and become easily infectious as vulnerabilities are discovered [19]. They can infect devices specifically or even the piconet [25]. According to Su et al., Bluetooth worms are different than other forms of worms as the infection source would have to be close to the victim since Bluetooth devices typically only have a range of around 10–20 m. Additionally, the two devices would have to be near each other for a prolonged amount of time in order for the worm to replicate itself on the victim's device [63].

– **Cabir Worms.** A Cabir worm is a malicious software that attacks mobile phones that use a Symbian OS [10,11]. This worm preys on social engineering by sending a .sis (Symbian Installation System) file to the victim's device disguised as a security management utility [72]. Su et al. note that while dangerous, Cabir worms are not able to infect a large number of devices because it requires user authorization [63].
– **CommWarrior.** The CommWarrior worm is dangerous as it remains silent or inactive in a device until a designated time. CommWarrior is even more dangerous than Cabir worms as it depletes the device battery and is able to propagate faster than Cabir worms [72].

4.3   BLE-Specific Attack

Noticeably in recent year, Bluetooth Smart or Bluetooth 4 technology has taken over the public usage of Bluetooth devices. Designed by Bluetooth SIG the Bluetooth Smart is a technology that works for shorter ranges and consumes very low energy thus allowing manufacturers to assimilate this technology into variety of IoT devices. Because of its lightweight technology and low consumption of energy it is referred to as Bluetooth Low Energy (BLE). In their paper, Pallavi and Narayanan describe BLE having similar protocol to Bluetooth, but these technologies are not compatible with each other [47]. Due to this, BLE is susceptible to specific attacks in addition to the attacks discussed above. In their paper, Streiff et al. demonstrate attack on BLE enabled smart toy and point out the vulnerabilities of IoT devices with BLE technologies [62]. Some recent BLE attacks documented in the literature are Key Negotiation Downgrade attack [7], battery exhaustion attack [22], BLE beacons attack [46,71] and most recently discovered BleedingTooth Attack which specifically targets Linux Bluetooth[1].

Overall, the distribution of the papers associated with the different types of attacks based on our thematic analysis is mentioned in Table 2.

---

[1] https://harborlabs.com/cybervigilance/Cybersecurity_Alert_BleedingTooth.pdf.

Table 2. Snapshot of the number of papers discussing bluetooth security threats published in ACM DL and IEEEXplore.

Types of attacks	Number of articles	
	ACM	*IEEEXplore*
BlueBugging	4	5
Denial of Service (DoS) attacks		
BlueSmack	2	3
BlueChop	1	2
MAC Address Spoofing	3	0
PIN Theft Attacks	1	1
Man In The Middle (MITM) Attacks	5	1
BlueSnarfing	3	5
Fuzzing	2	2
CarWhisperer	1	3
BlueJacking	4	5
BluePrinting	1	2
Malaware threats		
CabirWorms	1	3
CommWarrior	0	2
BLE Attacks	3	3

5 Analysis and Results: Mitigation Strategies

Bluetooth vulnerabilities come in various forms and can do a great deal of damage. In the 48 papers that we examined; we found many attacks that called for mitigation techniques. Specifically, 13 of the 48 articles, 30.9%, talked about mitigation techniques and their importance. Cope et al. explains that even if an exploit patch is sent out, Bluetooth devices require upgrades in firmware, which is not something an update can do [13,60,67]. Users need to mitigate these attacks on their own accord to stay secure. For this reason, it is important to understand the Bluetooth piconet and security modes so that we can understand how we can protect user data.

User Mitigation

– Users need to **be aware of all of the Bluetooth devices that are connected in their piconet**. Each device's addresses should be verified to ensure they are a recognized device by the user. The default setting of each of the device in the Bluetooth piconet must be changed to reflect the security policy of the piconet. For example, if there are multiple cars connected to one's phone, add a name for the car's Bluetooth. Once the car is gone, one can delete that Bluetooth device, helping prevent an attack in the future [10,27].

- Users should **consistently update their devices and be aware of potential vulnerabilities.** For example, Lonzetta et al. mentions that if a firmware upgrade is necessary, then the user should try to update it as soon as possible. The weaker and older a device/security there is, then the easier it is for a hacker to attack the device [38].
- **Turn off Bluetooth when it is not in use.** When users leave their Bluetooth on, they leave a roaming signal on. This is especially dangerous in public areas such as fast foods restaurants and shopping malls. Users should also turn off location data for their Bluetooth. Singelee and Preneel found that many users leave Bluetooth on because they are unaware of the security risks [59].
- **Use a long PIN for the authentication phase when connecting to another Bluetooth device**, as suggested by Cope et al. This PIN should also be long and random, which will be more resistant against brute-force attacks. This also means changing the PIN code as frequently as a phone password [13].
- **Do not enter PIN when randomly asked.** As Tan and Masagca discussed, many worms make it appear as if a user needs to enter code to 'update'. In reality, it is a corrupted file that is trying to download code onto the device. A user should not enter their PIN unless they know why they are doing so [65].
- **If you have an old device that runs Bluetooth versions 1.0 and 1.2, then upgrade your firmware**, or upgrade your device as a whole, as identified by Lonzetta et al. The most up-to-date Bluetooth version is BLE. You cannot change the PIN on legacy devices, so they can be difficult to secure [38,41].
- **Keep up to date with the encryption that is being used.** On many older devices, the E0 stream cipher algorithm is weak and needs to be updated. Velez and Shanblatt recommend v4.0 + LE, since this version uses AES-CCM cryptography [66].
- **When connecting devices, make sure you are at home or in a safe area.** Saltzstein finds that in a public location, it is easy for an attacker to mask their device to gain access to your device [55].
- **Remove, unpair, and delete access to devices that are lost or stolen.** This will prevent an attacker from accessing your devices through these other devices. Sethi et al. discusses how many users forget which devices they purchased in the past that may be connected to their newer devices. He discusses the importance of cloud connectivity between devices, so it is easier to know which devices are registered. Older devices on the cloud or block chain can then be deleted by users, or the software can be automatically used to detect and disconnect old devices [57].
- **Do not accept images or messages from unknown devices.** Cope et al. explains that if you hit accept, it can accept malicious code or software as well. You should never accept Bluetooth packages from anyone you are not expecting it from. This goes hand in hand with turning off your Bluetooth when it is not in use. Attackers know that users tend to use their Bluetooth devices when in the airport, thus it is important to be mindful in heavily populated areas [13].
- When Bluetooth devices save a link key, it is non-volatile memory to use in the future. When the same Bluetooth devices attempt to communicate

again, they use this stored link key. This is not safe because it increases the probability of an attacker eavesdropping and the PIN being exposed. To make this safer, it is important to **encrypt your devices and the link keys when you are connecting devices.** Hunt suggests using the E0 stream cipher for encryption which requires a unique session key to derive packet keys. This greatly reduces the risk of key reuse [30].

- **When two Bluetooth devices are being connected, ensure that authentication and authorization are required by both devices.** This helps you ensure that both network connections are legitimate [10,48]. Cope et al. mentions that users should never accept communication from unknown or suspicious devices. They should only accept transmissions from trusted devices and require mutual authentication for all devices [13].
- **Link keys used should be based on combination keys instead of unit keys.** For example, Bouhenguel et al. discuss about Bluetooth using two types of link keys: temporary keys and semi-permanent keys where the second one has both unit and combination keys. Thus, using the combination keys adds another layer of security allows to block MITM attacks [10].

Organizational Mitigation Strategies. In order to stop sniffing devices like BlueEar, there are scripting methods that can be used to counteract them. Albazrqaoe et al. discuss how implementing a user-space script on the Bluetooth master can flip the status of sub-channels. This script randomly selects $n - 20$ sub-channels for hopping, which makes it harder for a sniffer to learn the adaptive hopping technique. This technique is more suited for companies to implement as most users will not know how to implement the scripts to secure their devices. A positive about this technique is that it is a script so that new hardware is not needed so it can be used almost immediately [3].

Heinze et al. discuss a technique called MagicPairing, which has a higher level of security than traditional Bluetooth techniques. In current Bluetooth devices, once the permanent key is leaked, then all of the security levels are broken for previous and future connections. This is because the same key is used and changing a key is not easy. Apple solves this problem with Magic Pairing. Once a new Bluetooth device is added to the piconet, a fresh permanent key is created based on the iCloud keys for each session. This does mean the permanent key is not permanent, but it also means it changes often and is done seamlessly without the user knowing. The MagicPairing technique only works with certain Apple devices so this security technique can only secure Apple users [29].

6   Discussion and Implications

In this paper, we have examined literature published in ACM and IEEEXplore digital libraries, that discuss the security and privacy aspect of Bluetooth technology. In this process we examined 48 papers which helped us to consolidate the themes discussed in all these papers. Many of the papers have studied all the potential cyber-threats prevalent in the Bluetooth technology (e.g., [26,57,64]) and many others focus on risk mitigation measures (e.g., [10,13,27]). However, very less attention has been paid to understanding the user perspective regarding these security vulnerabilities and the proposed mitigation measures.

6.1   User Focused Studies

The outcome of the systematic literature review has been to highlight the importance of user-focus studies when discussing security aspect of Bluetooth technologies. The perception of privacy and threat is individualistic and varies from one person to another. Grace and Surridge argue it is important to create security systems that are user-focused as the level of privacy preferred by users is not universal [21]. Moreover, the risk mitigations measures should also be informed by general user behavior and experience, otherwise users will simply not use it. Tan and Masagaca show with their study that 74.68% (59 out of 79) of study population, which consists of educated college students who are also regular Bluetooth users, do not adopt any preventive risk mitigation measures [65]. Therefore, it is evident that user-focused studies are more necessary than ever to create better Bluetooth security systems and user-based risk mitigation measures. The systematic literature review was helpful in combing through the studies done so far and finding out the current status of research in regard to Bluetooth security in the industry.

6.2   Digital Literacy

An important theme touched by some papers examined in this review is the significance of information literacy. As ordinary users interact more with different electronics in our current digital age, it is evident that many are unaware of the security and privacy aspect of these electronics. As described by the widely accepted *weakest link phenomenon* ordinary uses are the weakest links in the cybersecurity chain [1]. In their paper Yan et al. have observed among college students that for the most part they are able to make good judgements when it comes to detecting spams or pop-ups, but it has a limit. Due to lack of good education and training in cybersecurity they are not able to make rational decisions when it comes to detecting complicated threats or risks [73]. Along these lines, providing good education on the Bluetooth technology and its vulnerabilities can help the ordinary people to understand the importance of mitigation measures, thus encouraging adoption of secure habits.

6.3   Risk Mitigation Measures

Finally, the mitigation measures are vital in warding off threats and attacks on Bluetooth devices. Although prior researchers (e.g. [3,29,30]) have been able to provide a list of precautionary measures that can prove to be immensely helpful, it must be noted that we need more measures that are well-informed by ordinary human behaviors. In daily life a lot of regular Bluetooth users are fairly careless and not so strict in checking authentication and authorization of every device they connect to. Sometimes it is simply not possible, for example connecting to a Bluetooth enabled device in a large conference, in foreign country and so on. As Woodhouse mentions in his paper the risk mitigation strategies should be intuitive enough so it can be integrated into corporate culture. The paper also points out the risk mitigation protocols should be informed by changing user attitudes and human behavior [70]. Although this paper focuses solely on organizational risk mitigation measures, it is clear to understand that users adopt new behaviours in a similar fashion in their personal life too.

7 Limitations and Future Research

We collected and analyzed academic literature focusing on Bluetooth technology, security threats on these devices, existing and less-explored vulnerabilities, and potential mitigation measures as studied by prior researchers. This literature review is critical as it provides a consolidated analysis of papers related to different cybersecurity aspects of Bluetooth technology. However, given the vastness of this research area and the prolific implementation in peripheral devices, we could have likely missed some papers, as we have focused our research on ACM and IEEE DLs. Additionally, manual analysis helped us in obtaining detailed qualitative analysis f the 48 papers, however, relying on human judgement. We acknowledge this limitation of our work and want to address this in the future extension of this research. Thus, we plan to conduct a large scale study on the evaluation of existing literature outside of the DLs selected for this work while utilizing text mining for automated analysis. Thereafter, our goal is to test the mitigation methods from the user perspective through detailed user studies to test the efficacy on the measures adapted by the users.

8 Conclusion

Bluetooth technologies impact our everyday life through connected devices, which has been immensely helpful for communication, exchange of data, connecting with other peripherals, and other purposes. However, such digital innovations have also opened new attack vectors, thus its security has become an important topic for research for Bluetooth connections and Bluetooth-enabled devices. To this aid, we conducted a systematic literature review on papers published in ACM and IEEEXplore DLs. Our detailed analysis collected a list of 48 academic papers focused on an overview of Bluetooth functionality, types of threats, and mitigations measures explored by prior researchers. Our findings reveal that there are several Bluetooth attacks that can lead to loss of user information and exploitation. This paper aimed to educate users on relevant attacks and provide them with useful ways of mitigating them by analyzing prior research. With the ease of hacking into a piconet, it is important for users to notice the signs of a potential breach in their piconet. There are numerous vulnerabilities from easy PINs to outdated Bluetooth security software on user devices.

Thus, we concluded by detailing the mitigation measures which can be implemented both on individual and organizational level. Our analysis revealed a need for far-reaching user knowledge on mitigations, evaluation of current security leaks, and more periodic Bluetooth security updates.

Acknowledgement. We would like to acknowledge the Inclusive Security and Privacy-focused Innovative Research in Information Technology: InSPIRIT lab at the University of Denver. We would also like to thank Lucas McLeod for their initial contribution on the editing of the paper. Any opinions, findings, and conclusions or recommendations expressed in this material are solely those of the authors and do not necessarily reflect the views of the University of Denver.

References

1. Adams, A., Sasse, M.A.: Users are not the enemy. Commun. ACM **42**(12), 40–46 (1999). https://doi.org/10.1145/322796.322806
2. Albahar, M.A., Haataja, K., Toivanen, P.: Bluetooth MITM vulnerabilities: a literature review, novel attack scenarios, novel countermeasures, and lessons learned. Int. J. Inf. Technol. Secur. **8**(4), 25–49 (2016)
3. Albazrqaoe, W., Huang, J., Xing, G.: Practical bluetooth traffic sniffing: systems and privacy implications. In: Proceedings of the 14th Annual International Conference on Mobile Systems, Applications, and Services, MobiSys 2016, p. 333–345. Association for Computing Machinery, New York (2016)
4. Albazrqaoe, W., Huang, J., Xing, G.: A practical Bluetooth traffic sniffing system: design, implementation, and countermeasure. IEEE/ACM Trans. Netw. **27**(1), 71–84 (2019). https://doi.org/10.1109/TNET.2018.2880970
5. Alfaiate, J., Fonseca, J.: Bluetooth security analysis for mobile phones. In: 7th Iberian Conference on Information Systems and Technologies (CISTI 2012), pp. 1–6 (2012)
6. Almiani, M., et al.: Bluetooth application-layer packet-filtering for blueborne attack defending. In: 2019 Fourth International Conference on Fog and Mobile Edge Computing (FMEC), pp. 142–148 (2019). https://doi.org/10.1109/FMEC. 2019.8795354
7. Antonioli, D., Tippenhauer, N.O., Rasmussen, K.: Key negotiation downgrade attacks on Bluetooth and Bluetooth low energy. ACM Trans. Priv. Secur. **23**(3), 1–28 (2020). https://doi.org/10.1145/3394497
8. Arney, T.O.: A literature review on the current state of security and privacy of medical devices and sensors with Bluetooth low energy. Ph.D. thesis, Michigan Technological University (2018)
9. Bitton, R., Boymgold, K., Puzis, R., Shabtai, A.: Evaluating the information security awareness of smartphone users. In: Proceedings of the 2020 CHI Conference on Human Factors in Computing Systems, pp. 1–13 (2020)
10. Bouhenguel, R., Mahgoub, I., Ilyas, M.: Bluetooth security in wearable computing applications. In: 2008 International Symposium on High Capacity Optical Networks and Enabling Technologies, pp. 182–186 (2008). https://doi.org/10.1109/ HONET.2008.4810232

11. Carettoni, L., Merloni, C., Zanero, S.: Studying Bluetooth malware propagation: the bluebag project. IEEE Secur. Priv. **5**(2), 17–25 (2007). https://doi.org/10.1109/MSP.2007.43
12. Classen, J., Hollick, M.: Happy MitM: fun and toys in every Bluetooth device. In: Proceedings of the 14th ACM Conference on Security and Privacy in Wireless and Mobile Networks, WiSec 2021, pp. 72–77. Association for Computing Machinery, New York (2021). https://doi.org/10.1145/3448300.3467822
13. Cope, P., Campbell, J., Hayajneh, T.: An investigation of Bluetooth security vulnerabilities. In: 2017 IEEE 7th Annual Computing and Communication Workshop and Conference (CCWC), pp. 1–7 (2017). https://doi.org/10.1109/CCWC.2017.7868416
14. Das, S., Kim, A., Tingle, Z., Nippert-Eng, C.: All about phishing exploring user research through a systematic literature review. In: Proceedings of the Thirteenth International Symposium on Human Aspects of Information Security & Assurance (HAISA 2019) (2019)
15. Das, S., Wang, B., Tingle, Z., Camp, L.J.: Evaluating user perception of multifactor authentication: a systematic review. In: Proceedings of the Thirteenth International Symposium on Human Aspects of Information Security & Assurance (HAISA 2019) (2019)
16. Dell, P., Ghori, K.S.H.: A simple way to improve the security of Bluetooth devices. In: 2008 International Symposium on Applications and the Internet, pp. 444–447 (2008). https://doi.org/10.1109/SAINT.2008.39
17. Dunning, J.: Taming the blue beast: a survey of Bluetooth based threats. IEEE Secur. Priv. **8**(2), 20–27 (2010). https://doi.org/10.1109/MSP.2010.3
18. Ficco, M., D'Arienzo, M., D'Angelo, G.: A Bluetooth infrastructure for automatic services access in ubiquitous and nomadic computing environments. In: Proceedings of the 5th ACM International Workshop on Mobility Management and Wireless Access, pp. 17–24. Association for Computing Machinery, New York (2007). https://doi.org/10.1145/1298091.1298095
19. Ghallali, M., El Ouadghiri, D., Essaaidi, M., Boulmalf, M.: Mobile phones security: the spread of malware via MMS and Bluetooth, prevention methods. In: Proceedings of the 9th International Conference on Advances in Mobile Computing and Multimedia, pp. 256–259 (2011)
20. Ghori, M.R., Wan, T.C., Anbar, M., Sodhy, G.C., Rizwan, A.: Review on security in Bluetooth low energy mesh network in correlation with wireless mesh network security. In: 2019 IEEE Student Conference on Research and Development (SCOReD), pp. 219–224. IEEE (2019)
21. Grace, P., Surridge, M.: Towards a model of user-centered privacy preservation. In: Proceedings of the 12th International Conference on Availability, Reliability and Security, ARES 2017. Association for Computing Machinery, New York (2017). https://doi.org/10.1145/3098954.3104054
22. Guo, Z., Harris, I.G., Jiang, Y., Tsaur, L.: An efficient approach to prevent battery exhaustion attack on BLE-based mesh networks. In: 2017 International Conference on Computing, Networking and Communications (ICNC), pp. 1–5 (2017). https://doi.org/10.1109/ICCNC.2017.7876092
23. Haataja, K., Hyppönen, K., Pasanen, S., Toivanen, P.: MITM attacks on Bluetooth. In: Haataja, K., Hyppönen, K., Pasanen, S., Toivanen, P. (eds.) Bluetooth Security Attacks. BRIEFSCOMPUTER, pp. 61–70. Springer, Heidelberg (2013). https://doi.org/10.1007/978-3-642-40646-1_5
24. Haataja, K., Hypponen, K., Toivanen, P.: Ten years of Bluetooth security attacks: lessons learned. Computer Science I Like, p. 45 (2011)

25. Haataja, K.M.J.: New efficient intrusion detection and prevention system for Bluetooth networks. In: Proceedings of the 1st International Conference on MOBILe Wireless MiddleWARE, Operating Systems, and Applications, MOBILWARE 2008. ICST (Institute for Computer Sciences, Social-Informatics and Telecommunications Engineering), Brussels (2008)

26. Hager, C.T., Midkiff, S.F.: An analysis of Bluetooth security vulnerabilities. In: 2003 IEEE Wireless Communications and Networking, WCNC 2003, vol. 3, pp. 1825–1831 (2003). https://doi.org/10.1109/WCNC.2003.1200664

27. Hale, M.L., Lotfy, K., Gamble, R.F., Walter, C., Lin, J.: Developing a platform to evaluate and assess the security of wearable devices. Digit. Commun. Netw. **5**(3), 147–159 (2019)

28. Hassan, S.S., Bibon, S.D., Hossain, M.S., Atiquzzaman, M.: Security threats in Bluetooth technology. Comput. Secur. **74**, 308–322 (2018)

29. Heinze, D., Classen, J., Rohrbach, F.: MagicPairing: Apple's take on securing Bluetooth peripherals. In: Proceedings of the 13th ACM Conference on Security and Privacy in Wireless and Mobile Networks, pp. 111–121 (2020)

30. Hunt, R.: Emerging wireless personal area networks (WPANs): - an analysis of techniques, tools and threats. In: 2012 18th IEEE International Conference on Networks (ICON), pp. 274–279 (2012). https://doi.org/10.1109/ICON.2012.6506569

31. Jamaluddin, J., Zotou, N., Edwards, R., Coulton, P.: Mobile phone vulnerabilities: a new generation of malware. In: 2004 IEEE International Symposium on Consumer Electronics, pp. 199–202 (2004). https://doi.org/10.1109/ISCE.2004.1375935

32. Jonsson, H., Olsson, C.M.: User privacy attitudes regarding proximity sensing. In: Proceedings of the 13th International Conference on Availability, Reliability and Security, ARES 2018. Association for Computing Machinery, New York (2018). https://doi.org/10.1145/3230833.3233270

33. Karim, I., Cicala, F., Hussain, S.R., Chowdhury, O., Bertino, E.: Opening Pandora's box through ATFuzzer: dynamic analysis of at interface for Android smartphones. In: Proceedings of the 35th Annual Computer Security Applications Conference, pp. 529–543 (2019)

34. Karim, I., Cicala, F., Hussain, S.R., Chowdhury, O., Bertino, E.: ATFuzzer: dynamic analysis framework of AT interface for Android smartphones. Digit. Threats Res. Pract. **1**(4), 1–29 (2020)

35. Kaur, S.: How to secure our Bluetooth insecure world! Pushing frontiers with the first lady of emerging technologies. IETE Tech. Rev. **30**(2), 95–101 (2013)

36. Kennedy, T., Hunt, R.: A review of WPAN security: attacks and prevention. In: Proceedings of the International Conference on Mobile Technology, Applications, and Systems, Mobility 2008. Association for Computing Machinery, New York (2008). https://doi.org/10.1145/1506270.1506342

37. Lee, H., Choi, K., Chung, K., Kim, J., Yim, K.: Fuzzing can packets into automobiles. In: 2015 IEEE 29th International Conference on Advanced Information Networking and Applications, pp. 817–821 (2015). https://doi.org/10.1109/AINA.2015.274

38. Lonzetta, A.M., Cope, P., Campbell, J., Mohd, B.J., Hayajneh, T.: Security vulnerabilities in Bluetooth technology as used in IoT. J. Sens. Actuator Netw. **7**(3), 28 (2018)

39. Jones, J.M., Duezguen, R., Mayer, P., Volkamer, M., Das, S.: A literature review on virtual reality authentication. In: Furnell, S., Clarke, N. (eds.) HAISA 2021. IAICT, vol. 613, pp. 189–198. Springer, Cham (2021). https://doi.org/10.1007/978-3-030-81111-2_16

40. Majumdar, R., Das, S.: SoK: an evaluation of quantum authentication through systematic literature review. In: Proceedings of the Workshop on Usable Security and Privacy (USEC) (2021)
41. Mantz, D., Classen, J., Schulz, M., Hollick, M.: InternalBlue-Bluetooth binary patching and experimentation framework. In: Proceedings of the 17th Annual International Conference on Mobile Systems, Applications, and Services, pp. 79–90 (2019)
42. Minar, N.B.N.I., Tarique, M.: Bluetooth security threats and solutions: a survey. Int. J. Distrib. Parallel Syst. **3**(1), 127 (2012)
43. Noah, N., Das, S.: Exploring evolution of augmented and virtual reality education space in 2020 through systematic literature review. Comput. Animation Virtual Worlds **32**(3–4), e2020 (2021)
44. O'Connor, T.J., Sangster, B.: HoneyM: a framework for implementing virtual honeyclients for mobile devices. In: Proceedings of the Third ACM Conference on Wireless Network Security, WiSec 2010, pp. 129–138. Association for Computing Machinery, New York (2010). https://doi.org/10.1145/1741866.1741888
45. Oliff, W., Filippoupolitis, A., Loukas, G.: Evaluating the impact of malicious spoofing attacks on Bluetooth low energy based occupancy detection systems. In: 2017 IEEE 15th International Conference on Software Engineering Research, Management and Applications (SERA), pp. 379–385. IEEE (2017)
46. Oliff, W., Filippoupolitis, A., Loukas, G.: Impact evaluation and detection of malicious spoofing attacks on BLE based occupancy detection systems. In: Proceedings of the 1st International Conference on Internet of Things and Machine Learning, IML 2017. Association for Computing Machinery, New York (2017). https://doi.org/10.1145/3109761.3109776
47. Pallavi, S., Narayanan, V.A.: An overview of practical attacks on BLE based IoT devices and their security. In: 2019 5th International Conference on Advanced Computing & Communication Systems (ICACCS), pp. 694–698. IEEE (2019)
48. Panigrahy, S.K., Jena, S.K., Turuk, A.K.: Security in Bluetooth, RFID and wireless sensor networks. In: Proceedings of the 2011 International Conference on Communication, Computing & Security, pp. 628–633 (2011)
49. Panse, T., Panse, P.: A survey on security threats and vulnerability attacks on Bluetooth communication. Int. J. Comput. Sci. Inf. Technol. **4**(5), 741–746 (2013)
50. Peters, T., Lal, R., Varadarajan, S., Pappachan, P., Kotz, D.: BASTION-SGX: Bluetooth and architectural support for trusted I/O on SGX. In: Proceedings of the 7th International Workshop on Hardware and Architectural Support for Security and Privacy. Association for Computing Machinery, New York (2018). https://doi.org/10.1145/3214292.3214295
51. Podhradsky, A.L., Casey, C., Ceretti, P.: The Bluetooth honeypot project. In: Wireless Telecommunications Symposium 2012, pp. 1–10 (2012). https://doi.org/10.1109/WTS.2012.6266078
52. Qu, Y., Chan, P.: Assessing vulnerabilities in Bluetooth low energy (BLE) wireless network based IoT systems. In: 2016 IEEE 2nd International Conference on Big Data Security on Cloud (BigDataSecurity), IEEE International Conference on High Performance and Smart Computing (HPSC), and IEEE International Conference on Intelligent Data and Security (IDS), pp. 42–48 (2016). https://doi.org/10.1109/BigDataSecurity-HPSC-IDS.2016.63
53. Ray, A., Raj, V., Oriol, M., Monot, A., Obermeier, S.: Bluetooth low energy devices security testing framework. In: 2018 IEEE 11th International Conference on Software Testing, Verification and Validation (ICST), pp. 384–393 (2018). https://doi.org/10.1109/ICST.2018.00045

54. Rijah, U.M., Mosharani, S., Amuthapriya, S., Mufthas, M., Hezretov, M., Dham-mearatchi, D.: Bluetooth security analysis and solution. Int. J. Sci. Res. Publ. **6**(4), 333–338 (2016)
55. Saltzstein, W.: Bluetooth wireless technology cybersecurity and diabetes technology devices. J. Diabetes Sci. Technol. **14**(6), 1111–1115 (2020)
56. Sandhya, S., Devi, K.S.: Contention for man-in-the-middle attacks in Bluetooth networks. In: 2012 Fourth International Conference on Computational Intelligence and Communication Networks, pp. 700–703. IEEE (2012)
57. Sethi, M., Peltonen, A., Aura, T.: Misbinding attacks on secure device pairing and bootstrapping. In: Proceedings of the 2019 ACM Asia Conference on Computer and Communications Security, pp. 453–464. Association for Computing Machinery, New York (2019)
58. Shaked, Y., Wool, A.: Cracking the Bluetooth pin. In: Proceedings of the 3rd International Conference on Mobile Systems, Applications, and Services, pp. 39–50. Association for Computing Machinery, New York (2005)
59. Singelée, D., Preneel, B.: Location privacy in wireless personal area networks. In: Proceedings of the 5th ACM Workshop on Wireless Security, pp. 11–18 (2006)
60. Snader, R., Kravets, R., Harris, A.F.: CryptoCoP: lightweight, energy-efficient encryption and privacy for wearable devices. In: Proceedings of the 2016 Workshop on Wearable Systems and Applications, WearSys 2016, pp. 7–12. Association for Computing Machinery, New York (2016). https://doi.org/10.1145/2935643.2935647
61. Stowell, E., et al.: Designing and evaluating mHealth interventions for vulnerable populations: a systematic review. In: Proceedings of the 2018 CHI Conference on Human Factors in Computing Systems, pp. 1–17 (2018)
62. Streiff, J., Das, S., Cannon, J.: Overpowered and underprotected toys empowering parents with tools to protect their children. In: 2019 IEEE 5th International Conference on Collaboration and Internet Computing (CIC), pp. 322–329 (2019). https://doi.org/10.1109/CIC48465.2019.00045
63. Su, J., et al.: A preliminary investigation of worm infections in a Bluetooth environment. In: Proceedings of the 4th ACM Workshop on Recurring Malcode, pp. 9–16. Association for Computing Machinery, New York (2006)
64. Sun, D.Z., Mu, Y., Susilo, W.: Man-in-the-middle attacks on secure simple pairing in Bluetooth standard V5.0 and its countermeasure. Pers. Ubiquit. Comput. **22**(1), 55–67 (2018). https://doi.org/10.1007/s00779-017-1081-6
65. Tan, M., Masagca, K.A.: An investigation of Bluetooth security threats. In: 2011 International Conference on Information Science and Applications, pp. 1–7. IEEE (2011)
66. Velez, D., Shanblatt, M.: Taxonomy of current medical devices for POCT applications and the potential acceptance of Bluetooth technology for secure interoperable applications. In: 2011 IEEE 13th International Conference on e-Health Networking, Applications and Services, pp. 288–295 (2011). https://doi.org/10.1109/HEALTH.2011.6026767
67. Walter, C., Hale, M.L., Gamble, R.F.: Imposing security awareness on wearables. In: Proceedings of the 2nd International Workshop on Software Engineering for Smart Cyber-Physical Systems, SEsCPS 2016, pp. 29–35. Association for Computing Machinery, New York (2016). https://doi.org/10.1145/2897035.2897038

68. Wang, J., Hu, F., Zhou, Y., Liu, Y., Zhang, H., Liu, Z.: BlueDoor: breaking the secure information flow via BLE vulnerability. In: Proceedings of the 18th International Conference on Mobile Systems, Applications, and Services, MobiSys 2020, pp. 286–298. Association for Computing Machinery, New York (2020). https://doi.org/10.1145/3386901.3389025

69. Willingham, T., Henderson, C., Kiel, B., Haque, M.S., Atkison, T.: Testing vulnerabilities in Bluetooth low energy. In: Proceedings of the ACMSE 2018 Conference, ACMSE 2018. Association for Computing Machinery, New York (2018). https://doi.org/10.1145/3190645.3190693

70. Woodhouse, S.: Information security: end user behavior and corporate culture. In: 7th IEEE International Conference on Computer and Information Technology (CIT 2007), pp. 767–774 (2007). https://doi.org/10.1109/CIT.2007.186

71. Yamamoto, D., Tanaka, R., Kajioka, S., Matsuo, H., Takahashi, N.: Global map matching using BLE beacons for indoor route and stay estimation. In: Proceedings of the 26th ACM SIGSPATIAL International Conference on Advances in Geographic Information Systems, SIGSPATIAL 2018, pp. 309–318. Association for Computing Machinery, New York (2018). https://doi.org/10.1145/3274895.3274918

72. Yan, G., Eidenbenz, S.: Bluetooth worms: models, dynamics, and defense implications. In: 2006 22nd Annual Computer Security Applications Conference (ACSAC 2006), pp. 245–256 (2006). https://doi.org/10.1109/ACSAC.2006.18

73. Yan, Z., et al.: Finding the weakest links in the weakest link: how well do undergraduate students make cybersecurity judgment? Comput. Hum. Behav. 84, 375–382 (2018). https://doi.org/10.1016/j.chb.2018.02.019. https://www.sciencedirect.com/science/article/pii/S0747563218300773

74. Yaseen, M., et al.: MARC: a novel framework for detecting MITM attacks in eHealthcare BLE systems. J. Med. Syst. 43(11), 1–18 (2019). https://doi.org/10.1007/s10916-019-1440-0

75. Zubair, M., Unal, D., Al-Ali, A., Shikfa, A.: Exploiting Bluetooth vulnerabilities in e-health IoT devices. In: Proceedings of the 3rd International Conference on Future Networks and Distributed Systems. Association for Computing Machinery, New York (2019)

JSLIM: Reducing the Known Vulnerabilities of JavaScript Application by Debloating

Renjun Ye[✉], Liang Liu, Simin Hu, Fangzhou Zhu, Jingxiu Yang, and Feng Wang

Nanjing University of Aeronautics and Astronautics, Nanjing 210000, Jiangsu, China
{renjunye,liangliu,siminhu,fangzhouzhu,jingxiuyang}@nuaa.edu.cn

Abstract. As the complexity of software projects increases, more and more developers choose to package various external dependency libraries into software projects to simplify software development. Unfortunately, these introduced dependent libraries are likely to introduce many potential security risks. This phenomenon is called software bloat. One way to handle this increased threat is through software debloating, i.e., the removal of dead code and code corresponding to vulnerabilities introduced from external dependency libraries. In our paper, we proposed JSLIM, an effective vulnerability-aware software debloating system. First, JSLIM processes the public vulnerability information through natural language processing technology, obtains the mapping relationship between the vulnerability and the NPM package, and determines which function in the package causes a specific vulnerability. Then, according to the generated function call graph, determine whether the program calls the method that generates the vulnerability in the dependent library. JSLIM removes the code that isn't called by the program and uses the sandbox to isolate the code that has vulnerabilities but cannot be removed. We conduct experiments on popular open-source JavaScript applications. The experimental results show that our method removes most of the code related to the known vulnerabilities of the application and effectively prevents attackers from exploiting known vulnerabilities in the NPM package to launch attacks on applications.

Keywords: JavaScript · Debloating · Vulnerability · Security · Static analysis

1 Introduction

In recent decades, the scale and complexity of software have increased astonishingly. Although this is beneficial to the development of the software indus-

This work is supported by the National Natural Science Foundation of China under Grant No. U20B2050 and the Science and Technology Funds from National State Grid Ltd. (The Research on Key Technologies of Distributed Parallel Database Storage and Processing based on Big Data).

© Springer Nature Switzerland AG 2022
W. Meng and S. K. Katsikas (Eds.): EISA 2021, CCIS 1403, pp. 128–143, 2022.
https://doi.org/10.1007/978-3-030-93956-4_8

try, it brings some performance problems to the application and causes many intractable security problems. For example, the development of software modularity has led to the excessive introduction of external dependency libraries by developers, causing the software to suffer performance and security problems. These problems are also called software bloat [6]. Furthermore, the bloated code introduced during software development brings many security risks, many serious vulnerabilities are rooted in the useless code in the imported dependency library [10, 15, 19]. Therefore, security researchers improved software security and performance by eliminating unnecessary functions and excess library code.

Previous works on software debloating have proposed different techniques, each tailored to use various analysis strategies to find out the unnecessary code of the application at runtime, then remove these unnecessary codes to speed up the execution of the application [18]. These current works are concentrate on removing unnecessary dead code in the application to optimizing the application. They did not consider removing useless code from a security perspective.

It is challenging to perform software debloating from the security level because we must consider the robustness of the application. In order to solve the problems, we have proposed a vulnerability-based software debloating technology for modern JavaScript applications-JSLIM. In general, JSLIM can be divided into three stages. First, we ascertain the various NPM packages that the application depends on from the NPM project files and clarify potential vulnerabilities in these NPM packages through data collected by search engines. The data collected by search engines includes commonly used vulnerability databases and blogs related to vulnerability disclosure. Because the information disclosed in the vulnerability database can only map CVE (Common Vulnerabilities & Exposures) to a specific version of the NPM package, in order to accurately map the CVE and source code to the function level, so we collected a large number of blogs from various technical forums. Furthermore, used natural language processing technology extracts essential information and determined the exact location of the code related to the vulnerability. Then, By statically analyzing the source code and using the collected code related to the vulnerability, we can build a function call graph for a specific function in a particular NPM package. According to the function call graph, we deleted the code that was not called by the main function. For the code with security risks but is still called by the main function, unlike existing work, we do not simply and radically remove these codes but use a sandbox for security isolation. Finally, After debloat the program, we need to perform corresponding functional verification and safety verification to ensure that the application can run normally. It is challenging to remove the unused parts of the dependent library because if part of the code is mistakenly deleted, it may affect the semantics of the entire application. Therefore, we use a progressive debloating strategy.

Our main contributions are the following:

- We propose a new software debloating ideology, which based on the perspective of security to analyze the known vulnerabilities in the application. Use natural processing technology to accurately map the relationship between vulnerabilities and source code to the function level, only remove or isolate pertient code that related to the vulnerability and not used in the dependent library.

- We have considered the safety of the code in the external dependency library that is called by the main function, we use sandboxes to isolate these codes from the application context and remove these security vulnerabilities to a certain extent.
- We designed and implemented JSLIM, a system for discovering related vulnerabilities in NodeJS applications. It uses a static analysis strategy to remove or isolate the code in dependent libraries. We have selected dozens of opensource JavaScript applications to experiment with these applications. The experimental results show that we can use this method to remove about 95% of the vulnerabilities in these applications.

The rest of the paper is organized as follows. In Sect. 2, we discuss the background knowledge of the research and list the related literature. Section 3 introduce the principle and process of each working stage of JSLIM in detail. In Sect. 4, we present the results of our quantitative, qualitative, and performance analysis of JSLIM. We conclude the paper in Sect. 5.

2   Background

In the past ten years, the problem of software bloat has been the center of research in performance tuning and optimization. Recently, due to the renewed interest in cyber defense-the main reason is that the need for active cyber defense expands the traditional software debloating technology to Reduce code size, improve runtime performance and eliminate unnecessary attack surfaces). Research work in this area has covered multiple research fields, including Java applications [6,9,11,13,18], Docker containers [17], and Internet of Things transport protocols.

Among all the research on application debloating, the discussion on C/C++ is the richest. Regehr et al. developed C-Reduce which is a tool that works at the source code level [4]. It reduces the C/C++ files in the application by defining some specific program conversion rules, but the definition of these rules takes a long time. Michael D. Brown proposed [5], a simple yet effective security-focused debloating technique that overcomes this problem. Sun et al. designed a framework called Perses that utilizes the grammar of any programming language to guide reduction [15]. Compared with applications written in C/C++, object-oriented languages such as Java applications are more prone to bloat problems. To solve problems such as bloat in object-oriented applications, Bobby R [10]. Bruce proposed [6], it augments traditional static reachability analysis with dynamic profiling and type dependency analysis and renovates existing bytecode transformations to account for new language features in modern Java. Gregor Wagner [13] use delayed code loading to transfer unused code, thereby reducing resource consumption when the application is running in this way.

In addition to removing useless code in the application through static analysis or dynamic analysis, Koo et al. [5] proposed configuration-driven debloating.

Their system removes unused libraries loaded by applications under a specific configuration. Rastogi et al. looked at debloating a container by partitioning it into smaller and more secure ones [14]. Although these past research works are very valuable, however, none target application's security, they only evaluate the security of the application after removing the useless code of the application, and do not design the debloating scheme based on the vulnerabilities in the application. This paper analyze the known vulnerabilities based on the perspective of security, only remove those code that related to the vulnerability and not used in the dependent library.

With the rapid development of web applications and the introduction of NPM [1,20] technology, dynamic interpreted languages JavaScript are entering all important areas of software development, including front-end, back-end and desktop applications, etc. The software bloat problem also appeared in the JavaScript application [7]. For how to solve these vulnerabilities loaded into the application through NPM, the solution given by the community is usually after the publisher of the relevant dependency package updates the version, the developer manually upgrades and applies the patch to the relevant vulnerability. However, due to the complex dependencies between NPM projects, the update of specific dependent packages will cause unexpected errors in the entire application. In order to ensure the stability of the entire system, developers will not be wronged by the updates of specific dependent packages. Therefore, the entire project undergoes dependency refactoring so that a large number of vulnerabilities known in the application cannot be repaired well [2]. Using the debloating software strategy can solve this problem because removing the vulnerability-related code in the dependent library will not destroy the dependencies between the dependent packages. Therefore, developers do not have to worry about the whole problem caused by repairing a particular vulnerability. Re-adjustment of application dependencies, Vázquez [12] et al. accelerated the construction of front-end projects by debloating the front-end application software [8]. While there exists many some JavaScript debloating tools [16], JSLIM differs because he considers the security of the application, and appropriately handles the malicious code that is directly called in the dependent library [3].

3 JSLIM

We have designed a debloating system JSLIM to find related vulnerabilities in JavaScript dependency libraries and delete or isolate these codes with vulnerabilities discovered. Our system aims to remove the known vulnerabilities in the NPM package, so find the vulnerability information in the NPM package of the application is a crucial step. The first phase is **analysis**, JSLIM parses source code to determine various external dependency libraries of the application and maps vulnerabilities to specific methods of source code through information publicly available on the Internet. In this process, we used natural processing technology to extract the data we need from the massive text information to determine the specific location of the vulnerability in the source code. The next phase is **debloat**, JSLIM static analysis source code to generate a function call graph, which is generated based on the vulnerability-related functions collected by JSLIM during the analysis phase. Then, JSLIM removes the code related to the vulnerability but not called by main function, and at the same time isolates the code related to the vulnerability and called by the main function. The last stage is **validate**. JSLIM verifies the application after debloating to ensure the safety and normal operation of the application. If the program's main functions are affected after debloating, mark the affected functions and debloating these affected functions more conservatively, the specific method will be given in detail later (Fig. 1).

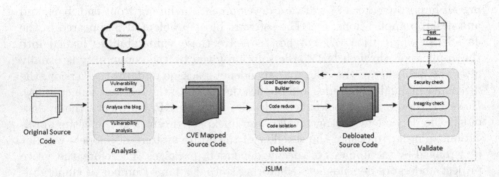

Fig. 1. The architecture of JSLIM.

3.1   Collect Vulnerabilities and Analyze Datas

The emergence of NPM technology allows JavaScript applications to load external JavaScript code from dependent libraries. In NPM, the dependencies are declared in a configuration file named package.json, which specifies the name and version of the dependent package.

After clarifying the various external libraries that the current application depends on, we can use the information available on the Internet to determine the vulnerability information of each version library and the vulnerability code. NLP (Natural Language Processing) technology is used in this process because most of the vulnerability reports collected on the Internet are text information, and these text data do not directly obtain critical information, such as the specific location of the vulnerability.

Collecting NPM vulnerability reports from the Internet and extracting specific knowledge from the collected reports for mapping relationship generation is a non-trivial task, with unique technical challenges. In order to address these challenges, in JSLIM, we use an NPM vulnerability extractor to eliminate irrelevant content and identify critical information that depends on security vulnerabilities in the dependency library (Fig. 2).

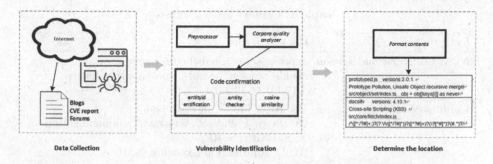

Fig. 2. Datas collect and extract.

The data collection process mainly collects vulnerability reports from the Internet, including commonly used forums, blogs, and mailing lists. More specifically, we grabbed popular online vulnerability leak sources and further ran a corpus quality analyzer to filter out documents unrelated to the vulnerability report. As mentioned earlier, we ran our crawler across the vulnerability reporting websites listed in Table 1, including a well-known technology forum (seclist.org/fulldisclosure), open-source community (github.com/gitlab.com).

After collecting and processing the vulnerability reports, we can scan and identify vulnerabilities. We first run a recognizer to discover related vulnerability reports and extract essential information (i.e., vulnerability types, CVE number, and NPM library name) and modeled the retrieval of vulnerability information as a named entity recognition problem in NLP [18]. More specifically, we first try to identify three entities related to vulnerabilities, including dependent library names and versions, common attack types, and CVE numbers. We then use the dependencies between them to confirm the existence of vulnerabilities. Then, considering the uniqueness of the description, we use a set of unique recognition technology of the JavaScript dependency library to retrieve them.

To identify these individual entities, we use a matching method based on keywords and regular expressions. For vulnerability types, CVE number and NPM library name. We believe that its corresponding entity exists as long as we find a word in the category (vulnerability types, CVE number, and NPM library name). We first determined the relevant dependency libraries by scanning the dependency configuration in the JavaScript application and then collected the vulnerability types from the Common Weakness Enumeration (CWE). Finally, the CVE generation strategy is used to determine the relevant CVE. Due to the extensive and challenging enumeration, we constructed a regular expression to identify each entity.

In this way, our method can identify all documents related to specific dependency library vulnerabilities. However, given the ubiquity of such entities (for example, the term "express" also appears in documents unrelated to library vulnerabilities), using them alone may lead to a large number of false positives. We use the dependencies between these entities to ensure that these vulnerabilities are correctly identified to solve this problem. Generally speaking, when these

Table 1. Context textual terms

Entity	Context terms
NPM Lib Name and version	express, sqlite3, babel-core, process, ejs, ajc cookie, session, accepts, aproba, array-flatten 4.17.1,0.11.10,2.3.4,0.2.4
Common Vuln Type	Use After Free, Out-of-Bounds, Prototype Pollution, Arbitrary Command Injection, XSS, CSRF, SSRF, RCE), Information Exposure, XML
CVE	CVE-[0-9]4-[0-9]4
Supplementary information	Attack, Javascript, NPM, NodeJS

entities describe JavaScript external dependency vulnerabilities, they usually do not appear independently. So we can conclude that when they appear in the same document, there is a dependency between them. For example, on the blog, the name and version number of the NPM dependent library will appear before the attack type, and the corresponding vulnerability description and sample code will usually appear after the vulnerability type. Finally, according to the entity name obtained by data analysis, the cosine similarity with the dependent library name and version number is calculated. If the similarity is extremely low (for example, 0.08), we think the document has nothing to do with our needs.

After determining some vulnerabilities related to a particular NPM package in the captured data, we can confirm the specific location of the vulnerability in the source code based on the open source information or the error report in the official public, that is, determine the JavaScript source file, function, or method that caused the vulnerability.

3.2   Debloating JavaScript Application

By collecting vulnerability reports related to the NPM package and grasp the exact location of the vulnerability in the source code, we should to determine whether the main function references the code that will cause security risks. If we directly remove the code with hidden security risks, it is very likely that some functions of the application cannot be used. Therefore, we need to use the code with hidden security risks as the initial position and use a reasonable program analysis strategy. Context search, if these methods do not have a main function reference, we can directly remove these codes. However, suppose the main function directly references these codes. In that case, we will load these codes into a sandbox, isolate these codes that pose security risks from the application context, and ensure the normal operation of the application without affecting the regular operation of the application safety.

Since JavaScript is a dynamic scripting language, it can generate code at runtime, dynamically add object properties, and even delete them during program execution. Nevertheless, it is precisely because of the dynamic characteristics and third-party code that will generate public events during compilation, making JavaScript analysis and modeling execution behavior an insurmountable difficulty. Our application only pays attention to the calling relationship of specific methods in the application and does not need to consider the specific program execution. Therefore, we do not need to consider the accuracy of the analysis, only the scalability of the analysis results. Therefore, we use the field-based analysis technique proposed by Asger Feldthaus [8] to determine the objective function call graph quickly. The experimental results also show that although the call graph constructed by our method is not accurate enough, it is sufficient to determine the relationship between the objective function and the main program.

When building our call graph, we first load all the JavaScript files in the application, use Parser to generate the corresponding AST for each javaScript file, collect the export object and require function in each AST file, and generate the corresponding dictionary. Then recursively visit all modules at the entry point of the application and mark them as used by Load Dependency Builder. We first construct a file-level dependency graph, and we can construct it based on the call method in the AST. Suppose the parameter type is literal when the call is called. In that case, Load Dependency Builder will use the Node.js default parsing algorithm to parse the required parameters to determine the dependency between the two. However, if some dependent libraries are dynamically imported into the file, we need to match the parameters require based on the dictionary information generated when traversing the AST. Suppose the similarity of the parameter is a simple identifier, and the dictionary contains the value of this identifier. In that case, Load Dependency Builder will traverse all possible values and resolve to possible modules in the application. This work is achieved with the help of the open-source tool detective. Suppose the identifier does not exist in the dictionary. In that case, Load Dependency Builder will mark this module as using a complex dynamic import, indicating that the dependency cannot be resolved reliably using only static technology. Suppose the application's dependency graph contains a module with complex dynamic imports. In that case, JSLIM will stop performing further analysis and exit because it cannot reliably reduce the application being analyzed without destroying its original behavior.

```
1   module.export = {
2       funcEval:function(req,res) {
3           var datas = eval(req.query.q);
4           return datas;
5       },
6       funcProp:function(obj,params,max) {
7           obj1.propetype.newFunction =
8           function(params,max){
9               for(var i=0;i<params.length;i++){
10                  max(params[i],i);
11              }
12          }
13      },
14      funcNew:function(obj,params,max) {
```

```
15              obj.newFunction(params,max)
16          },
17          funcSql:function(params,sql) {
18              const conn = createConnection(params);
19              conn.query(sql);
20          },
21          strTrim:function(params){
22              return params.map(String.trim);
23          },
24          createConnection:function(params){
25              params = strTrim(params);
26              conn = DataBase.createConnection(params);
27              return conn;
28          }
29  }
```

exam.js

After constructing the basic dependency graph based on the file, we need to be more precise to determine the internal calling relationship of each JavaScript file. Let us take the code in Fig. 3 as an example. This is a simple dependency library function exam.js. The external function can perform SQL operations on the database by loading this dependency (line 18) or using the funcEval method (line 2). Process the sent request. The entire library function can be divided into three parts: to perform processing on the received req, change the prototype method of the incoming object, receive the incoming parameters, and perform database operations. Although the level of the entire library function is apparent, due to the dynamic characteristics of JavaScript, such as the function funcProp (line 7), the prototype of the passed in object is set, so that the passed in obj has a new method, but this method The call must be called by funcProp before it can appear, so it is difficult to determine the call within the entire function directly.

```
1  const exam = require('./exam.js');
2  app.get('/eval',function(req,res){
3      exam.funcEval(req,res);
4  })
```

main.js

But we are concerned about the specific method in the external dependency library, not a variable. Because the main function must call specific methods after importing the dependent library instead of only introducing certain variables. Therefore, our granularity is based on the method and does not need to be accurate to a specific variable. We only need to find the node whose type is 'FunctionDeclaration' in the AST. Then, determine which methods in the entire dependency library call the target method we found in the mapping relationship. Finally, we can analyze the call graph from the information required to construct the AST, and the generated call graph is as follows.

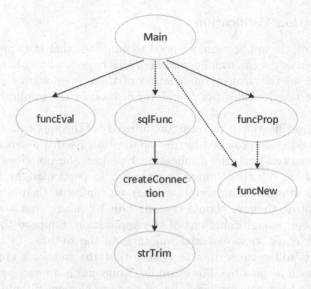

Fig. 3. Function call graph

According to the application, we construct the corresponding function call graph and combine the collected vulnerability and code mapping information. We can remove the code that is related to the vulnerability and is not called by the main function. When removing the code, we only need to delete the AST Mark the unused AST node while ensuring that the structure of the entire AST is not destroyed because we also need to build a new application from the AST after removing some nodes.

In order to better reflect the various situations in the display, we have designed three different slimming strategies, corresponding to the three scenarios of conservative, moderate, and aggressive.

Conservative. We remove the code related to known vulnerabilities and not called by the main function, and does not perform any processing on the code that has a security risk but is called by the main function.

Moderate. We remove the code related to known vulnerabilities and not called by the main function, and at the same time, isolate the code related to security vulnerabilities in the dependent library.

Aggressive. We remove the code with security risks and is not called by the main function and isolates the code related to security vulnerabilities in the dependent library. At the same time, remove the useless code that has no security risks and is not called by the main function during the static analysis.

3.3 Application Verification

After debloating the application, we need to judge whether the application after application debloating can usually work. For this reason, we test in an automated manner based on the project information of these open source projects. The content of the test includes functional verification of the application, security verification, etc.

Functional verification is to verify the integrity of the application, In addition to using the test code provided by the application itself, we can also simulate common interactions with the application based on the use cases provided by the application in the open-source community. In particular, we need to map these tutorials into Selenium scripts so that we can reuse them multiple times. It is worth noting that we should try our best to ensure that these Selenium scripts can cover enough functions of the application. Suppose these Selenium scripts do not cover some essential functions of the website. In that case, we will artificially add some scripts to ensure that the website's application can be cover as much as possible. For example, Node-elm is an excellent JavaScript application. Its front-end project is based on vue+element-ui, and its back-end is based on express+mongoose. It mainly provides many functions such as city selection, user configuration, registration, and log in. In addition to these tutorials, we also designed some more complex Selenium scripts based on the website's functions, such as the operation of items that have been added to the shopping cart, and the adjustment of the price of the goods the back-end administrator. By running the same test code and selenium script on the application before and after debloating, the application's functional integrity can be checked according to the results of the operation.

Security verification is to determine the security of the application after debloating. In the process of vulnerability identification, we analyze the data of open source communities and blogs to calculate whether a specific vulnerable dependency is part of the package's internal dependency chain and map the vulnerability to a specific location in the package. In the process of data collection, we can also collect some attack scripts with corresponding vulnerabilities. Through these attack scripts, we can verify the security of the application after debloating. Because these security-related codes are removed or isolated by operation, and attackers can no longer use these vulnerabilities in common dependent libraries to launch attacks.

4 Evaluation

In this section, we present an empirical analysis of known vulnerability removal in JavaScript applications. First, we introduced the target application. Second, we present the results of JSLIM apply in the selected application. Finally, we discuss the threats to the validity of our study.

4.1   Target Applications

We have selected more than 50 popular JavaScript applications, each application must meet the following conditions:

- It must depend on at least ten library.
- It must be open-source.
- It must have detailed information about how to compile and run the test.

Table 2 shows the direct libraries on which each application depends and the size of the application. According to the changes in the application size, we can determine the amount of code removed by JSLIM. Since JSLIM is removing the code in the external dependency library of the JavaScript application, the size of the application here refers to the size of the application in regular operation after the external dependency library specified in package.json is loaded. The applications we collect need to have particular functions, not a simple application framework, so we did not choose those trendy open-source frameworks (such as express, Aedes). Instead, we chose some large-scale applications built by JavaScript and some exquisite small-scale applications, such as wifi setting tools, web crawlers, etc. After selecting the required applications, we also need to download these applications from Github and ensure that the entire project can run normally.

4.2   Vulnerability Identification

Table 2. Vulnerability identification and remove

Application	The number of vulnerability	Vulnerabilities identified	Vulnerabilities removed	% of reduction vulnerabilities
node-elm	33	32	30	93.7%
Koa2 blog	15	15	15	100%
kite	37	35	34	97.1%
douban_Website	48	46	40	86.9%
booksearch	14	13	10	76.9%
react-music-webapp	62	59	58	98.4%
NewsAggregationWebsite	12	12	12	100%
qinVideo	16	16	15	93.8%
NodeShop	12	10	9	90%
node-crawler	11	11	9	81.8%
node-wifi	6	6	6	100%
hummusRecipe	8	8	7	87.5%
draw	5	5	5	100%
instagram-tools	10	10	9	90%
unsplash-downloader	8	8	8	100%

After download the source code of the selected application, we scan the package.json of the application one by one to identify the external dependency libraries required by the application, and then collect related vulnerability information based on the name and version information of the external dependent libraries. There are publicly disclosed and widely discussed vulnerabilities in the dependency libraries of our selected applications. The types of these vulnerabilities include Prototype Pollution, Improper Input Validation, Regular Expression Denial of Service (ReDoS), Timing Attack, Arbitrary Code Execution, etc. For a shopping website, Improper Input Validation may not be a serious problem, but privilege escalation may cause non-administrator users to perform some high-privileged operations. The number of vulnerabilities in each application is also in line with our basic understanding. The more third-party libraries an application depends on, the more vulnerabilities it has. It should be noted that these vulnerabilities are only vulnerabilities disclosed on the network in the external dependency library of the application, and do not represent the actual number of vulnerabilities contained in the application.

Since we need to collect information related to a certain NPM package from the website or forum shown in Table 1, the accuracy of the collected information is very important. Therefore, we first manually write a package.json file, and then use Collector to collect related vulnerability information. Finally, we randomly sampled 200 reports from those identified for manual validation and achieved a precision of 90%.

By collecting and analyzing the vulnerability information published on the Internet, we can map most of the vulnerabilities to the corresponding positions in the source code, but there are also some vulnerabilities that cannot be accurately found in the relevant code. The cause may be the vulnerability. The discloser did not give specific information about the vulnerability, or it may be because the vulnerability was not paid attention to by other researchers. In application node-elm, we found 33 vulnerabilities in the application's dependency library, and successfully mapped 32 of them to the specific location of the source code. For the only vulnerability that was not successfully mapped, we manually The analysis found that the related information of this vulnerability is very little, and it is a very low threat of information exposure vulnerability. We can ignore such vulnerabilities. In application kite, we found that the entire application is very large and bloated, that the entire application is very large and bloated. It introduces a large number of external dependent libraries, and even introduces a dependent library that is not used in the application, lowdb. Of the 37 known vulnerabilities, there are still 2 vulnerabilities that we cannot find the exact location of the source program. The main reason is that these two vulnerabilities were collected in issure on github. The researchers who discovered this problem only the problems that exist when the program is running are raised, and no detailed information is given. In application booksearch, the only vulnerability that has not been successfully mapped to a specific location in the source code is Arbitrary Code Execution, the only vulnerability that has not been successfully mapped to the specific location of the source code is Arbitrary Code Execution. This is a vulnerability with a medium risk level. Because it was announced a week ago, there is too little blog information about it, so we cannot get enough public information to analysis. In addition, for most of the other vulnerabilities, we can normally map the vulnerabilities to specific locations in the NPM package.

4.3 Vulnerability Remove

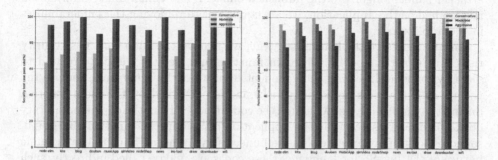

Fig. 4. Vulnerability removal rate and test pass rate under different strategies

After determining the exact location of the vulnerability in the dependent library, we can construct a function call graph based on the collected code to determine whether the main function directly calls the code related to the vulnerability. For example, suppose vulnerabilities were part of the program's core functionality. In that case, the debloater cannot remove the code associated with them, only use the code isolation strategy to isolate these vulnerable codes from the context of the application. However, if some vulnerabilities reside in parts of an application that are not commonly used, the process of debloating can effectively remove them (Fig. 4).

Due to the complexity of the application, we provide three different strategies for debloating, which represent different application scenarios. The specific differences have been explained in detail in Sect. 3.2. In each scenario, we debloating the application with JSLIM and build the resulting variant using the default package. All application and debloated variants were built on the same platform, with configurations kept constant for each build.

In the conservative debloating strategy, we only remove code related to vulnerability and not called by the main function. JSLIM does not perform any processing on code related to vulnerability but is not called by main function. Therefore, we can only remove some of the vulnerabilities in the external dependency library. Compared with the results of other slimming strategies, this result is more conservative, but it also means that JSLIM retains the application's land to the greatest extent under this strategy. Various functions. Because we remove all useless code that is not needed by the application, all the application functions are intact.

In a moderate debloating strategy, we remove the code that has security risks and is not called by the main function. At the same time, isolate the code related to security vulnerabilities in the dependent library. Because we use code isolation to isolate the vulnerabilities in external dependent libraries from the application context and "remove" the vulnerabilities in the application in a more elegant way. Although this is not thin in the traditional sense, we did not remove the code related to the vulnerabilities from the application. However, our goal is to destroy the known vulnerabilities in the application, as long as the attacker can no longer use the published online. If the vulnerability information is launched on the application, we are equivalent to removing the vulnerabilities in the application.

In an aggressive debloating strategy, we remove the code that has security risks and is not called by the main function and isolates the code related to security vulnerabilities in the dependent library. At the same time, remove the useless code that has no security risks and is not called by the main function during the static analysis. Although the code removed from the dependent library does not directly show that the application calls it in the function call graph, some test cases may execute these to unnecessary paths, and due to the dynamic nature of the JavaScript language, these codes are maybe called indirectly, such as funcNew in Fig. 3.

5   Conclusion

This paper presented a debloating system based on known JavaScript vulnerabilities-JSLIM, which measures and effectively removes unnecessary code and dependencies by statically analyzing JavaScript applications. Compared with the previous debloating technology that focused on the application's attack surface, our method is more accurate because we remove the known vulnerabilities instead of reducing the possibility of vulnerabilities. We selected dozens of popular javaScript applications and set up three different debloating strategies to experiment. Experimental results show that JSLIM can ensure the stable operation of the application after removing about 95% of the known vulnerabilities.

References

1. Official babel documentation (2015). https://www.npmjs.com/package/detective
2. Agten, P., Joosen, W., Piessens, F., Nikiforakis, N.: Esprima. In: ECMAScript Parsing Infrastructure for Multipurpose Analysis (2012)
3. Agten, P., Joosen, W., Piessens, F., Nikiforakis, N.: Seven months' worth of mistakes: a longitudinal study of typosquatting abuse. In: Network and Distributed System Security Symposium, 08–11 February 2015, San Diego, USA (2015)
4. Azad, B.A., Laperdrix, P., Nikiforakis, N.: Less is more: quantifying the security benefits of debloating web applications. In: 28th USENIX Security Symposium USENIX Security 19, pp. 1697–1714 (2019)
5. Brown, M.D., Pande, S.: Carve: practical security-focused software debloating using simple feature set mappings. In: Proceedings of the 3rd ACM Workshop on Forming an Ecosystem Around Software Transformation, pp. 1–7 (2019)
6. Bruce, B.R., Zhang, T., Arora, J., Xu, G.H., Kim, M.: Jshrink: in-depth investigation into debloating modern java applications. In: Proceedings of the 28th ACM Joint Meeting on European Software Engineering Conference and Symposium on the Foundations of Software Engineering, pp. 135–146 (2020)

7. Davis, J., Kildow, G., Lee, D.: The case of the poisoned event handler: weaknesses in the node.js event-driven architecture. In: Proceedings of the 10th European Workshop on Systems Security, p. 8 (2017)
8. Feldthaus, A., Schäfer, M., Sridharan, M., Dolby, J., Tip, F.: Efficient construction of approximate call graphs for javascript IDE services. In: 2013 35th International Conference on Software Engineering (ICSE), pp. 752–761. IEEE (2013)
9. Koo, H., Ghavamnia, S., Polychronakis, M.: Configuration-driven software debloating. In: Proceedings of the 12th European Workshop on Systems Security, pp. 1–6 (2019)
10. Landsborough, J., Harding, S., Fugate, S.: Removing the kitchen sink from software. In: Proceedings of the Companion Publication of the 2015 Annual Conference on Genetic and Evolutionary Computation, pp. 833–838 (2015)
11. Macias, K., Mathur, M., Bruce, B.R., Zhang, T., Kim, M.: Webjshrink: a web service for debloating java bytecode. In: Proceedings of the 28th ACM Joint Meeting on European Software Engineering Conference and Symposium on the Foundations of Software Engineering, pp. 1665–1669 (2020)
12. node-elm. https://github.com/bailicangdu/node-elm
13. Sharif, H., Abubakar, M., Gehani, A., Zaffar, F.: Trimmer: application specialization for code debloating. In: Proceedings of the 33rd ACM/IEEE International Conference on Automated Software Engineering, pp. 329–339 (2018)
14. Shin, Y., Williams, L.: An empirical model to predict security vulnerabilities using code complexity metrics. In: Proceedings of the Second ACM-IEEE International Symposium on Empirical Software Engineering and Measurement, pp. 315–317 (2008)
15. Sun, C., Li, Y., Zhang, Q., Gu, T., Su, Z.: Perses: syntax-guided program reduction. In: Proceedings of the 40th International Conference on Software Engineering, pp. 361–371 (2018)
16. Szurdi, J., Kocso, B., Cseh, G., Spring, J., Felegyhazi, M., Kanich, C.: The long "taile" of typosquatting domain names. In: 23rd USENIX Security Symposium USENIX Security 14, pp. 191–206 (2014)
17. Vázquez, H.C., Bergel, A., Vidal, S., Pace, J.D., Marcos, C.: Slimming javascript applications: an approach for removing unused functions from javascript libraries. Inf. Softw. Technol. **107**, 18–29 (2019)
18. Xu, G., Arnold, M., Mitchell, N., Rountev, A., Sevitsky, G.: Go with the flow: profiling copies to find runtime bloat. In: Proceedings of the 30th ACM SIGPLAN Conference on Programming Language Design and Implementation, pp. 419–430 (2009)
19. Xu, G., Mitchell, N., Arnold, M., Rountev, A., Sevitsky, G.: Software bloat analysis: finding, removing, and preventing performance problems in modern large-scale object-oriented applications. In: Proceedings of the FSE/SDP Workshop on Future of Software Engineering Research, pp. 421–426 (2010)
20. Zimmermann, M., Staicu, C.A., Tenny, C., Pradel, M.: Small world with high risks: a study of security threats in the NPM ecosystem. In: 28th USENIX Security Symposium USENIX Security 19, pp. 995–1010 (2019)

Digital Twin Monitoring for Cyber-Physical Access Control

Brian Greaves[✉] , Marijke Coetzee , and Wai Sze Leung

University of Johannesburg, Auckland Park 2006, South Africa
{bgreaves,marijkec,wsleung}@uj.ac.za

Abstract. Cyber-physical systems are defined by the integration of physical space entities and cyberspace information processing systems. Physical access control is generally perimeter-based, where assets can be vulnerable to a malicious entity once they have entered the perimeter of the space. Therefore, the relative distances between subjects and objects are needed to enforce cyber-physical access control within the perimeter of the physical space. The interplay between a physical entity and its virtual representation can be modelled using the concept of a digital twin. A digital twin enables the virtual monitoring of a physical entity to ensure better access control decision-making. This research presents a prototype indoor positioning and tracking system that can uniquely identify and track people and equipment in physical 3D space to create and maintain digital twins in real-time. The integration of 2D image processing and 3D depth-sensing technologies results in a system that can monitor a physical space where entities come into proximity to one another. Furthermore, the system can be used to prevent transgressions between physical entities within a relative distance of a few centimetres by tracking entities using human digital twin technology and reporting their relative proximity to an access control system for real-time enforcement.

Keywords: Cyber-physical systems · Human digital twins · Access control · 3D depth sensing · Stereovision

1 Introduction

The convergence of physical and logical access control is a recent research focus [1]. Sensitive documents on a device are protected by logical access control using access control rules, decision, and enforcement points [2]. To protect physical devices containing sensitive information, physical access control is defined over a real space such as a room or office with a locked door [3] that subjects can enter if they present an access card granting them access [1].

A person with sufficient clearance can enter a room without permission to interact with some specific equipment contained therein. Even though logical access control has permitted them access to the perimeter of the room, they may be able to misuse equipment that belongs to another employee once inside. In this case, there is a disparity between the protection provided by the cyber access control system and the reality of the

© Springer Nature Switzerland AG 2022
W. Meng and S. K. Katsikas (Eds.): EISA 2021, CCIS 1403, pp. 144–158, 2022.
https://doi.org/10.1007/978-3-030-93956-4_9

physical access control system. This calls for the convergence of physical and logical access control to eliminate the disparity between these two access control areas [1].

Accordingly, the matter of controlling proximity arises. In current research, physical access control is performed at the perimeter [4] of a physical space such as a door to the room [5]. These approaches do not cater toward proximity-based access control once within the room. To protect assets within the perimeter of the room, the access control system needs to know where each person is and how far they are from objects.

Current work utilizes Bluetooth beacons to accurately detect the proximity of objects to one another [6] and smartphone sensors to position devices in the space accurately [7]. Systems such as these require some form of costly device to be either carried or installed, making them susceptible to being circumvented if the device is lost or intentionally removed [1, 8]. Therefore, a gap in the body of knowledge exists, calling for inexpensive indoor positioning systems that can locate entities without circumvention.

This work proposes a prototype system that can determine the relative distance between tracked people and objects. Their physical representation is associated with a virtual representation as a digital twin in real-time using a stereovision camera-based system. The digital twin can then be used to report proximity information to a suitable access control model. If two entities are found to be located in close proximity to one another, access control is performed.

The remainder of the paper is laid out as follows: Sect. 2 introduces a motivating scenario. Section 3 discusses the concept of a digital twin that supports a real-time virtual representation of physical objects and compares it to human digital twins. Section 4 discusses proximity-based access control for cyber-physical systems. Section 5 describes current camera-based indoor positioning systems and image processing techniques to detect and track entities. Section 6 presents digital twin monitoring that supports real-time information for access control decision-making. A prototype system that can determine the relative distances between tracked objects is presented in Sect. 7. Section 8 concludes the paper.

2 Motivating Scenario

Consider scientists that work in a high-security laboratory space. Sensitive samples are stored, moved, and tested using delicate laboratory equipment. Confidential data is stored and processed on laptops in the venue that no one should view without the required clearance. If sensitive samples are carried between points, staff must be more than 1 m apart from each other to prevent accidental collisions. A set perimeter around laboratory samples and specific laboratory equipment must be maintained to avoid unwarranted access by unauthorized staff members. Currently, these constraints cannot be enforced within the physical space.

To protect equipment and laboratory samples, collisions between moving objects such as people need to be prevented. Furthermore, unauthorized physical access to laptops, equipment, or sensitive samples needs to be prevented. To address these conditions, an accurate representation of the topology of the space needs to be maintained. The location of each person, laptop, sample, and piece of equipment at any given time needs to be determined and maintained. To make access control decisions, the physical identity of an object or subject needs to be associated with its cyber identity. Even as the topology changes with entities moving about, tight coupling between the physical and cyberspace must be maintained [1].

To address the minimum distance between people, the system needs to determine their proximity to one another. Should they be too close, an access control system can deploy a countermeasure such as sounding an alarm as a warning and logging the transgression. To address the unauthorized access to laboratory equipment such as laptops and test equipment, the system needs to track all movements of persons, maintain associations between real-world objects and their cyber entities, and determine the relative distances between them.

The laboratory example can be modelled as a cyber-physical system [9]. Physical devices are integrated with cyber systems such as controllers and communication devices to monitor and control physical activities. Figure 1 shows a high-level overview of a cyber-physical system. At the bottom, the physical space consists of the building, its sensors responsible for data collection, the computers and equipment, and the physical human beings. The physical space connects to cyberspace using a computer network to facilitate data transmission. In cyberspace, there are data storage services and documents that humans use in work activities. There are also data processing capabilities, either from local or remote servers, to serve the system's users. Humans are represented by their user IDs or processes that act on their behalf. Cyber identities and other information represent physical objects such as computers or equipment.

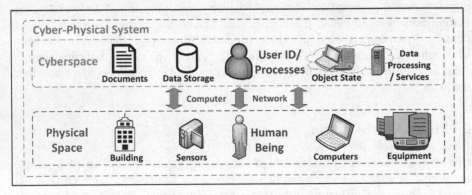

Fig. 1. A cyber-physical system

Physical and cyber entities are represented within the cyber system to use their information in relevant system operations, requiring tight coupling between related physical and cyber entities.

Next, the concept of a digital twin is introduced to support the tight coupling between physical and cyber entities.

3 Digital Twin

The first description of the digital twin concept was provided by Grieves [10] that stated that it consisted of three components, namely, a physical product in real space, a virtual representation of that product in the virtual space, and the connections of data and information that tie the virtual and real products together. A recent work [11] reviewed 46 definitions of a digital twin and presented the following definition – *"a virtual representation of a physical system (and its associated environment and processes) that is updated through the exchange of information between the physical and virtual systems."* This definition supports the cyber-physical example presented in this research.

For this research, a digital twin is defined by three components, namely a physical space and the physical entities that occupy it, their virtual representation, and the interconnections that enable a bidirectional exchange of information between the two. Figure 2 shows an example of digital twins created from the state of a human John and a physical office printer. The printer's state does not change much, whereas the state of John often changes as he moves around the room.

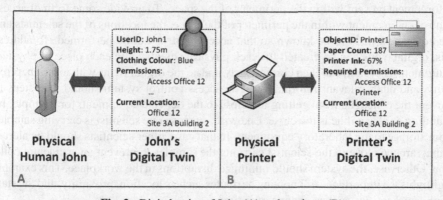

Fig. 2. Digital twins of John (A) and a printer (B)

The primary motivation for using a digital twin is monitoring a system over time to enable decision-making. Tao et al. [12] argue that if a digital twin's coupling is maintained, state information can be used in information security processes to prevent harm or damage. A tightly coupled physical person and its virtual representation ensure that a digital twin can be used to observe the behaviour of humans in the space. The virtual representation of a physical entity can be described by data such as properties, states, parameters, and attributes, as shown in Fig. 2. The types of data modelled depend on the level of abstraction required by the system [11].

However, human beings are not like machines: Each is unique and highly complex, more so than a piece of machinery. Machines can also directly receive information from a digital twin via networks; humans have no in-built mechanism for this [13]. Furthermore, human beings are not deterministic and are subject to their human agency which means that even if they are issued instructions, they can elect not to execute them [13]. This is problematic when trying to create digital twins for human beings.

Human digital twins are a variety of digital twins used to model parts of the human body as digital twins for use in medical procedures [14]. Human digital twins have been acknowledged as lacking in bidirectional information flow compared to their manufacturing counterparts [15]. One researcher goes so far as to propose that human digital twins have more in common with digital shadows that are automatically updated based on the state of the physical entity than a digital twin that requires the ability to alter the physical entity dynamically [15]. Despite the lack of bidirectional information flow, most human digital twin research still refers to them as a form of a digital twin. In light of this, this research also refers to human digital twins as a form of a digital twin but requires that actions are taken to alter the human's state if the human elects not to do so of their own accord when notified by the system.

For example, a specialist scientist needs to work on delicate laboratory equipment, which is not to be interacted with by anyone else in the laboratory. When the scientist is granted access to the laboratory space, he is merely granted access to the perimeter and not explicitly the delicate equipment. Therefore, if a colleague enters the space to work on his own equipment, it is possible that the colleague can walk over to the delicate equipment and accidentally or intentionally damage it as there is no access control enforcement present within the perimeter of the space. To provide some form of access control enforcement within the perimeter of the space, the locations of the scientists and the equipment need to be known so that access control can be performed. To address this, digital twins can be created for each physical scientist and each piece of physical equipment. A system can then continuously update the digital twins with location, proximity, and other relevant information. The access control system should take steps to prevent the colleague from getting too close to the delicate equipment, for example, by sounding an alarm if he is too close. Likewise, suppose one scientist is carrying samples from storage to the laboratory equipment. In that case, other scientists should be alerted if they are too close to the scientist carrying the samples to prevent an accidental collision. Otherwise, the system should minimize disruptions in the workplace. This example highlights the importance of knowing attributes such as location, proximity, and the state of physical entities as they change over time.

In the example above, a human digital twin can be used to monitor the state of humans as they move about the space and make decisions based on the state information. Should a problem be identified, the digital twin can be used to sound an alarm in the physical space to act as a deterrent [16]. Should the alarm be ignored by the scientist, then the digital twin can request a security response. In either case, the state of the human being will be altered to be more acceptable to the system, either if the human elects to change behaviour or if security forces them to change. This addresses the inherent lack of bidirectional information flow in human digital twins [15].

Thus, the system monitors a *physical* to *virtual* interaction [11] to update the state of a digital twin. Information is collected, processed to be consistent with the required level of abstraction needed, and updated to the digital twin. To collect information, sensor technology is deployed in the environment. At times, a *virtual to physical* transfer of information is required [11], closing the digital twin loop. The insights and decisions that are made by the virtual representation are fed back to the physical system. For example, by sounding an alarm or calling security if someone is too close to the equipment, they have not been permitted access to be there. The real-time update of information between the physical system and digital twin and vice versa needs to be at a sufficient frequency to enable the system to perform effectively. Consider the walking speed of a human being and how easily a collision can occur when walking around a small laboratory. Therefore, real-time updates are required to ensure the tight coupling of a digital twin to its physical counterpart [8].

A downside that needs to be considered for the use of digital twins is the matter of privacy. Due to the use of a camera-based system and a system that incorporates information about the inhabitants of a physical space derived from monitoring systems, occupants may feel uncomfortable being watched. Due to this, the researchers advocate that the camera feeds should not be viewable unless some form of problem arises. Even then, only the relevant information should be made available to appropriate security personnel to perform their duties. For example, only show a person's face if they are in a location that they should not be. This approach is employed by [17] to reduce the amount of exposed private information to the minimum required for system operation. Thus, the system can operate in a "black-box" mode until an irregularity is detected and only provide information to the required level of abstraction [11].

To address the protection of assets in the laboratory example, the role of proximity in cyber-physical access control is described next.

4 Proximity-Based Access Control for Cyber-Physical Systems

Proximity is the measure of how close two entities are to one another. As entities are active, their states are continuously changing. The closeness of entities can be defined as the physical distance that they are from each other. For this research, proximity is defined as the geospatial distance that entities are from each other in a three-dimensional physical space, often measured in centimetres or meters.

The location of a subject is used in Location-Based Access Control (LBAC) [18]. Once a subject's geographical location is verified, they are granted access to objects according to the policy governing that location. A recent form of LBAC proposed by Yamanaka et al. [19] supports using Geo-Fence technology to dynamically perform actions based on location events driven by subjects crossing a geofence perimeter. Proximity-Based Access Control (PBAC) [20] is a form of attribute-based access control where proximity is an attribute that indicates the distance between two proximity attributes, calculated using a distance function. Proximity does not necessarily refer to physical distance but can refer to many relative distance forms, including geospatial, temporal, risk, and other relative comparisons. Sensor-enhanced access control addresses the case where cyber objects are rendered in a physical space, and people come into close proximity with the device they are rendered on [21]. The approach uses a camera-based system but caters to fixed endpoints that track subjects' movement as they pass into or out of the line of sight of an endpoint.

Generally, in recent location and proximity-based access control, the convergence between physical and cyberspace is not addressed to support real-time changes in a three-dimensional space. This research contributes a method to determine the relative distance between physical entities monitored using human digital twins.

To perform proximity-based access control for cyber-physical systems, people, devices, and equipment need to be detected, identified and tracked in a three-dimensional space. Figure 3 gives the high-level components of such a system. It is important to note that the focus of this research is not the definition of an access control model. Instead, provide proximity information from digital twins as a set of attributes (access control policy information) that context or attribute-based access control models can use to make accurate decisions.

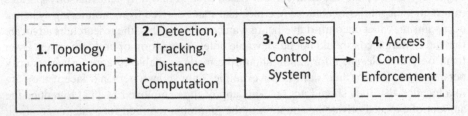

Fig. 3. High-level architecture of an access control system

The first two components provide access control information to an access control decision point. After a decision is made, access control is enforced.

Initially, *Topology Information* is collected from an environment such as the laboratory. Sensors are used to map the topology of the space to produce and maintain digital twins. For the physical space, the topology defines the physical characteristics of the space, such as physical locations and the proximity relationship among entities. In cyberspace, the topology establishes the location of digital files and the access states of subjects to objects such as equipment. For example, the location of the delicate laboratory equipment is determined and stored by the system. This information provides the baseline for the system against which to compare topology changes.

The second component performs *Detection, Tracking and Distance Computation* to determine locations and distances between people, laptops, and equipment using topology information of the space provided by the topology information component. This stage effectively maintains the coupling of the digital twin to its physical counterpart. The relative distances of each entity in the physical space are determined. Proximity information is defined by proximity attributes that express the proximity from one entity to another, defined as a physical distance in the space. Distance formulas are used to calculate the relative distance between two comparable proximity attributes. This research calculates the relative distance in a three-dimensional space and not between two geographical coordinates.

The *Access Control System* receives proximity and other related information from the digital twins to make access control decisions and enforce access control.

To the best of the researchers' knowledge, no capable system currently exists that is tailored specifically to determine relative distances between physical entities in a three-dimensional space using digital twins. Therefore, the focus of this research is on the first two components. A prototype system is presented that can detect and track entities by monitoring the changing topology information of physical entities in a space to determine the relative distances between them and maintain digital twins.

The following section discusses indoor positioning systems used to identify and track people and devices to provide a basis for coupling the states of the physical and cyberspaces of the laboratory as digital twins.

5 Indoor Positioning Systems for Detection and Tracking

The goal of an Indoor Positioning System (IPS) [22] is to provide distance information to prevent an unauthorized person, such as the scientist, from damaging delicate equipment or bumping into another while carrying samples to the lab equipment. Such distance information can be derived by computing the relative distance that two objects are from one another.

IPSs come in varied forms, such as token-based approaches that require a token in the form of an RFID card [23] to be carried and used at each authentication point. Other forms of IPS use active or passive localization techniques such as Bluetooth [23], Wi-Fi [24], or infrared [22] to locate entities. Previous work [25] explored various categories of IPSs to identify a suitable candidate to provide distance information. It was found that token-based systems such as RFID cards are not ideal as they can be removed or lost [8] and require all devices in a room to be protected by using the token as an authentication mechanism.

A sensory accuracy of centimetres is preferred to determine if someone can touch equipment that they do not have permission to use. The system needs to react if someone is within arm's reach of the delicate equipment. Therefore, high sensor accuracy is required to reduce the likelihood of false positives or negatives [8]. This eliminates most forms of triangulation as the expected accuracy is roughly 2 m [24]. Thus, two people could have already collided with each other, and the system would not register that they are in collision proximity—the greater the accuracy, the better.

The provision of a security perimeter around entities is of great importance. GeoFence [26] technologies allow for the specification of perimeters in the real world to perform actions if crossed. Outdoor GeoFences use systems such as GPS coordinates or 3G triangulation to mark static perimeters. These technologies, however, do not adapt well to indoor use as they are inaccurate due to large error margins or poor signal under concrete [27]. Therefore, traditional GeoFences are seldom used indoors. Many approaches [26, 27] adapt GeoFencing technology for indoor use by using IPSs as an alternative to GPS or 3G positioning systems [24]. The concept of a virtual perimeter [28] was presented as an indoor replacement for traditional GeoFence technology to enable perimeter-based actions to take place, using IPS technologies in an indoor space.

Computer-vision-based pattern recognition systems are the most viable candidates for an IPS [25] as they are accurate to sub 20 cm [29] and provide much context information. The exploration of many contemporary works has validated the consensus of camera use. For example, the works of Jensen et al. [21] and Yamanaka et al. [30] are of crucial importance as they demonstrate camera-based systems in similar use cases. The work of Hernández et al. [8] and Yap et al. [31] are also noteworthy because they demonstrate similar use cases to the defined scenario of this research.

Stereoscopic 3D cameras [32], often called stereovision or stereo cameras, have excellent capability to operate in 3D environments to produce depth maps and 3D point clouds representative of a space. Such technology can be beneficial to provide detection and tracking information using images to detect people and objects with 3D topology information to compute the relative distance between two objects in the space [24, 32].

Based on the abundance of works utilizing this method, the following section discusses image processing techniques used to detect and associate objects being monitored by a camera to update the virtual representation of a digital twin.

6 Digital Twin Monitoring

The *Detection, Tracking and Distance Computation* component in Fig. 3 produces relative distance measurements for the digital twin of each physical entity in a room. To monitor the physical to virtual interactions and update the state of a virtual representation of a digital twin, a camera-based system is defined to detect and track people and objects with 3D topology information. A 3D camera provides a 3D perception of the world. By triangulation, the human brain determines the distance or depth of objects relative to the observer position. Similarly, this principle is used to recreate a 3D scene representation based on the two images taken from different viewpoints. The result of the component is three major artefacts:

- A list of people and their associated cyber identities.
- A list of objects and their associated owners.
- A list of the relative distances between each of these entities in the scene.

Collectively, this information can be handed over to any suitable Access Control Service for access decisions to be made concerning the cyber credentials and clearance of entities based on their proximity to other entities in the room. For example, if a scientist is near the delicate equipment, it must be determined if that scientist has permission to use the equipment. Therefore, the scientist and the equipment are tracked in each frame produced by the camera and the relative distances. These distances are continuously reported as they change.

6.1 Detect and Track Physical Entities

Before relative distances between physical entities can be computed, the system must know which people and objects are present in the room. For example, an inexpensive and easily accessible Stereolabs ZED stereoscopic camera [33] can be used to capture images for this purpose. The camera-based indoor positioning system first detects entities of importance within a frame of an image. Once the detection is done, the detection information is used to track the individual objects as they move around [34]. Image processing culminates in a list of uniquely tracked people and objects detected in the room, as observed by the camera. Each of these is used to create initial digital twins.

6.2 Association of People with Cyber Identities

The system needs to differentiate between people who are in the view of the camera. A detected person needs to be associated with a known cyber-identity with a set of clearances or permissions to link the physical entity with its virtual representation. In modern access control, users prove their identity to the system by first authenticating themselves using a login, token, or biometric [3]. Due to the camera-based nature of the prototype, a person is authenticated as they enter a room. After that, they are tracked around the room, and their digital twins are updated accordingly. A biometric system such as facial or fingerprint recognition is preferred to authenticate a person as it is far more difficult to circumvent than a token such as RFID [8]. Once authentication is completed, applicable information is added to the appropriate digital twin.

6.3 Association of Physical Objects with Owners

Generally, physical objects such as laboratory equipment are static, and the state of their digital twins do not have to be associated with owners dynamically. They are statically assigned to subjects in the system. The system needs to cater to physical objects that can be moved around and have different users with different access rights. For example, physical objects such as laptops have the ability to restrict access by requiring a user to authenticate. This is useful; however, it does not explicitly enable a camera-based system to know which device is being authenticated to, mainly if multiple devices are observed simultaneously. If both scientists have laptops in the laboratory, the camera views them all at the same time.

To address the highlighted problem, the system associates a detected person with the closest detected laptop at the moment of authentication at the laptop. For example, suppose a scientist authenticates at a laptop. In that case, the system is notified of successful authentication and then finds the nearest laptop to him in the scene produced by the 3D camera. The closest laptop to the scientist is then associated with him via the digital twins. The system detects and identifies the laptop and the user with their associated identities and updates their digital twins. The system consequently knows who is in the environment and which laptop belongs to which person. Should the scientist leave the room and a different scientist attempt to access the other's laptop, the system would observe the scenario. The system can then respond reactively by locking the laptop, logging the transgression, sounding an alarm, or dispatching security.

6.4 Computation of Relative Distance

The focus of this step is to determine the relative distance between two identified objects, two people or an object and a person. The ZED camera extracts a point cloud matrix alongside an image matrix. A correlated point cloud provides a matrix containing a set of (x, y, z) coordinates representing real-world 3D locations relative to the camera [35]. The Cartesian coordinates produced by the ZED camera enable the computation of the Cartesian distance between any two points [35]. Due to the ZED being calibrated in metric units, points in the point cloud are stored in metric units. Therefore, the computation of cartesian distance yields a point-to-point distance in meters between any two selected points, P_1 and P_2. The relative distances between any two entities can then be computed.

The following section discusses the use of the ZED camera in the prototype.

7 Prototype Implementation

Python was chosen as the implementation language at the design stage of the prototype due to its widespread image processing ability. The experimentation was performed using an Intel i7-based laptop with an Nvidia Geforce GTX 1060 Graphical Processing Unit (GPU) with a CUDA compute power of 3.1. To enable GPU-centric ZED camera calculations, Tensorflow v2 [36] and DeepSort software libraries were integrated for 2D image processing. The prototype was run using CUDA 10.1 [37] and the ZED SDK for Python, PyZED [38] for inter-application compatibility between CUDA, Tensorflow v2 and DeepSort. The experimental setup used two volunteer test subjects who appear as "John" and "Mary" in the images below.

An image is extracted once the camera is ready. The camera must produce a standard colour or black and white image and a calibrated point cloud that represents the 3D space that the camera is observing [39]. An object detection component processes the image matrix. Figure 4 shows a graphical representation of the point cloud matrix associated with an image.

Fig. 4. Point cloud visualization

A list of all Person detections and Laptop detections are provided in the form of a set of bounding boxes. Figure 5 shows two people, and their respective devices present in a room, which the camera observes. Green bounding boxes are labelled as "A" and "B". To the right, a laptop is shown by the red bounding box labelled "C", and at the front right, a blue bounding box labelled "D" represents the authentication unit's location.

After the median point of every bounding box is computed, it is possible to calculate and display the relative distance between two objects. Figure 6 shows the relative distance that has been calculated between two people in the laboratory. The distance is shown as the white line connecting the center of each person's bounding box with the distance displayed in meters between them. Thus, the people are 1.39 m apart.

The next stage of the prototype solution is to provide the system with the ability to differentiate between people in the camera's view. The detected person needs to be associated with a known cyber-identity that has a set of clearances or permissions.

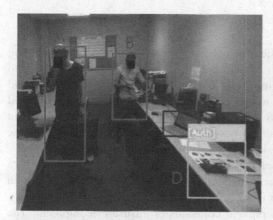
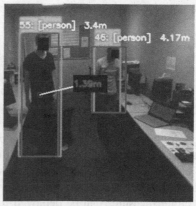

Fig. 5. Detection of people and laptops (Color figure online)

Fig. 6. Relative distance between persons

In the prototype, the scientists authenticate at the authentication unit biometrically to ensure their identity. Figure 7 shows the successful proximity-based authentication of a person and association with his user identity. The system associates the closest person in the scene to the authenticated cyber identity at the time of authentication.

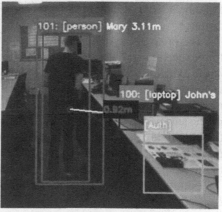

Fig. 7. Associate person with cyber identity

Fig. 8. Relative distance

In Fig. 8, a person comes in close proximity (0.92 m) to the other scientist's laptop. The system reports the relative distance between the person and the laptop to enable the access control system to make a decision. Even if a person is not authenticated, the system detects their movements and reports them to the access control system to make access decisions. Experimentation discovered that the accuracy of the proximity measurements falls within the 8 to 17 cm range, dependent on lighting conditions.

The following section concludes the research with a look to future work.

8 Conclusion

The research has contributed to the field of cyber-physical systems by amalgamating the two usually separate technologies of 2D object tracking and 3D depth sensing to form a prototype system capable of using 2D images to detect and track objects and the 3D information of the space to compute relative distance. The information gathered from the 2D and 3D systems enables a form of a digital twin to be created that can be updated in real-time using the camera-based systems. The system allows for the computation of the relative distance between two people or objects in the physical space using the information maintained in their digital twins. This enables the system to notify a suitable access control system when access needs to be computed, who is involved, which objects, and at what proximity. Then if the access control system deems it necessary, countermeasures can be deployed to prevent collisions or misuse of equipment. The accuracy of the system was determined by experimentation to be in the order of 8 to 17 cm per frame using a relatively inexpensive camera system. Usually, accuracy in the order of centimetres requires either expensive hardware or cumbersome tag-based systems that are subject to being removed or lost [8].

The prevention of misuse of equipment was shown using laptops as a form of lab equipment, and computing the relative proximity of all inhabitants of the space was demonstrated. Additionally, tracking ensured that the coupling was maintained even if a person or laptop moved about within the physical space.

The prototype system satisfies the required conditions of the scenario to produce a capable indoor positioning and tracking system that will enable the creation of a relative distance-based access control model.

The prototype system, however, is not perfect and has a number of limitations. Low frame rates are a problem for the accuracy of some tracking algorithms. During the course of the experimentation, framerates of between 3 and 8 frames per second were achieved using the defined hardware and software libraries. This led to some errors in tracking results, especially in the DeepSort algorithm. Several factors affect the framerate, such as processing power and the number of objects in the scene. This can be partially remedied by simplifying the pipeline by pre-filtering the Tensorflow object detection classes for detection. Furthermore, more powerful GPU image processing hardware can be utilized to raise framerates and improve the accuracy of the selected algorithms.

Future work aims to address an access control model to enable continuous access control using digital twins. A performance evaluation will be conducted against other approaches in the field, and security and privacy concerns will be addressed.

References

1. Tsigkanos, C., Pasquale, L., Ghezzi, C., Nuseibeh, B.: On the interplay between cyber and physical spaces for adaptive security **15**, 466–480 (2016)
2. Sandhu, R.S., Samarati, P.: Access control: principle and practice **32**, 40–48 (1994)
3. Sandhu, R.S.: Role-based access control. In: Advances in Computers, vol. 46, pp. 237–286 (1998)
4. Ullah, F., et al.: Barrier access control using sensors platform and vehicle license plate characters recognition. Sensors **19**(13), 3015 (2019)

5. Satoh, I.: Spatial connector: mapping access control models for pervasive computing and cloud computing. In: FNC/MobiSPC, pp.174–181 (2017)

6. Kouyoumdjieva, S.T., Karlsson, G.: Experimental evaluation of precision of a proximity-based indoor positioning system. In: 2019 15th Annual Conference on Wireless On-demand Network Systems and Services (WONS), pp. 130–137 (2019)

7. Jang, B., Kim, H., Kim, J.W.: IPSCL: an accurate indoor positioning algorithm using sensors and crowdsourced landmarks. Sensors **19**(13), 2891 (2019)

8. Hernández, J.L., Moreno, M.V., Jara, A.J., Skarmeta, A.F.: A soft computing based location-aware access control for smart buildings. Soft. Comput. **18**(9), 1659–1674 (2014). https://doi.org/10.1007/s00500-014-1278-9

9. Cook, D., Das, S.K.: Smart Environments: Technology, Protocols, and Applications, vol. 43. Wiley, Hoboken (2004)

10. Grieves, M.: Digital twin: manufacturing excellence through virtual factory replication. White Paper, vol. 1, pp. 1–7 (2014)

11. Van Der Horn, E., .Mahadevan, S.: Digital Twin: generalization, characterization and implementation. Decis. Support Syst. **145**, 113524 (2021)

12. Tao, F., Cheng, J., Qi, Q., Zhang, M., Zhang, H., Sui, F.: Digital twin-driven product design, manufacturing and service with big data. Int. J. Adv. Manuf. Technol. **94**(9–12), 3563–3576 (2017). https://doi.org/10.1007/s00170-017-0233-1

13. Barricelli, B.R., Casiraghi, E., Gliozzo, J., Petrini, A., Valtolina, S.: Human digital twin for fitness management. IEEE Access **8**, 26637–26664 (2020)

14. Sepasgozar, S.M.: Differentiating digital twin from digital shadow: elucidating a paradigm shift to expedite a smart, sustainable built environment. Buildings **11**(4), 151 (2021)

15. Sengan, S., Kumar, K., Subramaniyaswamy, V., Ravi, L.: Cost-effective and efficient 3D human model creation and re-identification application for human digital twins. Multimedia Tools Appl., 1–18 (2021). https://doi.org/10.1007/s11042-021-10842-y

16. Rajkamal, M., Swathi, D., Prabu, S., Mohanapriya, P.: Enhanced cyber physical security based automatic generation control with renewable energy system. Ann. Romanian Soc. Cell Biol. **25**, 15915–15925 (2021)

17. Skandhakumar, N., Reid, J., Dawson, E., Drogemuller, R., Salim, F.: An authorization framework using building information models. Comput. J. **55**(10), 1244–1264 (2012)

18. Ardagna, C.A., Cremonini, M., Damiani, E., di Vimercati, S.D.C., Samarati, P.: Supporting location-based conditions in access control policies. In: Proceedings of the 2006 ACM Symposium on Information, Computer and Communications Security, pp. 212–222 (2006)

19. Yamanaka, G., et al.: Geo-fencing in wireless LANs with camera for location-based access control. In: 2019 16th IEEE Annual Consumer Communications & Networking Conference (CCNC), pp. 1–4 (2019)

20. Lang, U., Schreiner, R.: Proximity-based access control (PBAC) using model-driven security. In: Reimer, H., Pohlmann, N., Schneider, W. (eds.) ISSE 2015, pp. 157–170. Springer, Wiesbaden (2015). https://doi.org/10.1007/978-3-658-10934-9_14

21. Jensen, C., Geneser, K., Willemoes-Wissing, I.: Sensor enhanced access control: extending traditional access control models with context-awareness. In: Fernández-Gago, C., Martinelli, F., Pearson, S., Agudo, I. (eds.) IFIPTM 2013. IAICT, vol. 401, pp. 177–192. Springer, Heidelberg (2013). https://doi.org/10.1007/978-3-642-38323-6_13

22. Liu, H., Darabi, H., Banerjee, P., Liu, J.: Survey of wireless indoor positioning techniques and systems **37**, 1067–1080 (2007)

23. Ijaz, F., Yang, H.K., Ahmad, A.W., Lee, C.: Indoor positioning: a review of indoor ultrasonic positioning systems. Presented at the 2013 15th International Conference on Advanced Communications Technology (ICACT), pp. 1146–1150 (2013)

24. Duque Domingo, J., Cerrada, C., Valero, E., Cerrada, J.A.: Indoor positioning system using depth maps and wireless networks. J. Sens. **2016** (2016)

25. Greaves, B., Coetzee, M., Leung, W.: A comparison of indoor positioning systems for access control using virtual perimeters. In: Yang, X.-S., Sherratt, S., Dey, N., Joshi, A. (eds.) Fourth International Congress on Information and Communication Technology. AISC, vol. 1041, pp. 293–302. Springer, Singapore (2020). https://doi.org/10.1007/978-981-15-0637-6_24

26. Young-Hyun, E., Young-Keun, C., Cho, S., Jeon, B.: FloGeo: a floatable three-dimensional geofence with mobility for the internet of things. Control Syst. **2017**, 114–120 (2017)

27. Pešić, S., Tošić, M., Iković, O., Radovanović, M., Ivanović, M., Bošković, D.: GEMAT-internet of things solution for indoor security geofencing. Presented at the Proceedings of the 9th Balkan Conference on Informatics, pp. 1–8 (2019)

28. Greaves, B., Coetzee, M., Leung, W.: Access control requirements for physical spaces protected by virtual perimeters. In: Furnell, S., Mouratidis, H., Pernul, G. (eds.) TrustBus. LNCS, vol. 11033, pp. 182–197. Springer, Cham (2018). https://doi.org/10.1007/978-3-319-98385-1_13

29. Deak, G., Curran, K., Condell, J.: A survey of active and passive indoor localization systems. Comput. Commun. **35**(16), 1939–1954 (2012)

30. Yamanaka, G., et al.: Geo-fencing in wireless LANs with camera for location-based access control. Presented at the 2019 16th IEEE Annual Consumer Communications & Networking Conference (CCNC), pp. 1–4 (2019)

31. Yap, R.H., Sim, T., Kwang, G.X., Ramnath, R.: Physical access protection using continuous authentication. Presented at the 2008 IEEE Conference on Technologies for Homeland Security, pp. 510–512 (2008)

32. Azarbayejani, A., Pentland, A.: Real-time self-calibrating stereo person tracking using 3-D shape estimation from blob features. Presented at the Proceedings of 13th International Conference on Pattern Recognition, vol. 3, pp. 627–632 (1996)

33. ZED Stereo Camera. https://www.stereolabs.com/zed. Accessed 11 Apr 2021

34. Wojke, N., Bewley, A.: Deep cosine metric learning for person re-identification. In: 2018 IEEE Winter Conference on Applications of Computer Vision (WACV), pp. 748–756 (2018)

35. ZED Spatial Mapping Module. https://www.stereolabs.com/docs/api/group__SpatialMapping__group.html. Accessed 11 Apr 2021

36. Tensorflow Object Detection API. https://github.com/tensorflow/models/tree/master/research/object_detection. Accessed 11 Apr 2021

37. CUDA 10.1. https://developer.nvidia.com/cuda-10.1-download-archive-base. Accessed 11 Apr 2021

38. ZED SDK. https://www.stereolabs.com/developers/release. Accessed 11 Apr 2021

39. Gupta, T., Li, H.: Indoor mapping for smart cities—an affordable approach: using Kinect Sensor and ZED stereo camera. In: 2017 International Conference on Indoor Positioning and Indoor Navigation (IPIN), pp. 1–8 (2017)

Improving Host-Based Intrusion Detection Using Thread Information

Martin Grimmer$^{(\boxtimes)}$, Tim Kaelble, and Erhard Rahm

Leipzig University, ScaDS.AI, Humboldtstraße 25, 04105 Leipzig, Germany
{grimmer,rahm}@informatik.uni-leipzig.de, tim_k@posteo.de
https://scads.ai/

Abstract. Host-based anomaly detection for identifying attacks typically analyzes sequences or frequencies of system calls. However, most of the known approaches ignore the fact that software in modern IT systems is multithreaded so that different system calls may belong to different threads and users. In this work, we show that anomaly detection algorithms can be improved by considering thread information. For this purpose, we extend seven algorithms and comparatively evaluate their effectiveness with and without the use of thread information. The evaluation is based on the LID-DS dataset providing suitable thread information.

1 Introduction

The frequency of cyber attacks and the associated damage are steadily increasing. This results in the interruption of various lines of business and services causing enormous financial losses (about 5.2 trillion USD) as shown in an Accenture study in 2019 [2]. In the event of loss of personal data, further financial penalties may be imposed on companies within the European Union due to the General Data Protection Regulation (GDPR) if adequate protection measures have not been taken, as required in Sect. 2 (Security of personal data), Article 32 (Security of processing) of the GDPR [8]. Another important point is the potential loss of customers' trust by losing their personal data. Restoring lost trust is a very long and difficult process. This all gets worse if you consider that in the past, on average, companies did not notice security incidents until weeks later as stated in the 2018 U.S. State of Cybercrime report [14]. For small and medium-sized companies, on average 56 d elapse between the time they notice a safety incident and the time when the incident is suspected to have occurred. For large enterprises, this time span is even 151 d on average.

A first step towards better IT security is to detect security incidents promptly. Only then can appropriate countermeasures be taken and potential security gaps be closed quickly. A possible technical solution for the fast identification of attacks is the use of intrusion detection systems. They can also help to address the requirements stated in article 32 (b) GDPR: *"Taking into account the state of the art [...], the controller and the processor shall implement appropriate technical [...] measures to ensure a level of security appropriate to the risk, [...] the*

© Springer Nature Switzerland AG 2022
W. Meng and S. K. Katsikas (Eds.): EISA 2021, CCIS 1403, pp. 159–177, 2022.
https://doi.org/10.1007/978-3-030-93956-4_10

ability to ensure the ongoing confidentiality, integrity, availability and resilience of processing systems and services [...]." [8]

Even if intrusion detection systems could only detect and avert 5% of all IT security incidents in time, this would correspond to an avoided loss of about 260 billion USD worldwide. It is therefore also worthwhile to examine approaches to enhance Intrusion Detection Systems (IDS).

1.1   Our Contribution

The aim of this work is to improve existing approaches for host-based intrusion detection systems (HIDS), in particular, anomaly-based approaches that evaluate system calls. These approaches mostly analyze sequences or frequencies of system calls. However, they do not consider the thread in which a system call has been executed, thereby ignoring the fact that software in modern IT systems is mostly multithreaded. Multiple runs of the same software, with identical input data, may thus result in different sequences of system calls due to the execution scheduling of the operating system. Since much current work on HIDS is focused on learning and analyzing subsequences of system calls, this can lead to incorrect results. This paper aims at answering the question whether considering the thread allocation of a system call can achieve better results in anomaly detection. For this purpose, we modify and evaluate seven known anomaly detection algorithms accordingly. We will show that the use of thread information increases the detection rate and reduces the number of false alarms in most cases. Our analysis also focuses on streams of system calls for a fast identification of anomalies while previous work mostly analyzes entire files in a batch-like manner.

1.2   Paper Outline

The remainder of this paper is structured as follows: First, we introduce a categorization of IDS to put the approaches of this paper into context. Then we present previous work for host-based anomaly detection. Following this, we discuss the available datasets and how they can be used to provide valid inputs for the algorithms. Afterwards we briefly introduce the considered algorithms and discuss how to determine a threshold for deciding whether an observation is normal or abnormal. We then describe the experimental setup, discuss the results of the experiments, and draw conclusions.

2   Host-Based Intrusion Detection

2.1   Categories of Intrusion Detection Systems

According to Milenkoski et al. [25] and Debar et al. [6] Intrusion Detection Systems can be categorized along the dimensions: the monitored platform, the method to detect attacks and the deployment architecture.

The Monitored Platform – If network data is evaluated, one speaks of network-based intrusion detection systems (NIDS). These systems analyse the incoming, outgoing and internal traffic of a network and can thus evaluate the externally "visible" behaviour of the systems within the monitored network. If, instead of network data, activities of the systems to be monitored are collected, this is referred to as host-based intrusion detection systems (HIDS). These systems have a vast amount of different data sources at their disposal to detect intrusions. Thus, characteristics such as CPU load, memory consumption or application logs can be examined. Another comprehensive and detailed source of the behavior are system calls executed on the host.

The Attack Detection Method – An intrusion detection system that checks monitored activity against a database of known attacks or predefined rules is called misuse- or signature-based. Such systems are not able to identify so-called zero-day attacks, i.e. attacks that were previously unknown. Unlike misuse-based systems, anomaly-based systems, also called behavior-based systems, detect deviations from a known normal behavior. They do not require attack signatures in advance allowing them to detect previously unknown attacks. The literature emphasizes that anomaly-based IDS often misinterprets normal behavior as anomalous, which is the greatest of their drawbacks [25].

The Deployment Architecture – Systems consisting of several subsystems that are used at different locations and communicate with each other to detect intrusions are called compound IDS. They can also detect coordinated attacks that have multiple targets. Otherwise they are called non-compound, i.e., IDS at a single location

Categories Considered in this Paper – In this paper, we focus on HIDS that can make use of rich information about the internal system behavior. We further focus on anomaly-based IDS as they can also detect previously unknown attacks. As mentioned before, they often have to contend with high error rates. Therefore we want to achieve low error rates and investigate whether this can be achieved by considering metadata such as the thread information of system calls as already suggested by Pendleton and Shouhuai in [29]. As a first step we want to investigate this for the simpler case of non-compound IDS and leave the more complex case of compound IDS for future work. Therefore we will deal with algorithms of non-compound anomaly-based host IDS.

2.2 Related Work

In 1996, an initial approach to intrusion detection called TIDE (time-delay embedding) was proposed based on a database of simple valid patterns (lookahead pairs) of system calls [9]. Using these patterns, the proportion of known patterns is determined to decide about whether a given trace is anomalous or not. STIDE (sequence time-delay embedding) expands this approach by considering contiguous sequences of system calls of fixed length instead of lookahead pairs [13]. Further work dealt with different evaluation possibilities of the underlying concept [11,33]. In 2001, Eskin proposed a method with dynamic window sizes using entropy modeling and context dependency to determine the optimal window size. [7] Another approach to eliminate the need of a fixed window size was introduced by Marceau using a finite state machine whose states represent predictive sequences of different lengths. [22] Jewell and Beaver investigated whether making the normal profile dependent on the user (uid) makes a difference [15]. They also considered dynamic sizes of system call sequences by dividing the input into sequences in which each system call occurs exactly once. In doing so, they defined the system calls for these types of sequences as (syscall, errno, args). [15] Since sequence-based approaches usually incur high computational and memory overheads, researchers also looked at the use of frequencies of individual system calls [1,16]. While these features are more lightweight in their computation, they are also less detailed so making it difficult to achieve similarly good detection and false alarm rates as sequential approaches. Other possibilities for feature extraction to improve anomaly detection include the use of parameter values of individual system calls. Kruegel et al. [19] created a separate model for each system call (e.g., write or open), which contains specific analyses for the parameters used. The model considers strings, characters, structure or tokens used. This approach was later extended with sequence analysis in 2006 and 2008 [21,28]. Many of the mentioned papers try to determine whether an attack occurs within a given trace which corresponds to a file of the used dataset. These papers determine their detection and false alarm rates accordingly at file level [7,9,11,13,16,19,28]. Some other works show that it can be done more detailed and determine the exact number of alarms and false alarms [1,15,21,22,33].

3 Datasets

Over the last two decades several datasets for evaluating HIDS using system calls have been published. The best known of these datasets include: The *KDD dataset*, to be more precise the BSM (Basic Security Module) of the DARPA Intrusion Detection Evaluation Data Set, from 1998 to 2000 [20], the Intrusion Detection Data Set from the University of New Mexico known as *UNM dataset* from 1999 [4,33], the data sets of the Australian Defence Force Academy, the *ADFA-LD* from 2013 [3,5] and the *NGIDS-DS* from 2017 [12].

All of the above mentioned datasets have critical drawbacks as discussed in [29] and [10]. The KDD and UNM datasets are outdated based on software older than 20 years that is hardly in use anymore. Furthermore, the hardware and the corresponding operating systems with their system calls have changed during this time. ADFA-LD is also several years old and lacks thread information. Since this paper deals with the question whether thread allocation of a system call can improve anomaly detection, this kind of information is needed in a suitable evaluation dataset. Only the NGIDS-DS and the newer LID-DS datasets [10,30] meet this requirement and are up to date. Therefore, these two datasets are considered further in this paper.

3.1 NGID-DS

The Next Generation Intrusion Detection System - Data Set (NGIDS-DS) consists of labeled network and host (system call) logs aiming to realistically reflect critical cyber infrastructures of enterprises in both normal and abnormal scenarios [12].

The Sequence Problem – In the host files of the NGIDS-DS each entry has a timestamp accurate to the second and an event id which indicates the order of the executed system call on the host system. Unfortunately we found that it is not possible to reliably determine a deterministic order of the system calls using this information. This is because there are in general several calls with the same timestamp and furthermore the order of event-ids sometimes contradicts the order of timestamps. We found that there are contracting entries in the files of NGIDS-DS, an example is shown in Table 1. Here the first entry has a smaller timestamp than the second one, while the event-ids are ordered the other way around. Therefore, unfortunately, it is not possible for us to reconstruct the correct sequence of system calls. Since all algorithms considered in this paper analyze the sequence of system calls, we cannot use the NGIDS-DS data.

Table 1. Extract from NGIDS-DS host file 1.csv with conflicting timestamp and event-id orders.

date	time	pid	process name	syscall	event id
11/03/2016	2:45:01	2114	/usr/bin/compiz	168	45357
11/03/2016	2:45:06	1804	/bin/dbus-daemon	256	45352

3.2 LID-DS

To address the observed shortcomings of the older datasets, Grimmer et al. created the LID-DS. It contains system calls, timestamps, thread ids, process names, arguments, return values and excerpts of data buffers from traces of normal and attack behaviour of several recent, multi-process, multi-threaded scenarios. Many of the included features are not available from previous datasets [10]. For this paper, the system calls, their unambiguous sequence and their thread assignment are of particular importance.

Structure of the LID-DS – The LID-DS consists of 10 different scenarios each representing a real vulnerability. They are named after the official Common Vulnerabilities and Exposures (CVE) [27] number, the corresponding Common Weakness Enumeration (CWE) number [26] or a specific name (e.g. ZipSlip). Each of these scenarios contains about 1137 files consisting of about 1021 normal and 116 attack sequences. The attack sequences consists of both normal behavior and attack behavior. What this means for the evaluation of the experiments will be explained in Sect. 6. The recordings are between 30 s and 60 s long (45 s on average). The first 200 normal sequences are used as *training data*, the next 50 are used as *validation data* and the remaining normal and attack sequences

Table 2. LID-DS scenarios, their abbreviation and their number of system calls.

scenario	abbr.	#syscalls	scenario	abbr.	#syscalls
Bruteforce-CWE-307	BF	5 696 050	CVE-2012-2122	2012	5 721 512
CVE-2014-0160	2014	4 009 668	CVE-2017-7529	2017	1 796 862
CVE-2018-3760	2018	19 160 009	CVE-2019-5418	2019	17 955 534
EPS-CWE-434	EPS	126 458 405	PHP-CWE-434	PHP	22 268 842
SQL-Injection-CWE-89	SQL	23 616 570	ZipSlip	ZIP	252 934 566

are used as *test data*. This leaves about 771 normal sequences $(771 \cdot 45\,\text{s})$ and about half the runtime of the attack sequences $(116/2 \cdot 45\,\text{s})$ that contain normal behavior. This corresponds to roughly $10\,\text{h}$ of runtime of normal behavior per scenario.

In the remainder of this paper, we abbreviate the individual scenarios of the LID-DS. The original names, our abbreviation and the number of system calls in the scenarios can be found in Table 2.

4 Feature Engineering

In the following, we present different concepts and preprocessing methods needed for the anomaly detection approaches.

n-gram – A n-gram is a contiguous sequence of n items, e.g., system calls, from a given input. If for example the sequence (a, b, c, d) is given, then following n-grams can be derived for $n = 2$: (a,b), (b,c) and (c,d).

n-grams using thread information – As mentioned before many IT systems nowadays are multi-threaded. As a result, multiple runs of the same software with identical input data can lead to different sequences of system calls across all threads due to the execution scheduling of the underlying operating system. Ignoring this fact as done in previous approaches can thus lead to incorrect results for anomaly detection. This is illustrated by the example in Table 3 where threads 1 and 1', 2 and 2', and 3 and 3', respectively each perform the same sequences of system calls. However, due to different scheduling, the resulting so-called *flat sequences* s and s' (the system call sequences without thread information) differ from each other.

Table 3. Two traces resulting from different runs of the same software and input in a multi-threaded environment.

thread t_1:		b		d		b		thread t_1':		b	d		b
thread t_2:			c		b			thread t_2':	c			b	
thread t_3:	a			a		c		thread t_3':	a		a		c
flat sequence s:	a	b	c	a	d	b	c	b	flat sequence s':	a	c	b	a	d	b	c	b

Ignoring this information can lead to learning incorrect data. As shown in Table 4 the resulting n-grams (here with $n = 2$) differ depending on the source sequence. The left side shows the n-gram frequencies for the flat sequence s, the middle shows the n-gram frequencies for flat sequence s' and the right side shows the frequencies in case they were determined from the underlying threads t_1, t_2 and t_3 (which is the same for t'_1, t'_2 and t'_3). For example, n-gram or subsequence (b c) occurs twice in flat sequence s but only once in s' and never in the thread-specific sequences.

Table 4. Frequencies of n-grams (n=2) from sequences s, s' and t_1, t_2, t_3.

	from s				from s'				from t_1, t_2, t_3			
	a	b	c	d	a	b	c	d	a	b	c	d
a	0	1	0	1	0	0	1	1	1	0	1	0
b	0	0	2	0	1	0	1	0	0	0	0	1
c	1	1	0	0	0	2	0	0	0	1	0	0
d	0	1	0	0	0	1	0	0	0	1	0	0

One Hot Encoding of Categorical Data – Machine learning (ML) algorithms usually require numerical (quantitative) inputs. However, system calls and n-grams of system calls are nominal qualitative (categorical) data but not quantitative information. One way to represent this type of data for an ML algorithm is one hot encoding (OHE). To represent a system call c_i from the set of m possible system calls $C = \{c_1, c_2, ..., c_m\}$, a one-hot vector v_i of length m is used. For system call c_i such a vector v_i is a bit vector with value 1 at position i and value 0 in all other positions. n-grams of system calls can be encoded by concatenating the one hot encoded system calls.

System Call Embeddings – The use of long OHE representations can lead to a large number of weights to be trained in neural networks. Therefore it is advisable to use shorter vectors. In the field of natural language processing, so called word embeddings have proven their value, e.g., based on the Word2Vec method proposed by Mikolov et al. [24]. Word2vec uses a neural network to learn word associations from a large corpus of text. A word is thereby mapped to a vector of a certain length, the word embedding. The cosine similarity between two such vectors indicates the degree of semantic similarity between the associated words. We have applied this principle to system calls. For each scenario of the LID-DS, we generated a system call corpus of the training data. We then used this to compute the corresponding word embeddings using the original implementation of Mikolov et al. [23]. We have calculated two variants of word embeddings. The first, "thread unaware" variant uses the system calls as they occur in the training data one after the other. The second, "thread aware" variant considers the system calls of the training data per thread, so that the system calls of different threads do not mix. With the system call embeddings computed in this way, the composite n-grams can be generated by simple concatenation, as before. We later call this embedding W x, where x corresponds to the length of the vector.

Duplicates in the Training Data – In this work, we decided to use the training data not as presented, but duplicate free. For all algorithms we discuss in Sect. 5, except SCG (since it should explicitly learn the distribution of node transitions) the training data is modified in a way, such that duplicate entries of the same n-grams are removed from the input to the training algorithm. This is done to reduce the size of the training matrices (and their used memory) and to speed up training time. By removing duplicates in the training data, the algorithms are trained in such a way that frequent and rare "patterns" in the training data are learned "equally" well.

5 Algorithms

In this paper we consider only algorithms or variants of algorithms that can process streams of system calls to enable a fast identification of anomalies at runtime. Hence we do not investigate a more batch-like retrospective analysis of entire collections of system calls. To process a stream of system calls, each algorithm always receives exactly one system call after another as input. It then builds n-grams as described above within a given **streaming window** of a predefined length. It then calculates a so-called **anomaly score** indicating how abnormal the determined n-gram is in relation to previously seen system call n-grams.

Each of the algorithms presented here basically consists of two phases: the training phase and the detection phase. In the following descriptions, we will discuss these two phases separately. In addition, for each of the algorithms, we specify how the final anomaly value is calculated for a streaming window.

The Bag of System Calls (**BOSC**) algorithm was introduced in [16] and later applied in [1]. It does not consider the order of system calls in a n-gram but only the frequency of occurrence.

Training: N-grams of the training data are built. Then the occurrences of every system call within each n-gram is counted. A bag of system calls in this sense is the assignment from all system calls to their frequency within a given n-gram. All these bags are then saved in a database for later use as normal bags.

Detection: In detection mode every n-gram is converted to a bag as described. Then for each bag it is checked if it is included in the normal database from the training phase. If the bag is included, we call it a match otherwise a mismatch.

Anomaly: An anomaly is detected if the anomaly score (ratio of mismatches to number of n-grams in the streaming-window) is greater than a predefined threshold.

In 1998 Hofmeyer et al. designed the Sequence Time-Delay Embedding (**STIDE**) [13] algorithm.

Training: The STIDE algorithm is similar to the BOSC algorithm, but rather looking only at the frequencies and ignoring the sequence of system calls the actual n-grams are stored and used as the normal database.

Detection: In the detection phase the STIDE algorithm checks whether the current n-gram is included in the normal database. Similar to the BOSC algorithm if the n-gram is included, we call it a match otherwise a mismatch.

Anomaly: As before an anomaly is detected if the anomaly score (ratio of mismatches to the number of n-grams in the streaming-window) is greater than a predefined threshold.

The method of System Call Graphs (**SCG**) is also called n-gram probability graph [11]. Here system calls are placed in a directed weighted graph, where the nodes describe n-grams of system calls and the edges represent the probabilities of transitions from one n-gram to another.

Training: In the training phase the n-gram probability graph is built as described above.

Detection: In the detection phase the transition probability from one n-gram to its successor n-gram is determined using the n-gram probability graph. If this transition is not present in the graph its probability is set to 0.

Anomaly: The resulting anomaly score is then given by the mean of all transition probabilities within the streaming window. If this anomaly score is greater than a predefined threshold an anomaly is detected.

The One Class Support Vector Machine (**SVM**), introduced in [31] and later applied in [34] is a variant of the Support Vector Machine. Simply put it tries to learn a function which classifies if a sample could have been drawn from the input distribution.

Training: The One Class SVM is trained for all n-grams from the training data.

Detection: The One Class SVM algorithm decides whether a given n-gram is part of the normal class (match) or not (mismatch).

Anomaly: As before an anomaly is detected if the anomaly score (ratio of mismatches to the number of n-grams in the streaming-window) is greater than a predefined threshold.

Different kinds of artificial neural networks are used to predict the next element of a given sequence. This for example was done in [35] on sequences of numbers and in [17] on sentences. We want to transfer the principle applied there to our application. Here it is used to predict the probability of each possible next system call after a given n-gram of system calls. We utilize two variants of artificial neural networks: The Multi Layer Perceptron (**MLP**) and Convolutional Neural Networks (**CNN**) which are known for their ability to identify patterns in data. As the two approaches just differ in the neural network architecture they are jointly summarized in the following.

Training: N-grams of system calls are being used as the input of the MLP/CNN. The expected output is the successor system call. The actual successor system call can be used for supervised learning.

Detection: With the given n-gram, the probability of every possible system call appearing in the next time step is predicted.

Anomaly: The anomaly score (one minus the mean probabilities of all n-grams in the streaming window) is then again compared to a predefined threshold. If it is greater than this threshold we count it as anomaly.

Autoencoders (**AE**) can learn to compress data through finding correlated features in the data. [18] With these features they are capable of reconstructing the compressed data with less noise. If the underlying features which it learned are less represented in the test data the reconstruction loss is greater. So with reconstructing an anomaly the loss is expected to be higher than with data from the training data.

Training: The Autoencoder tries to learn the features of all n-grams of the training data. By reconstructing this data through the Autoencoder, a loss can be determined which should be minimized.

Detection: The mentioned reconstruction loss between input and output of the Autoencoder is then used as the anomaly score of the specific n-gram.

Anomaly: If the average anomaly score of all n-grams in a streaming window is higher than a predefined threshold, an anomaly is detected.

6   Evaluation Approach

Before we come to the results of our investigation in the next section, we want to first outline how we determine the sucess of anomaly detection with streams of system calls and how we set the anomaly thresholds.

Anomaly Evaluation – As described before each algorithm produces an anomaly score for every new system call in a stream. How we interpret this score depends on the threshold value as well as the attack start time. The threshold value is used to distinguish between normal classifications (the anomaly score is less or equal the threshold) and abnormal classifications (the anomaly score is greater than the threshold) as described before. The expected attack start time t_{attack} is recorded in the LID-DS for each file containing an attack. Unfortunately t_{attack} is somewhat imprecise so that we soften this value a bit and use $t'_{attack} = t_{attack} - 2\,\text{s}$ instead. As visualised in Fig. 1, using the anomaly threshold and attack start time we obtain four areas (quadrants) that can be used for evaluation anomaly detection. In particular, one can classify a given anomaly score as a false alarm, FA (or FP, false positive), i.e., incorrectly classified as attack, if the score is in quadrant 2. An anomaly or false alarm may span more than one system call or n-gram. Therefore, an alarm should not be triggered for every single abnormal system call or every single abnormal n-gram. In reality, this would result in a too large number of alarms that have to be manually reviewed. Instead, alarms that directly follow each other should only counted as a single alarm. A score in quadrant 3 counts as normal behavior (TN, true negative). Unfortunately, its hard to make such statements for values with a timestamp greater then t'_{attack} since we don't know whether the attack has already started, it is already over and if in this case normal behavior has appeared again already. The only thing we know for this case is that after t'_{attack} an attack is expected. Therefore, to correctly classify an attack (TP, true positive) at least one anomaly score in quadrant 1 is needed for an attack file. Due to the given expected start times of all attacks in the LID-DS, we can determine false alarms in the files containing attacks up to t'_{attack}. This allows much more accurate statements than simply classifying an entire file as benign or malicious, as done for other datasets before. Additionally we calculate the detection rate $DR = TP/A$ with A, the number of attacks in the test data of a scenario, to improve the comparability of the individual scenarios, since they do not all contain the same number of attack files. To compare the results in this work we use DR and FA.

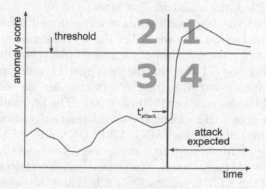

Fig. 1. Exemplary plot of anomaly scores (y axis) against time (x axis). It shows the threshold (horizontal blue line), attack start time (vertical red line) and the resulting four quadrants 1–4. (Color figure online)

Determining the Threshold Value – The choice of the anomaly threshold obviously is a critical parameter that impacts the overall quality of anomaly detection. We aimed at automatically finding suitable values. Given that anomalies are unknown beforehand we only use the data about normal behavior for this purpose. In particular, we use the maximum anomaly score from the corresponding validation part of the normal behavior as the threshold for the normal class. By using the validation data, we prevent overfitting compared to using the actual training data to determine the threshold.

Experiments – To investigate how the described thread information affects the different algorithms presented, we ran a grid search over a large set of possible configurations and all scenarios of the LID-DS. In total, we have trained and evaluated more than 30,000 different configurations of the presented algorithms.

7 Findings

In this section, we analyze how well the presented algorithms perform on the LID-DS without and with using thread information. We also analyse the impact for different scenarios.

7.1 Results per Algorithm over All Scenarios

We first evaluate the impact of using thread information (TI) on the average performance of the individual algorithms over all scenarios. For this purpose, we report for every algorithm results for three configurations, (1) the configuration achieving the best detection rate (DR) without thread information, (2) the results for the same configuration of (1) but with the use of thread information (i.e., after switching the "thread information flag"), and (3) the best configurations with thread information. The obtained results over all scenarios are summarized in Table 5 together with the used encodings for n-grams and the considered n-gram lengths n and window sizes l.

We observe that the best configuration using thread information (conf. 3) achieves a better detection rate for six of the seven algorithms and about the same detection rate for the autoencoder approach (AE). For BOSC and STIDE, even just switching the TI flag for the best non-TI configuration achieves a noticeable DR improvement despite the fact that for the use of threads the window size should be far smaller (1000 vs. 10000). The FA results for the number of false alarms are mixed. Here using thread information results in improvements for four of the seven algorithms (SCG, MLP, CNN and AE). Hence for these algorithms the use of thread information improves (or maintains) both detection rate and the number of false alarms. The overall best detection rates are achieved for the BOSC and the STIDE approaches (98,6%) and the lowest number of false alarms for AE and MLP.

We now want to illustrate the relative performance of the best algorithms for the different scenarios in more detail. Since it is difficult to rank configurations for multiple target criteria (DR, FA) one can use the concept of Pareto optimality, a condition in which no criterion can get better without making at least one other criterion worse. According to this concept, the configurations BOSC 1, STIDE 3, SCG 3, MLP 3 and AE 3 from Table 5 are Pareto optimal. Therefore in Tables 6 and 7 we show the results of these configurations and their corresponding configuration with altered TI flag for each scenario.

We observe that the different algorithms behave quite differently for the various scenarios. The STIDE approach excels in achieving high detection rates for all scenarios with use of TI. In contrast to the other algorithms and with the use of TI, STIDE and SCG are especially able to solve scenario 2014 with some and ZIP with only one respectively zero FA. On the downside, for STIDE and in particular BOSC using TI leads to relatively high FA values. From one scenario solved to nine, with almost no change in FA, the SCG algorithm also benefits greatly from *TI*. The two other algorithms achieve high detection rates only for six to eight of the ten scenarios. The MLP algorithm benefits strongly from using *TI*, now able to solve eight instead of four scenarios and fewer false alarms compared to not using thread information. Perfect results (DR 1, FA 0) are achieved for the 2019 and EPS scenarios. Finally, the AE approach achieves perfect detection rates in three scenarios. The use of *TI* does not affect DR, but it does reduce the number of false alarms, especially in the PHP, 2018 and SQL scenarios.

Table 5. Algorithm wise best average configuration over all scenarios. The columns are: algorithm, configuration, encoding, thread information, n-gram length, streaming window length, mean DR and mean FA.

alg.	con.	enc.	*TI*	n	l	$\overline{DR}$	$\overline{FA}$
BOSC	1	-	-	11	10000	0.885	17.4
BOSC	2	-	+	11	10000	0.949	519.5
BOSC	3	-	+	7	1000	0.986	110.4
STIDE	1	-	-	3	10000	0.879	12.5
STIDE	2	-	+	3	10000	0.981	118.6
STIDE	3	-	+	5	1000	0.986	61.5
SCG	1	-	-	9	10000	0.711	43.9
SCG	2	-	+	9	10000	0.686	166.4
SCG	3	-	+	5	10	0.895	29.1
SVM	1	OHE	-	5	100	0.562	13.3
SVM	2	OHE	+	5	100	0.292	13.3
SVM	3	OHE	+	9	100	0.595	42.7
MLP	1	OHE	-	11	100	0.614	18.1
MLP	2	OHE	+	11	100	0.605	34.7
MLP	3	OHE	+	7	1	0.789	4.2
CNN	1	OHE	-	7	100	0.686	35.4
CNN	2	OHE	+	7	100	0.694	28.2
CNN	3	OHE	+	22	10	0.702	20.0
AE	1	W 5	-	5	1	0.629	16.4
AE	2	W 5	+	5	1	0.622	2.3
AE	3	W 5	+	7	1	0.622	2.2

Table 6. Results for configuration 1 (without TI) and 2 (with TI) of BOSC and configuration 3 (with TI) and its variant without TI of STIDE.

| | BOSC | | | | STIDE | | | |
| | no TI (1) | | with TI (2) | | no TI | | with TI (3) | |
scenario	DR	FA	DR	FA	DR	FA	DR	FA
BF	0.94	32	0.94	29	0.94	66	0.94	24
2012	0.95	11	0.99	201	0.03	4	0.99	26
2014	0.00	1	0.59	210	0.00	3	0.95	44
2017	0.97	9	0.99	5	0.97	9	0.99	5
2018	0.99	19	0.99	5	0.99	25	0.99	12
2019	1.00	4	0.99	22	1.00	8	1.00	18
EPS	1.00	20	1.00	604	1.00	4	1.00	12
PHP	1.00	2	1.00	119	0.95	1	1.00	93
SQL	1.00	40	1.00	3183	0.15	18	1.00	380
ZIP	1.00	36	1.00	817	0.34	1	1.00	1
mean	0.89	17.4	0.95	519.5	0.64	13.9	0.99	61.5

Table 7. Results for configuration 3 (with TI) and its variant without TI of SCG, MLP and AE.

| | SCG | | | | MLP | | | | AE | | | |
| | no TI | | with TI (3) | | no TI | | with TI (3) | | no TI | | with TI (3) | |
scenario	DR	FA	DR	FA	DR	FA	DR	FA	DR	FA	DR	FA
BF	0.04	2	0.94	1	0.00	0	0.94	1	0.00	1	0.00	0
2012	0.01	25	0.10	67	0.01	16	0.98	10	0.03	19	0.00	0
2014	0.01	33	0.95	25	0.00	0	0.01	7	0.00	0	0.00	0
2017	0.97	17	0.97	9	0.97	11	0.97	14	0.97	8	0.97	8
2018	0.00	4	0.99	35	0.00	0	0.99	2	0.99	79	0.99	11
2019	0.00	9	1.00	11	1.00	36	1.00	0	1.00	0	1.00	3
EPS	0.27	5	1.00	40	0.00	0	1.00	0	1.00	0	1.00	0
PHP	0.02	0	1.00	19	1.00	31	1.00	6	1.00	169	1.00	0
SQL	0.09	113	1.00	84	1.00	31	1.00	2	1.00	25	1.00	0
ZIP	0.03	12	1.00	0	0.00	0	0.00	0	0.27	0	0.27	0
mean	0.14	22.0	0.90	29.1	0.40	12.5	0.79	4.2	0.63	30.1	0.62	2.2

7.2   Scenario Wise Best Results

We now analyze the influence of using thread information for each of the ten scenarios separately. Table 8 shows the best result regarding DR per scenario without and with the use of *TI* together with the applied configuration. For cases of several configurations with the same "best" result for a scenario, only one is shown. The table shows that in nine of the ten scenarios the use of *TI* results in a better or about equally good DR and FA values (only for scenario "2018" the FA value is increased). In general, the use of thread information enables very good solutions for all scenarios with perfect or almost perfect detection rates (0.94 to 1.0) and 0 false alarms for 6 of the ten scenarios. Compared to the configurations not using thread information, DR is especially increased for scenario 2014 (from 0.06 to 0.95) and the FA value is improved or kept at 0 for nine scenarios. Table 8 also reveals that the AE algorithm is able to provide a perfect result with 100% DR and no FA for 4 scenarios, for both without and with using TI. For using *TI*, the ZipSlip scenario can also be perfectly solved by the BOSC algorithm (as well as SCG, not shown in the table). Overall the best results are mostly achieved by the AE, CNN, MLP and STIDE algorithms while the SVM approach is not among the top-performing approaches.

7.3 Overall Best Practical Configurations

The presented results show that in many cases it is not possible to achieve both very high detection rates and a very low number of false alarms with the same configuration over all scenarios. However configurations optimizing only one of the two goals are not sufficient and can be ineffective in practice. This

Table 8. Scenario-wise best configurations over all algorithms without and with *TI*. The columns are: scenario, algorithm, encoding, thread information, n-gram length, streaming window length, DR and FA.

scenario	alg.	enc.	*TI*	n	l	DR	FA
BF	CNN	OHE	-	9	100	0.95	97
BF	MLP	OHE	+	5	1	0.94	0
2012	AE	OHE	-	5	100	0.97	33
2012	STIDE	-	+	5	1000	0.99	26
2014	MLP	OHE	-	22	10000	0.06	22
2014	STIDE	-	+	9	10	0.95	18
2017	CNN	OHE	-	5	100	0.99	13
2017	CNN	OHE	+	9	100	0.99	4
2018	CNN	OHE	-	7	100	1.00	5
2018	MLP	OHE	+	7	100	1.00	28
2019	AE	W 2	-	3	1	1.00	0
2019	AE	W 2	+	3	1	1.00	0
EPS	AE	W 2	-	3	1	1.00	0
EPS	AE	W 2	+	7	1	1.00	0
PHP	AE	W 2	-	3	1	1.00	0
PHP	AE	W 2	+	3	1	1.00	0
SQL	AE	W 2	-	3	1	1.00	0
SQL	AE	W 2	+	3	1	1.00	0
ZIP	STIDE	-	-	5	10000	1.00	4
ZIP	BOSC	-	+	3	10	1.00	0

is especially the case when IDS alarms need to be handled by a security expert to prevent possible damage to the monitored system. This asks for reducing the number of false alarms as much as possible while aiming for a detection rate as high as possible. For example a configuration with $DR = 0.80$ and $FA = 10$ might be more effective than one with $DR = 0.90$ and $FA = 100$ or even $DR = 0.99$ and $FA = 1000$ since manually dealing with 100 or even 1000 false alarms can make the system impractical to use.

At this point the concept of Pareto optimality shall be applied again. One possible approach to limit the number of possible Pareto-optimal results is to define certain levels of the accepted number of false alarms and ranking the configurations according to their DR results within each level. For example, we might be interested in the following five FA levels: Level 1: $\overline{FA} < 40$, level 2: $\overline{FA} < 20$, level 3: $\overline{FA} < 10$, 4: $\overline{FA} < 5$ and 5: $\overline{FA} < 2.5$.

For each of these levels, Table 9 shows the configuration with the best DR result (average over all scenarios) with their FA average for the case with TI and without TI, respectively. We observe again that the TI configurations achieve better DR values for all five levels. As observed before, algorithm AE supports the lowest FA values for using thread information followed by MLP while the STIDE and BOSC algorithms achieve better DR values when FA levels 1 and 2 are still manageable.

Table 9. Top configurations for level 1 to 5 with and without TI.

| | | | with TI | | | | | | | without TI | | | | |
	alg.	enc.	TI	n	l	$\overline{DR}$	$\overline{FA}$	alg.	enc.	TI	n	l	$\overline{DR}$	$\overline{FA}$
1	STIDE	-	+	5	100	0.983	23.7	BOSC	-	-	7	100	0.710	14.9
2	BOSC	-	+	3	10	0.982	18.9	BOSC	-	-	7	100	0.710	14.9
3	MLP	OHE	+	7	1	0.788	4.2	AE	W 2	-	3	1	0.624	8.2
4	MLP	OHE	+	7	1	0.788	4.2	MLP	W 5	-	3	1	0.528	3.1
5	AE	W 5	+	7	1	0.622	2.2	MLP	W 2	-	3	1	0.526	2.3

8   Conclusion

Summary – We made it our task to check whether thread information is helpful to improve anomaly-based HIDS. In the search for a suitable data set, we ended up with the LID-DS. We then evaluated 7 algorithms on the LID-DS. For each of these algorithms, many different configurations (n-gram length, streaming window length, encoding of the input data, and thread information) were experimentally tested. Particular emphasis has been placed on the difference between the variants with and without thread information. As a result, it can be said that for most cases the use of thread information increases the detection rate and reduces the number of false alarms. In addition, we performed a thought experiment in which different levels of error rates were defined as acceptable. For each of these levels, the best solution was an algorithm that uses thread information. For comparison, we additionally searched for the best matching algorithm without thread information for each of these levels. The results were worse in almost every respect.

Outlook and Open Questions – In future work, we plan to investigate additional algorithms and how they can make use of thread information, in particular based on self organizing maps (SOMs), long short-term memory networks (LSTMs) and the Transformer [32] architecture.

Given that several algorithms have complementary strengths and limitations regarding different scenarios and regarding DR and FA results we also want to investigate whether combined approaches can perform better than single algorithms.

Acknowledgment. This work was supported by the German Federal Ministry of Education and Research within the project Competence Center for Scalable Data Services and Solutions (ScaDS) Dresden/Leipzig (BMBF 01IS18026B) and by the German Federal Ministry for Economic Affairs and Energy (BMWi - ZIM, 16KN061130) based on a resolution of the German Parliament within the project "Anomaly-based attack detection on data- and control flow-based sensors". Computations for this work were done with resources of Leipzig University Computing Centre.

References

1. Abed, A.S., Clancy, C., Levy, D.S.: Intrusion detection system for applications using Linux containers. In: Foresti, S. (ed.) STM 2015. LNCS, vol. 9331, pp. 123–135. Springer, Cham (2015). https://doi.org/10.1007/978-3-319-24858-5_8
2. Accenture: Securing the digital economy (2019). https://www.accenture.com/gb-en/insights/cybersecurity/_acnmedia/Thought-Leadership-Assets/PDF/Accenture-Securing-the-Digital-Economy-Reinventing-the-Internet-for-Trust.pdf
3. Australian Center for Cyber Security (ACCS): The ADFA intrusion detection datasets (2013). https://www.unsw.adfa.edu.au/australian-centre-for-cyber-security/cybersecurity/ADFA-IDS-Datasets/
4. Computer Science Department Farris Engineering Center; University of New Mexico: Computer immune systems - data sets and software (1999). https://www.cs.unm.edu/~immsec/systemcalls.htm
5. Creech, G., Hu, J.: Generation of a new ids test dataset: time to retire the KDD collection. In: 2013 IEEE Wireless Communications and Networking Conference (WCNC), pp. 4487–4492. IEEE (2013)
6. Debar, H., Dacier, M., Wespi, A.: Towards a taxonomy of intrusion-detection systems. Comput. Netw. **31**(8), 805–822 (1999)
7. Eskin, E., Lee, W., Stolfo, S.J.: Modeling system calls for intrusion detection with dynamic window sizes. In: Proceedings DARPA Information Survivability Conference and Exposition II, DISCEX 2001, vol. 1, pp. 165–175. IEEE (2001)
8. European Union: Regulation (eu) 2016/679 of the european parliament and of the council of 27 April 2016 on the protection of natural persons with regard to the processing of personal data and on the free movement of such data, and repealing directive 95/46/ec (general data protection regulation) (2016). https://eur-lex.europa.eu/legal-content/EN/TXT/?uri=CELEX:02016R0679-20160504
9. Forrest, S., Hofmeyr, S.A., Somayaji, A., Longstaff, T.A.: A sense of self for unix processes. In: Proceedings 1996 IEEE Symposium on Security and Privacy, pp. 120–128. IEEE (1996)

10. Grimmer, M., Röhling, M.M., Kreusel, D., Ganz, S.: A modern and sophisticated host based intrusion detection data set. IT-Sicherheit als Voraussetzung für eine erfolgreiche Digitalisierung, pp. 135–145 (2019)
11. Grimmer, M., Röhling, M.M., Kricke, M., Franczyk, B., Rahm, E.: Intrusion detection on system call graphs. Sicherheit in vernetzten Systemen, pp. G1–G18 (2018)
12. Haider, W., Hu, J., Slay, J., Turnbull, B.P., Xie, Y.: Generating realistic intrusion detection system dataset based on fuzzy qualitative modeling. J. Netw. Comput. Appl. **87**, 185–192 (2017)
13. Hofmeyr, S.A., Forrest, S., Somayaji, A.: Intrusion detection using sequences of system calls. J. Comput. Secur. **6**(3), 151–180 (1998)
14. International Data Group: CSO: 2018 u.s. state of cybercrime (2018). https://www.idg.com/tools-for-marketers/2018-u-s-state-of-cybercrime/
15. Jewell, B., Beaver, J.: Host-based data exfiltration detection via system call sequences. In: ICIW2011-Proceedings of the 6th International Conference on Information Warfare and Secuirty: ICIW, p. 134. Academic Conferences Limited (2011)
16. Kang, D.K., Fuller, D., Honavar, V.: Learning classifiers for misuse and anomaly detection using a bag of system calls representation. In: Proceedings from the Sixth Annual IEEE SMC Information Assurance Workshop, pp. 118–125. IEEE (2005)
17. Kim, Y.: Convolutional neural networks for sentence classification. arXiv preprint arXiv:1408.5882 (2014)
18. Kramer, M.A.: Nonlinear principal component analysis using autoassociative neural networks. AIChE J. **37**(2), 233–243 (1991)
19. Kruegel, C., Mutz, D., Valeur, F., Vigna, G.: On the detection of anomalous system call arguments. In: Snekkenes, E., Gollmann, D. (eds.) ESORICS 2003. LNCS, vol. 2808, pp. 326–343. Springer, Heidelberg (2003). https://doi.org/10.1007/978-3-540-39650-5_19
20. Lincoln Laboratory MIT: Darpa intrusion detection evaluation data set (1998–2000). https://www.ll.mit.edu/r-d/datasets
21. Maggi, F., Matteucci, M., Zanero, S.: Detecting intrusions through system call sequence and argument analysis. IEEE Trans. Dependable Secur. Comput. **7**(4), 381–395 (2008)
22. Marceau, C.: Characterizing the behavior of a program using multiple-length n-grams. In: Proceedings of the 2000 Workshop on New Security Paradigms, pp. 101–110 (2001)
23. Mikolov, T., Chen, K., Corrado, G., Dean, J.: Word2vec - tools for computing distributed representation of words, https://github.com/tmikolov/word2vec
24. Mikolov, T., Chen, K., Corrado, G., Dean, J.: Efficient estimation of word representations in vector space. arXiv preprint arXiv:1301.3781 (2013)
25. Milenkoski, A., Vieira, M., Kounev, S., Avritzer, A., Payne, B.: Evaluating computer intrusion detection systems: a survey of common practices. ACM Comput. Surv. **48**(1), 1–49 (2015). https://doi.org/10.1145/2808691
26. MITRE: Common weakness enumeration - a community-developed list of software and hardware weakness types. https://cwe.mitre.org/
27. MITRE: Cve - common vulnerabilities and exposures. https://cve.mitre.org/
28. Mutz, D., Valeur, F., Vigna, G., Kruegel, C.: Anomalous system call detection. ACM Trans. Inf. Syst. Secur. (TISSEC) **9**(1), 61–93 (2006)
29. Pendleton, M., Xu, S.: A dataset generator for next generation system call host intrusion detection systems. In: MILCOM 2017-2017 IEEE Military Communications Conference (MILCOM), pp. 231–236. IEEE (2017)

30. Röhling, M.M., Grimmer, M., Kreubel, D., Hoffmann, J., Franczyk, B.: Standardized container virtualization approach for collecting host intrusion detection data. In: 2019 Federated Conference on Computer Science and Information Systems (FedCSIS). pp. 459–463. IEEE (2019)

31. Schölkopf, B., Williamson, R.C., Smola, A., Shawe-Taylor, J., Platt, J.: Support vector method for novelty detection. Adv. Neural Inf. Process. Syst. **12**, 582–588 (1999)

32. Vaswani, A., et al.: Attention is all you need. In: Advances in Neural Information Processing Systems, pp. 5998–6008 (2017)

33. Warrender, C., Forrest, S., Pearlmutter, B.: Detecting intrusions using system calls: Alternative data models. In: Proceedings of the 1999 IEEE Symposium on Security and Privacy (Cat. No. 99CB36344), pp. 133–145. IEEE (1999)

34. Xie, M., Hu, J., Yu, X., Chang, E.: Evaluating host-based anomaly detection systems: application of the frequency-based algorithms to ADFA-LD. In: Au, M.H., Carminati, B., Kuo, C.-C.J. (eds.) NSS 2014. LNCS, vol. 8792, pp. 542–549. Springer, Cham (2014). https://doi.org/10.1007/978-3-319-11698-3_44

35. Zhao, Y., Chu, S., Zhou, Y., Tu, K.: Sequence prediction using neural network classiers. In: International Conference on Grammatical Inference, pp. 164–169 (2017)

Database Intrusion Detection Systems (DIDs): Insider Threat Detection via Behaviour-Based Anomaly Detection Systems - A Brief Survey of Concepts and Approaches

Muhammad Imran Khan[1(✉)], Simon N. Foley[2], and Barry O'Sullivan[1]

[1] Insight Centre for Data Analytics, School of Computer Science and Information Technology, University College Cork, Cork, Ireland
imran.khan@insight-centre.org
[2] Department of Information Security and Communication Technology, Norwegian University of Science and Technology, Gjøvik, Norway

Abstract. One of the data security and privacy concerns is of insider threats, where legitimate users of the system abuse the access privileges they hold. The insider threat to data security means that an insider steals or leaks sensitive personal information. Database Intrusion detection systems, specifically behaviour-based database intrusion detection systems, have been shown effective in detecting insider attacks. This paper presents background concepts on database intrusion detection systems in the context of detecting insider threats and examines existing approaches in the literature on detecting malicious accesses by an insider to Database Management Systems (DBMS).

Keywords: Relational Database Management Systems · Insider threat · Intrusion Detection Systems · Anomaly detection systems · Behaviour-based anomaly detection systems

1 Introduction

The recent past has witnessed an exponential increase in the volume of data being stored and accessed through Database Management Systems (DBMS) and this comes along security and privacy concerns. Organizations need to take extra care in the management and storage of sensitive application data. Misuse or leakage of such data can lead to an organization suffering from damages in terms of reputation and financial loss. The harm caused by data breaches has routinely been reported in the popular press.

Threats to an organization's data come from external attackers - *outsider attacks* or internal attackers - *insider attacks*. Traditional security controls such as authentication, role-based access control, data encryption and physical-security can help to control access to this data. However, there is a persistent

© Springer Nature Switzerland AG 2022
W. Meng and S. K. Katsikas (Eds.): EISA 2021, CCIS 1403, pp. 178–197, 2022.
https://doi.org/10.1007/978-3-030-93956-4_11

concern of insider attacks whereby legitimate users of the system abuse the access privileges they hold. Therefore, effective security controls to mitigate insider attacks are desirable.

An Intrusion Detection Systems (IDS), in particular, behaviour-based intrusion detection systems (also referred to as behaviour-based anomaly detection systems) [38,43,48], can play a role in detecting insider attacks. Behaviour-based anomaly detection systems model normative behaviour of the system user and look for deviations in the run-time behaviour of the users.

This paper examines existing literature on detecting malicious accesses by an insider as anomalies, we refer to these anomalies as security-anomalies. Section 2 considers the threats to contemporary organizations, while Sect. 2.1 and 2.2 defines and discusses the impact of an *insider threat*. Section 3 explores the detection methods for insider attacks. Section 4 presents a taxonomy of anomaly-based detection methods and reviews the well-known techniques reported in the literature.

2   Threats to Contemporary Organizations

Threats to an organization can be classified as external (outsider attack) or internal (insider attack). External threats come from attackers outside of the organization who discover network and/or system vulnerabilities and use this information to penetrate the organization. Outside attackers may, for example, utilize social engineering techniques to accomplish a malicious goal, such as stealing confidential information or making some resources unavailable using a Denial-of-Service attack. Much research exists on dealing with external threats, and many security defences have been proposed, including host-based access controls, Intrusion Detection Systems (IDSs), and access control mechanisms [24]. On the other hand, an insider is a person who belongs to an organization and is authorized to access a range of its data and services. We are particularly interested in insider attacks as the nature of these attacks make them challenging to detect. The next section reviews how the understanding and definition of insider has evolved in the literature and provides the definition used in this work.

2.1   Defining Insiders

Several definitions can be found in the literature for an insider [16,17,58]; however, there is no consensus for a single definition [37]. In the 2008 paper, "Defining the Insider Threat", Bishop and Gates considered three definitions of insiders [16]. The first definition was from a RAND report [19] that defines an insider to be *"an already trusted person with access to sensitive information and information systems"*. The second definition was also from the same RAND report, which defines an insider to be *"someone with access, privilege, or knowledge of information systems and services"*. The third definition, originating from [60], defines an insider to be *"anyone operating inside the security perimeter"*. In the first definition, a person needs to be trusted in order to be called an insider, however, in the second definition, a person having knowledge of the system and services is also considered as an insider while the third definition considers everyone within the security perimeter to be an insider.

The first three definitions are regarded as binary definitions because if the person satisfies one of these definitions, then that person is called an insider, otherwise, the person is not an insider. Bishop and Gates [16] also provided a fourth, non-binary, definition for an insider. The non-binary notion of an insider is based upon a measure of the damage that an organization would suffer if entities such as resources, important documents, e-mails, source code, etc. are compromised or leaked. Each entity is assigned an impact value that specifies this measure of damage. Entities with the same impact value are grouped in protection domain groups. These protection domain groups are then paired with groups of users having access to entities in protection domain groups. Users having access to protection domain groups with the highest impact-value pose the highest risk of insider threat. This model provides a spectrum on which the degree to which an insider poses a threat can be identified. We believe that such a model is useful in developing more fine-grained security mechanisms by taking into account the threat-level that an insider poses. This proposed model for insider threat that Bishop and Gates presented is useful in understanding how threats may be traced and aggregated through a system. However, the model does not define what is meant by an insider.

In a 2008 cross-disciplinary workshop on *"Countering Insider Threats"* [17], a more specific definition was proposed. In this workshop, the insider was defined as *"a person that has been legitimately empowered with the right to access, represent, or decide about one or more assets of the organization's structure"*. There is a growing consensus over the definition put forwards in a 2008 cross-disciplinary workshop on *"Countering Insider Threats"* [17] and therefore we consider this definition for this paper.

A famously reported case of an insider attack was of an employee at an office that issues driving licences. The employee exploited access privileges to issue fraudulent licenses [58]. It has been reported that insider attacks can be unintentional as well. For instance, the breach resulted from the carelessness of an employee [8].

Once we've defined who an insider, we look at the definition of an insider threat is defined. The definition for insider threat that has consensus on it is put forward by Predd et al. in [61] that defines insider threat as *"[...] an insider's action that puts an organization or its resources at risk"* [61].

Masqueraders and Masquerade Attacks. It is worth mentioning that the chosen definition of an insider does not cover the *masqueraders*. A masquerader is defined as an attacker who has gained (steals) the credentials of an employee (insider) of a contemporary organization and subsequently, uses those credentials to maliciously access organization resources (includes databases) by impersonating as a legitimate employee of that organization. A masquerade attack can take one of the two following forms (i) - a masquerader is an insider who gains control of credentials of another employee of the same organization having different privilege level than that being held by the masquerader, (ii) - the masquerader is an outside attacker who somehow gains control of legitimate employee's credentials. A distinction, in-terms knowledge base, can be drawn between an *internal masquerader* and *external masquerader*. Intuitively, an insider masquerader knows more about the organization as compared to an external masquerader though this is not necessarily always be the case. Additionally, an internal masquerader can mimic behaviour similar to the behaviour of other employees of the organization, whereas an external masquerader's behaviour is likely to manifest differently because of the lack of knowledge about employee behaviours. Figure 1 a depiction of insiders, outsiders, and internal and external masqueraders in an organizational setting.

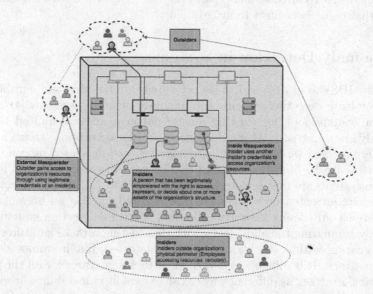

Fig. 1. Figure depicting insiders, outsiders, internal and external masqueraders in organizational settings.

2.2   The Impact of an Insider Attack

A 2015 report titled *Insider Threat Report* by Vormetric [3] reported that globally 89% of the respondent organizations are at risk of insider attack and that among these respondent organizations 34% of them felt extremely vulnerable to this kind of attack. Of the respondent organizations, 56% plan to increase their spending on tackling the challenge of insider threat. The 2015 *Cost of Cyber Crime: Global Report* from the Ponemon Institute [2] reported that insiders cause the costliest cyber-crimes. Information Systems Audit and Control Association (ISACA), reported that, globally, insider threat was among the top three threats for 2016 [5]. In the context of healthcare, insiders have reported as the cause of most health-care data breaches [20]. For example, a health-care data security report from IBM Managed Security Services reported that insiders were responsible for 68% of all network attacks targeting health-care data in 2016 [6]. Insider attacks are on the rise, as reported in a 2015 survey report [4] that internal factors caused 43% of data breaches as compared to 2004 where it was reported in [1] that insiders caused 29% of the crimes.

Nonetheless, the reporting rate of insider attacks remains very low for a variety of reasons compared to the actual number of instances, including inconsequential impact or lack of evidence [1]. Another reason is that organizations are sometimes hesitant to report insider attacks due to loss of reputation and liability; however, legislations are now in place directing organizations to report data breaches such as the recently passed Privacy Amendment (Notifiable Data Breaches) Act 2016 in Australia [7] and the EU's General Data Protection Regulation that came into effect from 2018 [29].

3   Anomaly Detection in Systems

Originally, IDSs were designed to detect network intrusions and can be classified into misuse detection systems and anomaly detection systems [41]. Misuse detection systems look for existing misuse patterns and are limited to detect previously known attacks [41,49]. In general, misuse detection systems have also been referred to as *signature-based systems* or *knowledge-based intrusion detection systems* in the literature [12,54,57]. The majority of commercial intrusion detection systems are misuse detection systems [15,39,72]. Misuse detection systems are circumvented by sophisticated attackers targeting an organization as these systems only detect known attacks [50]. A misuse detection system detects attacks by comparing the audit trails with the existing attack signatures. It provides a guarantee that the known attack is detected, but it cannot detect an unknown attack. It is difficult to determine attack signatures for all the variants of a particular attack as different ways exist to exploit vulnerability or weakness.

In contrast to misuse detection systems, anomaly detection (also known as *behaviour-based*) systems look for a deviation from normative behaviour. In principle, anomaly detection systems have the potential to detect zero-day attacks – attacks for which there is not a known predefined pattern. However, in practice, it is a challenge to model normative behaviour accurately. Existing work has generally focused on identifying anomalous system operations [28], malicious network events [26] or malicious application system events [9]. The anomaly detection systems can be distinguished on the basis of the way in which normative behaviour is modelled, that is, either the system learns the normative behaviour by automatically mining the past behaviours (learning-based anomaly detection systems) or the normative behaviour (specification-based anomaly detection systems) is specified manually [45,65].

It has been reported that the attacker can evade the anomaly detection system by carefully mimicking normative behaviour while exploiting a vulnerability. Such attacks are known as *mimicry attacks* [18,46,70,71,73].

The effectiveness of IDSs is evident in domains like computer networking, operating systems, and industrial control systems thus making them a favourable choice to be deployed to protect databases against intrusions [13, 21–23, 25, 27, 31, 33, 35, 36, 52, 59, 68, 69, 74, 76]. However, IDSs deployed to protect systems in the above-mentioned domains are not adequate for databases; therefore, IDSs tailored to databases are desirable. Such a tailored IDS for DBMS is known as *Database Intrusion Detection System (DIDS)*. The literature has shown that intrusion detection systems tailored to databases are effective in the detection of these malicious queries made by an insider [14, 38, 56, 63]. The following sections of this paper review DIDS research and proposes a taxonomy of IDS in the context of DBMS.

An anomaly-based detection system is further classified into learning-based or specification-based. While remaining within the scope of detecting malicious access to DBMS, the literature lacks any specification-based detection system. A naïve way to design a specification-based detection system would be to list all the legitimate SQL queries. However, it is impractical to a priori specify every potentially legitimate query. The development of a complete specification in the case of DBMS is unattainable, essentially for the inherent flexibility of SQL, that is, a SQL statement can be written in different ways to query the information. In our opinion, the notion of the specification-based detection system is immaterial in the context of databases intrusion detection because of its impracticality. In the literature in general, within the context of DIDS research, the anomaly-based detection systems imply that it is a learning-based system. In literature and commercially, the DIDS solutions are routinely referred to as Data Loss Prevention (DLP) solutions.

4   A Taxonomy for DBMS Anomaly Detection

This section introduces a taxonomy of methods that detect anomalous access to a DBMS. Anomaly-based DIDS research has remained a centre of focus of the research community, while less attention is being paid on misuse (or signature)-based DIDSs. The proposed taxonomy is shown in Fig. 2 that broadly categorizes IDSs to detect anomalous access in a DBMS. An aspect to keep in consideration while performing classification of anomaly-based DIDS is the set of features used to model normative behaviour of a user, for example, time of access, attributes in projection clause, relations/tables queried etc. Section 4.2 and its following sections discuss these classifications. To address these classifications, we first present the prevalent architecture of anomaly-based database intrusion detection systems in the following section.

4.1   Prevalent Architecture of Anomaly-Based Database Intrusion Detection Systems

Figures 3 and 4 depict the prevalent architecture of an anomaly-based database intrusion detection system. The architecture involves two phases: a training phase and a detection phase. A profile of normative behaviour is constructed during the training phase and is compared against the run-time profile that is constructed in the detection phase. The future deviations of the run-time profile from normative profiles are labelled as anomalies and necessitate attention. The architecture consists of two fundamental components: feature extraction (abstraction) and profile constructor. In feature extraction, the features required to construct the profile are extracted. The profile construction component is the technique to construct the profile using selected features.

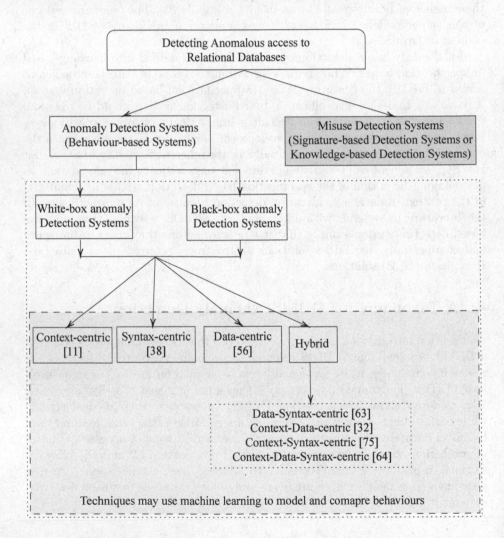

Fig. 2. Taxonomy of anomalous DBMS-access detection systems.

Profiling "normative behaviour" is non-trivial as many features about queries can be taken into consideration while constructing profiles, and identifying significant determinant features is a challenge. The classification based on features and the techniques to construct profiles is discussed in the following next sections.

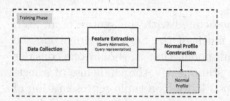

Fig. 3. Training phase of an anomaly detection system.

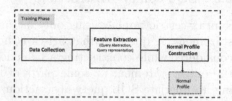

Fig. 4. Detection phase of an anomaly detection system.

4.2 Feature Classification

Anomaly-based intrusion detection techniques for detecting malicious access to databases can be further distinguished based on what features they extract from a DBMS audit log of SQL queries to model behaviours. The modelled behaviour is represented as a behavioural profile [38,43]. These features can be syntax-centric, context-centric, and data-centric, which is sometimes is referred to as result-centric in the literature [38,56,63].

Techniques using syntax-centric features construct behavioural profiles by using syntax features of the SQL query included but are not limited to the attributes in a projection clause, the relations queried, the attributes in selection clause, and/or the type of SQL command [38]. Techniques using data-centric or result-centric features construct behavioural profiles using data returned in response to an SQL query or any other statistical measurement on returned data, for instance, the minimum and maximum value in case of numeric data. For example, one could use the amount of information (the percentage of data returned) returned in response to a query or the returned values of attributes to model behaviour or a user [56]. The context-centric techniques construct behavioural profiles using contextual features. Contextual features are associated with the context of the query, for example, the time at which the query was made, the user ID of the person making the query, or the number of queries made in a specified time period, etc. [11]. A combination of the context, syntax and data-centric features, can be used while modelling normative behaviours. One such anomaly detection technique that uses syntax and data-centric features is proposed in [63].

An anomaly-based detection system building behavioural profiles that are not understandable by humans in a meaningful way is known as a *Black-Box* anomaly detection system. On the other hand, an anomaly-based detection system building behavioural profiles that are understandable by humans are known as *White-Box* anomaly detection system. Understandability implies that the actual root cause of the anomaly can be identified by the administrators (security officer, database administrator, etc.) when they inspect the anomaly. Intuitively, white-box approaches have the potential to help explain anomalies.

4.3 SQL Query Abstraction

Syntax-centric implies using only factors associated with the syntax of an SQL statement. A question that arises is how much of the SQL statement can be considered while constructing a behavioural model, that is, should one consider the entire statement or some parts of the statement – the challenge of selecting appropriate SQL query abstraction. Abstraction is a tuple representation of an SQL statement and consists of query features like relation name, attribute names, the amount of returned data or any statistics on the returned data. A number of techniques [38,40,48,51,53,62,63] have been proposed that transform the syntax of an SQL statement into a more abstract fingerprint that can be used for comparing queries. SQL query abstractions are also referred to as SQL query fingerprints [51,53], SQL query signatures [38] or SQL query skeletons in the literature [48]. The query abstractions used by existing anomaly-based detection approaches are also described in this paper.

Other than DIDS research, the use of abstraction in practice has also been studied by audit log summarization research as typically audit logs encompass a large number of queries and methods to summarize logs in a meaningful way are sought [47]. For instance, it has been reported in a recent study that within the time period of 19 hours, approximately 17 million SQL queries were made in a major US bank [48].

4.4 Syntax-Centric Features-Based Techniques

Several anomaly detection approaches to detect malicious accesses to DBMS use syntax-centric features of the SQL queries to construct behavioural profiles [38]. For instance, the approach *DetAnom* [38] detects malicious DBMS-accesses by application programs. SQL queries executed by an application program are represented in the form of SQL query abstractions to generate a normative profile of an application. In [38], a SQL query abstraction consists of the following elements, (c, t, r, q, n), where c is SQL command type, for instance, SELECT. Attribute t is the list of attribute identifiers projected in the query and are relative to the relation to which they belong. Attribute r is the list of relation identifiers. Attribute q is the list of attribute identifiers in the WHERE clause and n is the number of predicates in the WHERE clause. For example, consider the following SQL query:

```
SELECT bankdb.acc_number, bankdbacc.current_amount,
FROM bankdbacc, bankdb,
WHERE bankdb.acc_number=7594
AND bankdb.acc_number = bankdbacc.account;
```

The corresponding identifiers for relations and the attributes are shown in Table 1. This query is then represented as follows:

$$\{\langle 1 \rangle \, \langle 100:10, 200:20 \rangle \, \langle 100, 200 \rangle \, \langle 100:20, 200:30 \rangle \, \langle 2 \rangle\}.$$

The generation of a query abstraction is followed by the exploration of all execution paths of the application program accomplished by Concolic execution (Concolic testing) which is a technique for program analysis [55,66,67]. Once all the paths are explored, the branching condition is then paired with the SQL query that falls under that branching condition that was discovered in the process of concolic testing. This *(branch condition, SQL query)* pair is referred to as a query record.

In the detection phase of DetAnom, a query is intercepted, and its branch condition is matched with the branch condition in the corresponding a query record. If the branch condition is satisfied, then matching of query abstraction is carried out. In case of a mismatch, the query is said to be malicious. DetAnom works only for application programs where the SQL queries are embedded in program code, and it is not extendible to capture users behaviours manifested in a variety of SQL queries made to the database.

Table 1. Identifiers example for the query abstraction approach proposed in [38].

Command type	Representation
SELECT	1
UPDATE	2
INSERT	3
DELETE	4
Relation name	Relation identifier
bankdb	100
bankdbacc	200
Attribute name	Attribute identifier
acc_number	10
current_amount	20
account	30

Another early approach based on syntax-centric features is presented in [14]. The approach uses three query abstractions each having different level of granularities, coarse triplet, medium-grain triplet, fine triplet. A Naïve Bayes classifier was used to predict a role for the SQL query. If the predicted role is not the same as from the one SQL query was originated then an alarm is raised. This approach has several limitations including, considering each query in isolation and it does not consider the sequence of queries, Second, the approach constructed profiles of roles while ignoring the case where one user can belong to multiple roles.

The proposed approach in [43] demonstrates that one can build behaviour-based anomaly detection systems by considering the sequence of queries (query correlations) to model insider's querying behaviour to detect malicious accesses manifested in sequences of queries rather than a query in isolation, to DBMS. The approach [43] models querying behaviour of an insider using n-grams that capture short-terms SQL query correlations. The model used abstractions of SQL query audit logs to construct insider profiles, a normative profile using safe logs and a run-time profile using run-time audit logs. The run-time profile is compared with normative profile and deviations are an indication of anomalies.

This model proposed in [42] introduced the notion that behaviours that are rare (infrequent) represent potentially malicious access by an insider, and frequent behaviours are possibly safe behaviours. The domain of item-set mining was explored. Item-set mining algorithms including PrePost+, Apriori-Inverse, and Apriori-Rare were adopted to mine frequent and rare query-sets to model querying behaviours (in terms of SQL query abstractions). Results point towards the potential effectiveness of modelling insiders malicious querying behaviour as rare behaviour that also enables detection of insider's malicious databases accesses as anomalies.

Syntax-centric approaches, in general, are useful in detection masquerader attacks as well as SQL injection attacks both these attacks lead to structural changes in SQL statement.

4.5   Data (Result)-Centric Features-Based Techniques

Little research has been reported on using data-centric features as the basis for anomaly detection in the context of DIDS. Data-centric features include the amount of data returned in response to a query or returned values of attributes or any other statics performed on the returned set of attribute values.

In [56], it is argued that syntax-centric features of a query alone are a poor discriminator of intent. Syntactically different queries can potentially give the same result while syntactically similar queries can potentially yield different results. Therefore, a user can craft a legitimate SQL query to retrieve results from the database which the user is authorized to retrieve, yet a purely syntax-centric anomaly-based detection system might label this as anomalous behaviour.

In the approach proposed in [56], user profiles are clusters that are specified in terms of an *S-Vector* that provides a statistical summary of the results (tuples/rows). In the detection phase, clustering algorithms were adopted, that are, as supervised learning methods, Euclidean k-means clustering, Support Vector Machines (SVM), Decision Tree Classifier, and Naïve Bayes, and as unsupervised methods, Cluster-Based Outlier Detection (based on Euclidean distance clustering) and Attrib-Deviation, using L_∞-norm. If a query belongs to the cluster, then it is considered normal else it is regarded as anomalous. The presented approach is suitable for the detection of a query in isolation and does not take a sequence of queries into account.

The approach in [44] looked at the modelling of behaviour from a DBMS's perspective. A record/DBMS oriented approach (also referred to as a semantic approach) is presented in [44] that considers frequency-based correlations to detect insiders malicious accesses as anomalies. The construction of the profiles utilizes control charts from statistical process control as a way to detect anomalies. Two scenarios were considered, in the first scenario, the training data for modelling normative behaviour contains outlier. In the second scenario, the training data for modelling normative behaviour is free from outliers. The experiments demonstrated the effectiveness of the approach in the detection of frequent observation attacks by insiders as anomalies. It was discovered that the semantic approach not only identified unseen behaviours but also identified behaviours that should have been present in the current behaviours as anomalies, which we refer to as oversight-anomalies. Oversight-anomalies are the anomalies introduced due to human negligence or human errors, for example, an instance where the doctor or the nurse (caregiver) missed a daily check-up of a patient. To the best of our knowledge, this is the first time the oversight-anomalies are considered in the DBMS setting. It was also demonstrated that the proposed model for the construction of record-oriented profiles could be transformed into a model for the construction of role-oriented profiles.

Data-centric approaches are capable of detecting sophisticated attacks as well. For instance, data harvesting attacks involving retrieval of a large amount of data, therefore, exceeding what is retrieved by a legitimate user.

4.6 Context-Centric Features-Based Techniques

Few purely context-centric approaches are reported in the literature. One such context centric approach is presented in [11] in which contextual features are considered in modelling user behaviours. The approach took the deployment of anomaly-based IDS in the medical sector as its use-case and studied the Break-The-Glass (BTG) procedure which is a procedure that breaks the traditional access control mechanism and enable access of patients data in case of emergency to employees of different departments. In this approach in [11], users who supposed to behave similarly are divided into groups and profiles are constructed for groups. The feature space comprised of contextual features like access type, time, division, date. Profiles were represented as the sequence of histograms and were constructed using the concept of *Bins*. Bins represent the frequency of features. In the detection phase, the distance between the histogram of a user and the existing profile is measured, and a larger distance is an indication as an anomaly. The approach represented user and group profile in terms of a sequence of histograms of features that can easily be interpreted by a concerned individual like a security officer. Therefore, the approach in [11] can be classified as a white-box anomaly detection approach.

Context-centric approaches typically increase the detection effectiveness of an ID approach when combined with syntax or data-centric approach.

4.7   Hybrid Techniques

An example of an approach using data and syntax-centric features to construct behavioural profiles is presented in [63]. Machine learning techniques, in particular, Naïve Bayes classifiers and multi-labelling classifiers, were also deployed in the profile generation process. User profiles are built in the training phase from logs containing user activities.

The approach transforms an SQL query into an SQL query abstraction called a quadruplet. A quadruplet $QT(c, P_R, P_A, S_R)$ is composed of data-centric and syntax-centric features including the command type c; the list of relations accessed by the query P_R; the list of attributes accessed by query relative to the relation P_A; and the amount of selected information from the relation S_R. This hybrid approach is demonstrated in two settings that is role-based anomaly detection and unsupervised anomaly detection. In the detection phase the role of a querier was predicted using a Naïve Bayes classifier. Multi-labelling classification was used in case of an overlap of roles that results in more than one role. If the predicted role is different from the actual role then the query is labelled as anomalous. In the unsupervised settings, the COBWEB [30, 34] clustering algorithm was selected. The query is treated as anomalous if a query made by a user falls into a cluster that does not contain any query made by this user. This approach is promising for the detection of a single malicious query in isolation; however, it ignores sequences of queries while modelling behaviour.

The approach presented in [32] uses context-centric and data-centric features. Normative profiles are constructed by discovering association rules between context-centric features and data-centric features using frequent item-set mining [10]. The basic idea of the approach is to tie the results retrieved by the SQL query with the context in which they were retrieved. For instance, a transaction made in London in the morning typically retrieves records for employees of the human resource department. Therefore, human resource department employees records are tied with the context that they are normally retrieved in the morning from London. In the detection phase, for any incoming query, context-centric features were extracted, and rules conforming to these features are matched, and then the result of the query is matched with the results associated with the retrieved rules. A drawback of this approach is that large databases result in large profiles. Additionally, this approach is too restrictive and less likely to be scalable. Another drawback of this approach is in general the drawback of context-centric approaches that is the context can be easily mimicked.

The approach in [75], also employed context and syntax-centric features to model behaviours and forms some assumptions for instance that every department in an organization has a unique IP space, employees work in shifts (there are three shifts in a day). The features collected for modelling include Employee ID, Role ID, time, IP address, Access Type (direct or through an application). The approach also records the SQL query associated with the contextual features. The profile consists of the probability of each feature's occurrence observed for every user. In the detection phase, a new transaction is compared against the constructed profiles to check the closest issuer (user) of that transaction.

The transaction is labelled as an anomaly in case the issuer of the transaction is different from the one computed. This approach also considered Role Hierarchy, meaning, if role $\ddot{r}_1$ is above Role $\ddot{r}_2$ in the hierarchy, then the access privileges of Role $\ddot{r}_2$ is a subset of Role $\ddot{r}_1$. For instance, if a query made by $\ddot{r}_1$ is labelled as malicious, but the same query is legitimate for $\ddot{r}_2$ then this' is not considered as a malicious query. The focus of this approach is to augment Role-Based Access Control (RBAC) to ensure that the query is made only by the authorized users. Similar to approaches discussed above, this approach also detects only single malicious DBMS transaction where later in the paper it is argued that a single query may be legitimate, however, a group of them made together might result in malicious or illegitimate action.

In [64] contextual, data and syntax-centric features are considered in modelling. The database intrusion detection approach in [64] is tailored for Data Warehouses in which applications are enabled to access Data Warehouses via the web. The profiles are constructed by considering various features, as shown in Fig. 5 and are represented in terms of the probabilistic distribution of each feature for each user and for the entire population. In the detection phase for this approach, testing is done to match features distribution with the distributions obtained in the training phase using statistical hypothesis tests like Chi-square, Shapiro-Wilk, and Kolmogorov-Smirnov tests [64]. In case of a non-conformity, the activity involving that feature is labelled as an anomaly. The approach is focused on web-based

F#	FeatureName	Description
Features per User/IPAddress		
F_1	#ConsFailedLoginAttempts	The number of consecutive failed database login attempts by a UserID or from an IPAddress (accumulated or in a given timespan)
F_2	#SimultSQLSessions	The number of active simultaneous database connections
F_3	#UnauthorAccessAttempts	The number of consecutive user requests to execute an unauthorized actions (e.g. request to modify data when the database is read-only, or requesting to query data to which does not have access privileges)
Features per User/IPAddress per Command		
F_4	CPUTime	CPU time spent by the DBMS to process the command
F_5	ResponseSize	Size (in bytes) of the result of the command's execution
F_6, F_7	#ResponseLines, #ResponseColumns	Nr. of lines and columns in the result of the command's execution
F_8, F_9	#ProcessedRows, #ProcessedColumns	Nr. of accessed rows and columns for processing the command
F_{10}	CommandLength	Number of characters
F_{11}	#GroupBy	Number of GROUP BY columns
F_{12}	#Union	Number of UNION clauses
$F_{13}...F_{17}$	#Sum, #Max, #Min, #Avg, #Count	Nr. of SUM, MAX, MIN, AVG and COUNT functions
F_{18}, F_{19}	#And, #Or	Nr. of AND and OR operators in the command's WHERE clause(s)
F_{20}	#LiteralValues	Nr. of literal values in the command's WHERE clause(s)
Features per User/IPAddress per Session		
F_{21}	#GroupBy	Number of GROUPBY columns in all SELECT statements, p/ session
F_{22}	#Union	Number of UNION clauses in all SELECT statements, per session
$F_{23}...F_{27}$	#Sum, #Max, #Min, #Avg, #Count	Nr. of appearances of SUM, MAX, MIN, AVG and COUNT functions in all commands, per session
F_{28}	TimeBetwCommands	Time period (in seconds) between exec. of commands, per session
F_{29}	#SimultaneousCommands	Number of commands simultaneously executing, per session

Fig. 5. List of features considered. Figure cropped from *Securing Data Warehouses from Web-Based Intrusions* by Santos et al. [64]

malicious access to Data Warehouses though insiders remain unaddressed. Table 2 shows a consolidated presentation of discussed and well-known approaches proposed in the literature.

Table 2. An overview of the characteristics discussed and well-known approaches proposed in the literature. ⊛, ⊙, and ⊘ represents syntax, data (result), and context-centric features respectively.

Approach	Features	White-box / Black-box	Single Query detection	Sequence of Queries detection	Profiles	Detection Style
Hussain et al. [38]	⊛	■	✓	✗	Tuples of SQL-branch condition	Tuple matching
Khan et al. [44]	⊙	□	✓	✓	Record Access Frequency	Control Charts
Mathew et al. [56]	⊙	■	✓	✗	Clusters / Classes of S-Vector	**Supervised:** Euclidean k-mean SVM, Decision Tree Classifier Naïve Bayes **Unsupervised:** Cluster-Based Outlier Detection Attrib-Deviation
Khan et al. [43]	⊛	□	✓	✓	n-grams of SQL query Abstraction	n-gram profile comparison mismatches labelled as anomalies
Alizadeh et al. [11]	⊘	□	✓	✗	Histograms	Distance b/w histograms
Sallam et al. [63]	⊛ ⊙	■	✓	✗	Classes / Clusters of Quadruplet	**Supervised:** Naïve Bayes. Multi-labelling classifier **Unsupervised:** COBWEB
Gafny et al. [32]	⊙ ⊘	■	✓	✗	Association Rules	FIM, rule matching
Kamra et al. [14]	⊛	■	✓	✗	quiplets,	Naïve Bayes
Wu et al. [75]	⊛ ⊘	■	✓	✗	Probabilities of Feature's Observed Values	Naïve Bayes
Santos et al. [64]	⊛ ⊙ ⊘	■	✓	✗	Probability Distribution	Distribution Matching (statistical hypothesis tests i.e. Chi-square, Shapiro-Wilk, Kolmogorov-Smirnov tests)
Khan et al. [42]	⊛	□	✓	Sets of queries	query-sets of SQL query Abstraction	Mined Rare query-sets Mismatched frequent query-sets

5   Conclusions

Database intrusion detection, specifically behaviour-based database intrusion detection approaches have seen to be effective in detecting insider attacks. Two significant aspects in the design of behaviour-based approaches are what level of features (and in the case of SQL statement then what level of abstraction) are selected for modelling behaviours and the technique (algorithm) selected for constructing profiles. The literature contains approaches using syntax-centric, data-centric, or context-centric features or a combination of these features. To construct profiles, machine learning approach like classification, clustering, as well as distance functions, rule matching algorithms are adopted. In the existing literature, pure data-centric, and context-centric approaches are not prevalent.

Some of the approaches are tailored for specific applications, i.e., data warehouses; second, these approaches do not allow for regularly updating normative profiles. Majority of these approaches reported in the literature are focused on the detection of a single malicious SQL query in different settings by considering only single SQL query in modelling behaviours [11,32,38,56,63,64,75]. Little attention has been paid on the detection of malicious queries sequences. As a single query might not be malicious, but a sequence of SQL queries might be an indication of malicious activity. Therefore, such approaches that can detect the malicious sequence of SQL queries are desirable.

Acknowledgement. This publication has emanated from research conducted with the financial support of Science Foundation Ireland under Grant number 12/RC/2289-P2 which is co-funded under the European Regional Development Fund.

References

1. 2014 US state of cybercrime survey. Technical report, CERT, Software Engineering Institute, Carnegie Mellon University (2014). https://resources.sei.cmu.edu/library/asset-view.cfm?assetid=298318
2. 2015 Cost of cyber crime: Global. Technical report, Ponemon Institute (2015). http://www.cnmeonline.com/myresources/hpe/docs/HPE_SIEM_Analyst_Report_-_2015_Cost_of_Cyber_Crime_Study_-_Global.pdf
3. 2015 Vormetric insider threat report. Technical report, Vormetric (2015). http://go.thalesesecurity.com/rs/480-LWA-970/images/2015_Vormetric_ITR_European_R3.pdf
4. Grand theft data data exfiltration study: Actors, tactics, and detection. Technical report, Intel security and McAfee (2015). https://www.mcafee.com/enterprise/en-us/assets/reports/rp-data-exfiltration.pdf
5. Cybersecurity snapshot global results. Technical report, ISACA (2016)
6. Security trends in the healthcare industry data theft and ransomware plague healthcare organizations. Technical report, IBM Security, IBM (2016). https://www.ibm.com/downloads/cas/PLWZ76MM
7. Privacy amendment (notifiable data breaches) act 2017 (2017). https://www.legislation.gov.au/Details/C2017A00012
8. 2018 insider threat report. Technical report, ca Technologies (2018). https://crowdresearchpartners.com/wp-content/uploads/2017/07/Insider-Threat-Report-2018.pdf
9. Amr, S., Abed, T., Clancy, C., Levy, D.S.: Applying bag of system calls for anomalous behavior detection of applications in linux containers. In: 2015 IEEE Globecom Workshops, San Diego, CA, USA, 6–10 December 2015, pp. 1–5 (2015)
10. Agrawal, R., Imieliński, T., Swami, A.: Mining association rules between sets of items in large databases. SIGMOD Rec. **22**(2), 207–216 (1993)
11. Alizadeh, M., Peters, S., Etalle, S., Zannone, N.: Behavior analysis in the medical sector: theory and practice. In: Proceedings of the 33rd Annual ACM Symposium on Applied Computing, SAC 2018, pp. 1637–1646, ACM, New York (2018)
12. Anjum, F., Subhadrabandhu, D., Sarkar, S.: Signature based intrusion detection for wireless ad-hoc networks: a comparative study of various routing protocols. In: 2003 IEEE 58th Vehicular Technology Conference. VTC 2003-Fall (IEEE Cat. No.03CH37484), vol. 3, pp. 2152–2156, October 2003

13. Ramos, R., Barbosa, R., Pras, A.: Intrusion detection in Scada networks. In: Stiller, B., De Turck, F. (eds.) Mechanisms for Autonomous Management of Networks and Services, pp. 163–166. Springer, Berlin (2010)
14. Bertino, E., Terzi, E., Kamra, A., Vakali, A.: Intrusion detection in CHAC-administered databases. In: 21st Annual Computer Security Applications Conference (ACSAC 2005), pp 10–182, December 2005
15. BeyondTrust. PowerBroker for Databases. https://www.beyondtrust.com/resources/brochures/powerbroker-for-databases
16. Bishop, M., Gates, C.: Defining the insider threat. In: Proceedings of the 4th Annual Workshop on Cyber Security and Information Intelligence Research: Developing Strategies to Meet the Cyber Security and Information Intelligence Challenges Ahead, CSIIRW 2008, pp. 15:1–15:3. ACM, New York (2008)
17. Bishop, M., Gollmann, D., Hunker, J., Probst, C.W. (eds): Countering Insider Threats, 20.07. - 25.07.2008, volume 08302 of Dagstuhl Seminar Proceedings. Schloss Dagstuhl - Leibniz-Zentrum für Informatik, Germany (2008)
18. Bouche, J., Hock, D., Kappes, M.: On the performance of anomaly detection systems uncovering traffic mimicking covert channels. In: Proceedings of the Eleventh International Network Conference, INC 2016, Frankfurt, Germany, July 19–21, 2016. pp. 19–24 (2016)
19. Brackney, R.C., Anderson, R.H.: Understanding the insider threat. In:Proceedings of a March 2004 Workshop, vol. 196. Rand Corporation (2004)
20. Brenner, B.: Healthcare data breaches mostly caused by insiders (2017). Naked Security by Sophos. https://nakedsecurity.sophos.com/2017/02/23/healthcare-data-breaches-mostly-caused-by-insiders/
21. Burguera, I., Zurutuza, U., Nadjm-Tehrani, S.: Crowdroid: Behavior-based malware detection system for android. In: Proceedings of the 1st ACM Workshop on Security and Privacy in Smartphones and Mobile Devices, SPSM 2011, pp. 15–26, ACM, New York (2011)
22. Butun, I., Morgera, S.D., Sankar, R.: A survey of intrusion detection systems in wireless sensor networks. IEEE Commun. Surv. Tutor. 16(1), 266–282 (2014)
23. Caselli, M., Zambon, E., Kargl, F.:Sequence-aware intrusion detection in industrial control systems. In: Proceedings of the 1st ACM Workshop on Cyber-Physical System Security, CPSS 2015, pp. 13–24. ACM,New York(2015)
24. Chari, S.N., Cheng, P.-C.: Bluebox: A policy-driven, host-based intrusion detection system. ACM Trans. Inf. Syst. Secur. 6(2), 173–200 (2003)
25. Tsang, C.H., Kwong, S.: Multi-agent intrusion detection system in industrial network using ant colony clustering approach and unsupervised feature extraction. In: 2005 IEEE International Conference on Industrial Technology, pp. 51–56, December 2005
26. Chung, C.-J., Khatkar, P., Xing, T., Lee, J., Huang, D.: NICE: network intrusion detection and countermeasure selection in virtual network systems. IEEE Trans. Dependable Sec. Comput. 10(4), 198–211 (2013)
27. Creech, G., Hu, J.: A semantic approach to host-based intrusion detection systems using contiguous and discontiguous system call patterns. IEEE Trans. Comput. 63(4), 807–819 (2014)
28. Creech, G., Jiankun, H.: A semantic approach to host-based intrusion detection systems using contiguous and discontiguous system call patterns. IEEE Trans. Comput. 63(4), 807–819 (2014)

29. Regulation (EU) 2016/679 of the European Parliament and of the Council of 27 April 2016 on the protection of natural persons with regard to the processing of personal data and on the free movement of such data, and repealing Directive 95/46/EC (General Data Protection Regulation). Offi. J. Eur. Union **L119**, 1–88 (2016)
30. Fisher, D.H.: Knowledge acquisition via incremental conceptual clustering. Mach. Learn. **2**(2), 139–172 (1987)
31. Forrest, S., Hofmeyr, S.A., Somayaji, A., Longstaff, T.A. :A sense of self for unix processes. In: Proceedings 1996 IEEE Symposium on Security and Privacy, pp. 120–128, May 1996
32. Gafny, M., Shabtai, A., Rokach, L., Elovici, Y.: Poster: applying unsupervised context-based analysis for detecting unauthorized data disclosure. In: Proceedings of the 18th ACM Conference on Computer and Communications Security, CCS 2011, pp. 765–768. ACM, New York, NY (2011)
33. Garcia-Teodoro, P., Diaz-Verdejo, J., Macia-Fernandez, G., Vazquez, E.: Anomaly-based network intrusion detection: techniques, systems and challenges. Comput. Secur. **28**(1), 18–28 (2009)
34. Gennari, J.H., Langley, P., Fisher, D.: Models of incremental concept formation. Artif. Intell. **40**(1), 11–61 (1989)
35. Hashemi, S., Yang, Y., Zabihzadeh, D., Kangavari, M.: Detecting intrusion transactions in databases using data item dependencies and anomaly analysis. Exp. Syst. **25**(5), 460–473 (2008)
36. Hofmeyr, S.A., Forrest, S., Somayaji, A.: Intrusion detection using sequences of system calls. J. Comput. Secur. **6**(3), 151–180 (1998)
37. Hunker, J., Probst, C.W.: Insiders and insider threats - an overview of definitions and mitigation techniques. J. Wirel. Mobile Netwo. Ubiquit. Comput. Depend. Appl. **2**, –27 (2011)
38. Hussain, S.R., Sallam, A.M., Bertino, E.: Detanom: detecting anomalous database transactions by insiders. In: Proceedings of the 5th ACM Conference on Data and Application Security and Privacy, CODASPY 2015, pp. 25–35. ACM, New York, NY (2015)
39. IBM. Guardium. http://www-01.ibm.com/software/data/guardium/
40. Kamra, A., Terzi, E., Bertino, E.: Detecting anomalous access patterns in relational databases. VLDB J. **17**(5), 1063–1077 (2008)
41. Kemmerer, R.A., Vigna, G.: Intrusion detection: a brief history and overview. Computer **35**(4), 27–30 (2002)
42. Khan, M.I., Sullivan, B.O., Foley, S.N.: Towards modelling insiders behaviour as rare behaviour to detect malicious RDMBS access. In 2018 IEEE International Conference on Big Data (Big Data), pp. 3094–3099 (2018)
43. Khan, M.I., Foley, S.N.: Detecting anomalous behavior in DBMS logs. In: Cuppens, F., Cuppens, N., Lanet, J.-L., Legay, A. (eds.) CRiSIS 2016. LNCS, vol. 10158, pp. 147–152. Springer, Cham (2017). https://doi.org/10.1007/978-3-319-54876-0_12
44. Imran Khan, M., O'Sullivan, B., Foley, S.N.: A semantic approach to frequency based anomaly detection of insider access in database management systems. In: Cuppens, N., Cuppens, F., Lanet, J.-L., Legay, A., Garcia-Alfaro, J. (eds.) Risks and Security of Internet and Systems, pp. 18–28, Springer International Publishing, Cham (2018). https://doi.org/10.1007/978-3-319-76687-4
45. Ko, C., Ruschitzka, M., Levitt, K.: Execution monitoring of security-critical programs in distributed systems: a specification-based approach. In: Proceedings. 1997 IEEE Symposium on Security and Privacy (Cat. No. 97CB36097), pp. 175–187, May 1997

46. Kruegel, C., Kirda, E., Mutz, D., Robertson ,W., Vigna, G.: Automating mimicry attacks using static binary analysis. In: Proceedings of the 14th Conference on USENIX Security Symposium - Vol. 14, SSYM 2005, pp. 11–11, USENIX Association, Berkeley (2005)

47. Kul, G., Luong, D.T.A., Xie, T., Chandola, V., Kennedy, O., Upadhyaya, S.: Similarity metrics for SQL query clustering. IEEE Trans. Knowl. Data Eng. **30**(12), 2408–2420 (2018)

48. Kul, G., et al.: Ettu: Analyzing query intents in corporate databases. In: Proceedings of the 25th International Conference Companion on World Wide Web, WWW 2016 Companion, pp. 463–466, Republic and Canton of Geneva, International World Wide Web Conferences Steering Committee, Switzerland (2016)

49. Kumar, S., Spafford, E.H.: A pattern matching model for misuse intrusion detection. In: Proceedings of the 17th National Computer Security Conference, pp. 11–21 (1994)

50. Lazarevic, A., Kumar, V., Srivastava, J.: Intrusion detection: a survey. In: Kumar, V., Srivastava, J., Lazarevic, A. (eds.) Managing Cyber Threats. Massive Computing, vol. 5, pp. 19–78. Springer, Boston (2005). https://doi.org/10.1007/0-387-24230-9_2

51. Lee, S.Y., Low, W.L., Wong, P.E.: Learning fingerprints for a database intrusion detection system. In: Proceedings of the 7th European Symposium on Research in Computer Security, ESORICS 2002, pp. 264–280, Springer-Verlag, London (2002)

52. Lee, V.C.S., Stankovic, J.A., Son, S.H.: Intrusion detection in real-time database systems via time signatures. In: Proceedings Sixth IEEE Real-time Technology and Applications Symposium. RTAS 2000, pp. 124–133 (2000)

53. Low, W.L., Lee, J., Teoh, P.: DIDAFIT: detecting intrusions in databases through fingerprinting transactions. In: ICEIS 2002, Proceedings of the 4st International Conference on Enterprise Information Systems, Ciudad Real, Spain, 2–6 April 2002, pp. 121–128 (2002)

54. Lunt, T.F., Jagannathan, R., Lee, R., Whitehurst, A., Listgarten, S.: Knowledge-based intrusion detection. In: [1989] Proceedings. The Annual AI Systems in Government Conference, pp. 102–107, March 1989

55. Majumdar, R., Sen, K.: Hybrid concolic testing. In: Proceedings of the 29th International Conference on Software Engineering, ICSE 2007, pp. 416–426. IEEE Computer Society,Washington, DC (2007)

56. Mathew, S., Petropoulos, M., Ngo, H.Q., Upadhyaya, S.: A data-centric approach to insider attack detection in database systems. In: Jha, S., Sommer, R., Kreibich, C. (eds.) RAID 2010. LNCS, vol. 6307, pp. 382–401. Springer, Heidelberg (2010). https://doi.org/10.1007/978-3-642-15512-3_20

57. Mishra, A., Nadkarni, K., Patcha, A.: Intrusion detection in wireless ad hoc networks. IEEE Wirel. Commun. **11**(1), 48–60 (2004)

58. Nurse, J.R.C., et al.: Understanding insider threat: a framework for characterizing attacks. In: 2014 IEEE Security and Privacy Workshops, pp. 214–228, May 2014

59. Parter, D.W.(ed.): Proceedings of the 13th Conference on Systems Administration (LISA-99), Seattle, WA, USA, November 7–12, 1999. USENIX (1999)

60. Patzakis, J.: New incident response best practices: Patch and proceed is no longer acceptable incident response procedure. Technical report, Guidance Software, Pasadena, CA

61. Pfleeger, S.L., Predd, J.B., Hunker, J., Bulford, C.: Insiders behaving badly: addressing bad actors and their actions. Trans. Info. For. Sec., **5**(1), 169–179 (2010)

62. Sallam, A., Bertino, E., Hussain, S.R., Landers, D., Lefler, R.M., Steiner, D.: Dbsafe:an anomaly detection system to protect databases from exfiltration attempts. IEEE Syst. J., **99**, 1–11 (2015)
63. Sallam, A., Fadolalkarim, D., Bertino, E., Xiao, Q.: Data and syntax centric anomaly detection for relational databases. Wiley Interdiscipl. Rev. Data Min. Knowl. Discov. **6**(6), 231–239 (2016)
64. Santos, R.J., Bernardino, J., Vieira, M., Rasteiro, D.M.L.: Securing data warehouses from web-based intrusions. In: Wang, X.S., Cruz, I., Delis, A., Huang, G. (eds.) WISE 2012. LNCS, vol. 7651, pp. 681–688. Springer, Heidelberg (2012). https://doi.org/10.1007/978-3-642-35063-4_53
65. Sekar, R., et al.: Specification-based anomaly detection: a new approach for detecting network intrusions. In: Proceedings of the 9th ACM Conference on Computer and Communications Security, CCS 2002, pp. 265–274. ACM, New York (2002)
66. Sen, K.: Concolic testing. In: Proceedings of the Twenty-second IEEE/ACM International Conference on Automated Software Engineering; ASE 2007, pp. 571–572. ACM, New York (2007)
67. Sen, K., Marinov, D., Agha, G.: Cute: a concolic unit testing engine for c. In: Proceedings of the 10th European Software Engineering Conference Held Jointly with 13th ACM SIGSOFT International Symposium on Foundations of Software Engineering, ESEC/FSE-13, pp. 263–272. ACM, New York (2005)
68. Somayaji, A., Forrest, S.: Automated response using system-call delays. In: Proceedings of the 9th Conference on USENIX Security Symposium - Volume 9, SSYM 2000, pp. 14–14, USENIX Association, Berkeley (2000)
69. Srivastava, A., Sural, S., Majumdar, A.K.: Weighted Intra-transactional Rule Mining for database intrusion detection. In: Ng, W.-K., Kitsuregawa, M., Li, J., Chang, K. (eds.) PAKDD 2006. LNCS (LNAI), vol. 3918, pp. 611–620. Springer, Heidelberg (2006). https://doi.org/10.1007/11731139_71
70. Tang, A., Sethumadhavan, S., Stolfo, S.J.:Unsupervised anomaly-based malware detection using hardware features. In: Stavrou, A., Bos, H., Portokalidis, G. (eds.) Research in Attacks, Intrusions and Defenses, pp. 109–129, Springer, Cham (2014). https://doi.org/10.1007/978-3-642-33338-5
71. Tapiador, J.E., Clark, J.A.: Masquerade mimicry attack detection: a randomised approach. Comput. Secur. **30**(5), 297–310 (2011)
72. Trustwave.   DbProtect.   https://www.trustwave.com/en-us/services/security-testing/dbprotect/
73. Wagner, D., Soto, P.: Mimicry attacks on host-based intrusion detection systems. In: Proceedings of the 9th ACM Conference on Computer and Communications Security, CCS 2002, pp. 255–264. ACM, New York (2002)
74. Gao, W., Morris, T., Reaves, B., Richey, D.: On Scada control system command and response injection and intrusion detection. In: 2010 eCrime Researchers Summit, pp. 1–9, October 2010
75. Wu, G.Z., Osborn, S.I., Jin, X.: Database Intrusion Detection Using Role Profiling with Role Hierarchy, pp. 33–48. Springer, Berlin (2009)
76. Zhang, Y., Lee, W.: Intrusion detection in wireless ad-hoc networks. In: Proceedings of the 6th Annual International Conference on Mobile Computing and Networking, MobiCom 2000, pp. 275–283. ACM, New York (2000)

Author Index

Printed in the United States
by Baker & Taylor Publisher Services

Printed in the United States
by Baker & Taylor Publisher Services